CLASSIC SCIENCE FICTION WRITERS

Writers of English: Lives and Works

Classic Science Fiction Writers

Edited and with an Introduction by

Harold Bloom

CHELSEA HOUSE PUBLISHERS
New York   Philadelphia

Jacket illustration: Konstantin Juon (1875–1958), *The New Planet* (courtesy of the Tretyakov Gallery, Moscow).

CHELSEA HOUSE PUBLISHERS

Editorial Director Richard Rennert
Executive Managing Editor Karyn Gullen Browne
Picture Editor Adrian G. Allen
Copy Chief Robin James
Art Director Robert Mitchell
Manufacturing Director Gerald Levine
Assistant Art Director Joan Ferrigno

Writers of English: Lives and Works

Senior Editor S. T. Joshi
Senior Designer Rae Grant

Staff for CLASSIC SCIENCE FICTION WRITERS

Assistant Editor Mary Sisson
Research Peter Cannon, Stefan Dziemianowicz
Picture Researcher Pat Burns

Library of Congress Cataloging-in-Publication Data

Classic science fiction writers / edited and with an introduction by Harold Bloom.
       p.   cm.—(Writers of English)
    Includes bibliographical references (p.).
    ISBN 0-7910-2211-0.—ISBN 0-7910-2236-6 (pbk.)
  1. Science fiction, English——History and criticism. 2. Science fiction, American—History and criticism. 3. Science fiction, American—Bio-bibliography. 4. Science fiction, English—Bio-bibliography. I. Bloom, Harold. II. Series.
PR830.S35C58 1994   94-5901
823'.0876209—dc20   CIP
[B]

▨ Contents

◈ User's Guide

THIS VOLUME PROVIDES biographical, critical, and bibliographical information on the twelve most significant classic science fiction writers. Each chapter consists of three parts: a biography of the author; a selection of brief critical extracts about the author; and a bibliography of the author's published books.

The biography supplies a detailed outline of the important events in the author's life, including his or her major writings. The critical extracts are taken from a wide array of books and periodicals, from the author's lifetime to the present, and range in content from biographical to critical to historical. The extracts are arranged in chronological order by date of writing or publication, and a full bibliographical citation is provided at the end of each extract. Editorial additions or deletions are indicated within carets.

The author bibliographies list every separate publication—including books, pamphlets, broadsides, collaborations, and works edited or translated by the author—for works published in the author's lifetime; selected important posthumous publications are also listed. Titles are those of the first edition; variant titles are supplied within carets. In selected instances dates of revised editions are given where these are significant. Pseudonymous works are listed, but not the pseudonyms under which these works were published. Periodicals edited by the author are listed only when the author has written most or all of the contents. Titles enclosed in square brackets are of doubtful authenticity. All works by the author, whether in English or in other languages, have been listed; English translations of foreign-language works are not listed unless the author has done the translation.

◈ *The Life of the Author*

Harold Bloom

NIETZSCHE, WITH EXULTANT ANGUISH, famously proclaimed that God was dead. Whatever the consequences of this for the ethical life, its ultimate literary effect certainly would have surprised the author Nietzsche. His French disciples, Foucault most prominent among them, developed the Nietzschean proclamation into the dogma that all authors, God included, were dead. The death of the author, which is no more than a Parisian trope, another metaphor for fashion's setting of skirt-lengths, is now accepted as literal truth by most of our current apostles of what should be called French Nietzsche, to distinguish it from the merely original Nietzsche. We also have French Freud or Lacan, which has little to do with the actual thought of Sigmund Freud, and even French Joyce, which interprets *Finnegans Wake* as the major work of Jacques Derrida. But all this is as nothing compared to the final triumph of the doctrine of the death of the author: French Shakespeare. That delicious absurdity is given us by the New Historicism, which blends Foucault and California fruit juice to give us the Word that Renaissance "social energies," and not William Shakespeare, composed *Hamlet* and *King Lear*. It seems a proper moment to murmur "enough" and to return to a study of the life of the author.

Sometimes it troubles me that there are so few masterpieces in the vast ocean of literary biography that stretches between James Boswell's great *Life* of Dr. Samuel Johnson and the late Richard Ellmann's wonderful *Oscar Wilde*. Literary biography is a crucial genre, and clearly a difficult one in which to excel. The actual nature of the lives of the poets seems to have little effect upon the quality of their biographies. Everything happened to Lord Byron and nothing at all to Wallace Stevens, and yet their biographers seem equally daunted by them. But even inadequate biographies of strong writers, or of weak ones, are of immense use. I have never read a literary biography from which I have not profited, a statement I cannot make about any other genre whatsoever. And when it comes to figures who are central to us—Dante, Shakespeare, Cervantes, Montaigne, Goethe, Whitman, Tolstoi, Freud, Joyce, Kafka among them—we reach out eagerly for every scrap that the biographers have gleaned. Concerning Dante and Shakespeare we know much too little, yet when we come to Goethe and Freud, where we seem to know more than everything, we still want to know more. The death of the author, despite our current resentniks, clearly was only a momentary fad. Something vital in every authentic lover of literature responds to Emerson's battle-cry sentence: "There is no history, only biography." Beyond that there is a deeper truth, difficult to come at and requiring a lifetime to understand, which is that there is no literature, only autobiography, however mediated, however veiled, however transformed. The events of Shakespeare's life included the composition of *Hamlet*, and that act of writing was itself a crucial act of living, though we do not yet know altogether how to read so doubled an act. When an author takes up a more overtly autobiographical stance, as so many do in their youth, again we still do not know precisely how to accommodate the vexed relation between life and work. T. S. Eliot, meditating upon James Joyce, made a classic statement as to such accommodation:

> We want to know who are the originals of his characters, and what were
> the origins of his episodes, so that we may unravel the web of memory
> and invention and discover how far and in what ways the crude material
> has been transformed.

When a writer is not even covertly autobiographical, the web of memory and invention is still there, but so subtly woven that we may never unravel it. And yet we want deeply never to stop trying, and not merely because we are curious, but because each of us is caught in her own network of memory and invention. We do not always recall our inventions, and long before we age we cease to be certain of the extent to which we have invented our memories. Perhaps one motive for reading is our need to unravel our own webs. If our masters could make, from their lives, what we read, then we can be moved by them to ask: What have we made or lived in relation to what we have read? The answers may be sad, or confused, but the question is likely, implicitly, to go on being asked as long as we read. In Freudian terms, we are asking: What is it that we have repressed? What have we forgotten, unconsciously but purposively: What is it that we flee? Art, literature necessarily included, is regression in the service of the ego, according to a famous Freudian formula. I doubt the Freudian wisdom here, but indubitably it is profoundly suggestive. When we read, something in us keeps asking the equivalent of the Freudian questions: From what or whom is the author in flight, and to what earlier stages in her life is she returning, and why?

Reading, whether as an art or a pastime, has been damaged by the visual media, television in particular, and might be in some danger of extinction in the age of the computer, except that the psychic need for it continues to endure, presumably because it alone can assuage a central loneliness in elitist society. Despite all sophisticated or resentful denials, the reading of imaginative literature remains a quest to overcome the isolation of the individual consciousness. We can read for information, or entertainment, or for love of the language, but in the end we seek, in the author, the person whom we have not found, whether in ourselves or in others. In that quest, there always are elements at once aggressive and defensive, so that reading, even in childhood, is rarely free of hidden anxieties. And yet it remains one of the few activities not contaminated by an entropy of spirit. We read in hope, because we lack companionship, and the author can become the object of the most idealistic elements in our search for the wit and inventiveness we so desperately require. We read biography, not as a supplement to reading the author, but as a second, fresh attempt to understand what always seems to evade us in the work, our drive towards a kind of identity with the author.

This will-to-identity, though recently much deprecated, is a prime basis for the experience of sublimity in reading. *Hamlet* retains its unique position in the Western canon not because most readers and playgoers identify themselves with the prince, who clearly is beyond them, but rather because they find themselves again in the power of the language that represents him with such immediacy and force. Yet we know that neither language nor social energy created Hamlet. Our curiosity about Shakespeare is endless, and never will be appeased. That curiosity itself is a value, and cannot be separated from the value of *Hamlet* the tragedy, or Hamlet the literary character. It provokes us that Shakespeare the man seems so unknowable, at once everyone and no one as Borges shrewdly observes. Critics keep telling us otherwise, yet something valid in us keeps believing that we would know Hamlet better if Shakespeare's life were as fully known as the lives of Goethe and Freud, Byron and Oscar Wilde, or best of all, Dr. Samuel Johnson. Shakespeare never will have his Boswell, and Dante never will have his Richard Ellmann. How much one would give for a detailed and candid *Life of Dante* by Petrarch, or an outspoken memoir of Shakespeare by Ben Jonson! Or, in the age just past, how superb would be rival studies of one another by Hemingway and Scott Fitzgerald! But the list is endless: think of *Oscar Wilde* by Lord Alfred Douglas, or a joint biography of Shelley by Mary Godwin, Emilia Viviani, and Jane Williams. More than our insatiable desire for scandal would be satisfied. The literary rivals and the lovers of the great writers possessed perspectives we will never enjoy, and without those perspectives we dwell in some poverty in regard to the writers with whom we ourselves never can be done.

There is a sense in which imaginative literature *is* perspectivism, so that the reader is likely to be overwhelmed by the work's difficulty unless its multiple perspectives are mastered. Literary biography matters most because it is a storehouse of perspectives, frequently far surpassing any that are grasped by the particular biographer. There are relations between authors' lives and their works of kinds we have yet to discover, because our analytical instruments are not yet advanced enough to perform the necessary labor. Perhaps a novel, poem, or play is not so much a regression in the service of the ego, as it is an amalgam of *all* the Freudian mechanisms of defense, all working together for the apotheosis of the ego. Freud valued art highly, but thought that the aesthetic enterprise was no rival for psycho-analysis, unlike religion and philosophy. Clearly Freud was mistaken; his own anxieties about his indebtedness to Shakespeare helped produce the weirdness of his joining in the lunacy that argued for the Earl of Oxford as the author of Shakespeare's plays. It was Shakespeare, and not "the poets," who was there before Freud arrived at his depth psychology, and it is Shakespeare who is there still, well out ahead of psychoanalysis. We see what Freud would not see, that psychoanalysis is Shakespeare prosified and systematized. Freud is part of literature, not of "science," and the biography of Freud has the same relations to psychoanalysis as the biography of Shakespeare has to *Hamlet* and *King Lear*, if only we knew more of the life of Shakespeare.

Western literature, particularly since Shakespeare, is marked by the representa-tion of internalized change in its characters. A literature of the ever-growing inner self is in itself a large form of biography, even though this is the biography of imaginary beings, from Hamlet to the sometimes nameless protagonists of Kafka and Beckett. Skeptics might want to argue that all literary biography concerns imaginary beings, since authors make themselves up, and every biographer gives us a creation curiously different from the same author as seen by the writer of a rival *Life*. Boswell's Johnson is not quite anyone else's Johnson, though it is now very difficult for us to disentangle the great Doctor from his gifted Scottish friend and follower. The life of the author is not merely a metaphor or a fiction, as is "the Death of the Author," but it always does contain metaphorical or fictive elements. Those elements are a part of the value of literary biography, but not the largest or the crucial part, which is the separation of the mask from the man or woman who hid behind it. James Joyce and Samuel Beckett, master and sometime disciple, were both of them enigmatic personalities, and their biographers have not, as yet, fully expounded the mystery of these contrasting natures. Beckett seems very nearly to have been a secular saint: personally disinterested, heroic in the French Resistance, as humane a person ever to have composed major fictions and dramas. Joyce, self-obsessed even as Beckett was preternaturally selfless, was the Milton of the twentieth century. Beckett was perhaps the least egoistic post-Joycean, post-Proustian, post-Kafkan of writers. Does that illuminate the problematical nature of his work, or does it simply constitute another problem? Whatever the cause, the question matters. The only death of the author that is other than literal, and that matters, is the fate only of weak writers. The strong, who become canonical, never die, which is what the canon truly is about. To be read forever is the Life of the Author.

◈ Introduction

VICTOR FRANKENSTEIN, Mary Shelley's "Modern Prometheus," by universal agreement is not nearly so interesting as the tragic daemon, his creature, whom he has made, marred in making, and failed to love. At one of the origins of science fiction, the scientist is truly more a Narcissus than a Prometheus, and the "monster," ancestor of so many cyborgs, is a High Romantic Promethean: Byronic, Shelleyan (Percy more than Mary), and in a profound sense Miltonic-Satanic. When the nameless daemon, in our contemporary popular, cinematic imagination, usurped the name of his creator, then the daemon's moral victory over Victor Frankenstein became complete. A "generous and self-devoted being" is the creature's pragmatically ironic epitaph for his creator, who in formidable ignorance dies still not recognizing his own moral idiocy. Frankenstein cannot bear to acknowledge that the daemon is his own, his alternative self, even his child. Prospero in *The Tempest* at last accepts Caliban, aquatic and monstrous, as being his, but Mary Shelley's scientist lacks Prospero's tardy wisdom.

In these days of cyberpunk, *Frankenstein* scarcely seems to be approaching nearly two centuries of age. Rereading the book, we are very much immersed in contemporary, quite aggressive feminism, though more restrained in its statement than is the going thing. Mary Shelley's rather dialectical rebellion against her father, the radical philosopher William Godwin, and her husband, most revolutionary of poets, has been studied by many critics, yet cannot be exhausted by analysis. But the implicit sexual politics of the book seem to me less prophetic than are its spiritual and aesthetic implications. Science fiction and fantasy, as we approach Millennium, more and more reveal their Gnostic contours. The Canadian poet Jay Macpherson (descendant of the bard Ossian), in her superb *The Spirit of Solitude* (1982), traces the ancestry of Frankenstein's daemon to the homunculus of Hermetic alchemy and to the Golem of Kabbalistic tradition. Hermetism, a secular gnosis, and the Kabbalah both belong to the long, diffuse history of Gnosticism, and so does science fiction and fantasy, except when it goes against the grain in the neo-Christian mode of the Inklings (C. S. Lewis, Tolkien, Charles Williams). Sometimes the Gnostic patterns are overt, as in Philip K. Dick; sometimes, they are concealed, as in *Frankenstein*. The poet Shelley was versed in Gnosticism, and Mary Shelley hints that the daemon is a new version of Primordial Man, who comes crashing down in the Demiurge's catastrophe-creation. Milton's Satan and Milton's Adam fuse in the daemon, whose bondage has in it the peculiar intensity of the Gnostic horror of time.

Science fiction, even in its utopias, always has courted temporal nightmares: The protagonists of the genre tend to be versions of Macbeth rather than of Hamlet. The poor daemon of *Frankenstein* inherits Macbeth's dread of being a bad actor, always in danger of missing his cues. But indeed all the agonists of science fiction, down to the feminist heroines of cyberpunk, essentially are poor players who know all too well their own belatedness. The formula of science fiction, from *Frankenstein* on, is that the dreadful has already happened. There are only negative quests in this genre, and they are more in the vein of Narcissus than of Prometheus. Perhaps alchemical fables always resolve themselves by mirror images; the ancient Gnostic myths of Divine degradation involve the catastrophe of Primordial Man descending into his own watery self-reflection, in an embrace that shatters the image of self. Melville, who was deeply affected by Shelley's poetry, wrote a kind of science fiction in his extraordinary story "The Bell-Tower," in *The Piazza Tales*, where another engineer-demiurge is ruined by his own creation. *Moby-Dick*, which is not science fiction or even apocalyptic fantasy, but an extraordinary fusion of the *Odyssey* and the Book of Job, has usurped *Frankenstein*'s bid to be the classic prose work of nineteenth-century Gnosticism. What abides for *Frankenstein* is its equivocal splendor as one of the mothering forces in modern science fiction, in those chronicles that prophesy the Cyborg Age now rushing upon us.

—H. B.

Edward Bellamy
1850–1898

EDWARD BELLAMY was born at Chicopee Falls, Massachusetts, on March 26, 1850. Raised by a very religious family, he experienced a profound religious experience at the age of fourteen and was baptized; he came to believe in the universality of sinfulness and at the same time in the need to alleviate humanity's sufferings through social action. Some of these beliefs may have been engendered by his close familiarity with the grim conditions of down-trodden workers at factories and a cotton mill near his home.

Bellamy wished to attend West Point but failed the physical examination; instead, he took courses for a year (1867–68) at Union College in Schenectady, New York, then studied in Germany for the next term (1868–69). Returning to the United States, Bellamy worked at a law office in Springfield, Massachusetts. He was admitted to the bar in 1871, but abandoned law practice after a single case because he came to believe that it was morally repugnant. After a period spent in New York working as a freelance journalist, Bellamy became an associate editor of the *Springfield Union* in 1872, staying there for the next five years. He also gave many lyceum lectures at this time, two of which contained the germ of the political ideas that would later be expressed in his best-known novel, *Looking Backward*.

Bellamy began publishing short stories in 1875. In 1878 he published his first novel, *Six to One: A Nantucket Idyl*, followed by the psychological novel *Dr. Heidenhoff's Process* (1880) and *Miss Ludington's Sister: A Romance of Immortality* (1884). An historical novel, *The Duke of Stockbridge*, was serialized in 1879 but not published as a book until 1900. In 1880 Bellamy and his brother Charles founded the *Penny News* (later the *Daily News*), where he remained until 1884. In 1882 he married Emma Sanderson; they had a son and a daughter.

Looking Backward, 2000–1887 (1888) established Bellamy's reputation. In this utopian romance a young Bostonian, Julian West, falls into a hypnotic trance in 1887 and awakens in the year 2000 to find a perfectly organized socialist society in which poverty and warfare have been eliminated. The book was an immense grass-roots popular success, and was eventually translated into almost every foreign language in the world. "Bellamy Clubs" sprang up around the country, and a Nationalist party was formed to advocate the principles set forth in the novel. In 1891 Bellamy founded the *New Nation*, a newspaper in Boston, to spread his ideas. The Nationalist party became associated with the Populist movement, and in 1892 the Populist candidate for president, General James B. Weaver, won a remarkable twenty-two electoral votes. Both the Populist and the Nationalist parties faded as independent entities when they merged with the Democratic party in 1896, which took over many planks of their platforms.

Bellamy was forced to suspend publication of the *New Nation* in 1894 because of ill health. In 1897 he published an exhaustive sequel to *Looking Backward* entitled *Equality*, in which he attempted to answer the objections of many critics to the utopian scheme he had depicted; in that same year he and his family moved to Denver for the sake of his health, but Bellamy returned to Chicopee Falls in 1898 and died there on May 22, 1898. A posthumous collection of his short stories, *The Blindman's World and Other Stories*, appeared later in 1898; it contains a few stories that could now be classified as science fiction.

▣ *Critical Extracts*

WILLIAM DEAN HOWELLS   With a work in the region of pure romance, with a frank allegory, like Mr. Bellamy's *Looking Backward*, one can have no such quarrel as with one portraying realistic people with unreal motives. You concede the premises, as in a poem, and after that you can hold the author only to a poetic consistency; he has no allegiance to the waking world. You may say that this is not the time of day for romances, for allegories, but that does not affect the quality of the kind of work which the author has chosen to do. Besides, the extraordinary effect which Mr. Bellamy's present romance has had with the public may well give pause to the doctor of literary laws, and set him carefully to revising his most cherished opinions. For here is a book which in the sugar-coated form of a dream has exhibited a dose of undiluted socialism, and which has been gulped by some of the most vigilant opponents of that theory without a suspicion of the poison they were taking into their systems. They have been shown the world as it is fancied to be a hundred years hence, when the state shall perform all the offices of manufacture, transportation, and distribution now abandoned to the chances of competition or combination, and they have accepted it as the portrait of a very charming condition of things, instead of shuddering at the spectacle in every fibre.

Mr. Bellamy's allegoric state of A.D. 2000 is constructed almost exactly upon the lines of Mr. Gronland's *Co-operative Commonwealth;* and it is supposed to come into being through the government acquisition of the vast trusts and monopolies, just as the collectivist author teaches. These grow, the larger absorbing the smaller, till the nation finally perceives their significance, and by a peaceful assertion of power possesses itself of them, and remains its own sole capitalist, producer, and distributor. The conditions which in Mr. Bellamy's book present themselves to a man of our time, carried far into the next century by a somewhat abnormal nap, are such as to make him heartily ashamed of our competitive civilization; but it is not our affair to reproduce the smiling picture. One cannot deny the charm of the author's art, which has made itself felt before now in *Dr. Heidenhoff's Process* and in *Miss Ludington's Sister.* The present story, compared with these, is no story, and the character-drawing is of the slightest; there are in fact only a number of personages who explain to the survivor of the nineteenth century the nature and extent of the economic change which has taken place. But there is a force of appeal in the book which keeps the attention, and which appears in the case of so many critics to have captivated the reason; and whether Mr. Bellamy is amusing himself or not with his conceit of the socialistic state as an accomplished fact, there can be no doubt that he is keenly alive to the defects of our present civilization.

William Dean Howells, "Editor's Study," *Harper's New Monthly Magazine* No. 457 (June 1888): 154–55

WILLIAM MORRIS   The only safe way of reading a utopia is to consider it as the expression of the temperament of its author. So looked at, Mr. Bellamy's utopia must be still called very interesting, as it is constructed with due economical knowledge, and with much adroitness; and of course his temperament is that of many thousands of people. This temperament may be called the unmixed, modern one, unhistoric and unartistic;

it makes its owner (if a Socialist) perfectly satisfied with modern civilization, if only the injustice, misery, and waste of class society could be got rid of; which half-change seems possible to him. The only ideal of life which such a man can see is that of the industrious *professional* middle-class men of to-day purified from their crime of complicity with the monopolist class, and become independent instead of being, as they are now, parasitical. It is not to be denied that if such an ideal could be realised, it would be a great improvement on the present society. But can it be realised? It means in fact the alteration of the machinery of life in such a way that all men shall be allowed to share in the fulness of that life, for the production and upholding of which the machinery was instituted. There are clear signs to show us that that very group whose life is thus put forward as an ideal for the future are condemning it in the present, and that they also demand a revolution. ⟨. . .⟩

Mr. Bellamy's ideas of life are curiously limited; he has no idea beyond existence in a great city; his dwelling of man in the future is Boston (U.S.A.) beautified. In one passage, indeed, he mentions villages, but with unconscious simplicity shows that they do not come into his scheme of economical equality, but are mere servants of the great centres of civilisation. This seems strange to some of us, who cannot help thinking that our experience ought to have taught us that such aggregations of population afford the worst possible form of dwelling-place, whatever the second-worst might be.

In short, a machine-life is the best which Mr. Bellamy can imagine for us on all sides; it is not to be wondered at then that his only idea of making labour tolerable is to decrease the amount of it by means of fresh and ever fresh developments of machinery. This view I know he will share with many Socialists with whom I might otherwise agree more than I can with him; but I think a word or two is due to this important side of the subject. Now surely this ideal of the great reduction of the hours of labour by the mere means of machinery is a futility. The human race has always put forth about as much energy as it could in given conditions of climate and the like, though that energy has had to struggle against the natural laziness of mankind: and the development of man's resources, which has given him greater power over nature, has driven him also into fresh desires and fresh demands on nature, and thus made his expenditure of energy much what it was before. I believe that this will always be so, and the multiplication of machinery will just—multiply machinery; I believe that the ideal of the future does not point to the lessening of men's energy by the reduction of *labour* to a minimum, but rather to the reduction of *pain in labour* to a minimum, so small that it will cease to be a pain; a gain to humanity which can only be dreamed of till men are even more completely equal than Mr. Bellamy's utopia would allow them to be, but which will most assuredly come about when men are really equal in condition; although it is probable that much of our so-called "refinement," our luxury—in short, our civilisation—will have to be sacrificed to it. In this part of his scheme, therefore, Mr. Bellamy worries himself unnecessarily in seeking (with obvious failure) some incentive to labour to replace the fear of starvation, which is at present our only one, whereas it cannot be too often repeated that the true incentive to useful and happy labour is and must be pleasure in the work itself.

William Morris, [Review of *Looking Backward*] (1889), *Science-Fiction Studies* 3, No. 3 (November 1976): 287–89

JOHN DEWEY   It is not surprising that during the present bankruptcy of economic class control, there is a great revival of interest in Bellamy. It is an American communism that he depicts, and his appeal comes largely from the fact that he sees in it the necessary means of realizing the democratic ideal. Limitations of space compel me to pass by in silence a multitude of interesting points, but I hope that what I have said will lead some to consult his *Equality* which is more thorough than the more popular *Looking Backward*, as he himself intended. The chapters on the "Suicide of the Profit System" and "The Parable of the Water Tank" are priceless— and not in its slang sense. The chapter on "What Started the Revolution" and its sequel are extraordinary summaries of contemporary history. It is encouraging to know that Bellamy Societies are starting almost spontaneously, but with the aid of a central organization, all over the country. It is a good omen and I do not believe that a mirage of prosperity will again bring about the collapse of Bellamy's teachings that occurred in the postwar period. In this country the problem of industrial socialization is much more of a psychological problem than, it seems to me, it is in any European country. The worth of Bellamy's books in effecting a translation of the ideas of democracy into economic terms is incalculable. What *Uncle Tom's Cabin* was to the anti-slavery movement Bellamy's book may well be to the shaping of popular opinion for a new social order. Moreover there is one difference. Bellamy's work is definitely constructive. While it is filled with fundamental criticisms of the present anarchy (which the demands of language have compelled me to refer to at times as an order or system!) there is no tinge of bitterness in it. It accords with American psychology in breathing the atmosphere of hope.

John Dewey, "A Great American Prophet," *Common Sense* 3, No. 4 (April 1934): 7

JOSEPH SCHIFFMAN   Bellamy made an important effort to "get at the truth" about "moral defects" in his little-known novel, *Dr. Heidenhoff's Process,* published originally in serialized form in the Springfield *Daily Union* from December 18, 1878 through March, 1879. ⟨. . .⟩

Dr. Heidenhoff's Process tells the story of Madeline Brand, a promising young person whose life is destroyed by a sense of unworthiness. The story is laid in a Massachusetts town, typical of nineteenth-century New England, where moral codes are rigidly enforced. Madeline has felt their sting. A victim of seduction, she finds life intolerable. Lacerated by the constant accusation in her mother's eyes, she escapes to Boston where she is followed by Henry Burr, a devoted beau whom she had spurned for her lover. Henry offers her love and marriage, but, unable to accept him because of her feelings of guilt and unworthiness, she sinks into deep depression. ⟨. . .⟩

Society had taught the price of sin too well to Madeline. Painfully, Henry watches her sink into unrelieved depression until she almost loses consciousness of his presence. Exhausted and distraught, Henry falls asleep and dreams of a magical process that restores Madeline to health—Dr. Heidenhoff's process.

In a magazine article, "The Extirpation of Thought Processes. A New Invention," Dr. Heidenhoff advertises his "galvanic battery" for the annihilation of "morbid ideas." A firm believer in the "physical basis of the intellect," Dr. Heidenhoff offers to see patients at his office for treatment. After listening to Henry's account of Madeline's case, the doctor exclaims:

> [In time] the mental physician will be able to extract a specific
> recollection from the memory. . . . Macbeth's question, "Canst
> thou not minister to a mind diseased; pluck from the memory a
> rooted sorrow; raze out the written troubles of the brain?" was a
> puzzler to the sixteenth century doctor, but he of the twentieth,
> yes, perhaps of the nineteenth, will be able to answer it
> affirmatively.

Dr. Heidenhoff describes his treatment, explaining that success depends on how severely morbidity has affected the material structure of the brain. The treatment itself is simple, and in no way painful. The patient's head is secured by padded clamps connected to a galvanic battery. A switch is thrown, giving the patient only a sensation of warmth, a bubbling sound in the ears, and an unpleasant taste in the mouth. The patient then falls into a deep sleep, and if he responds favorably to the treatment, awakes with a temporary feeling of slight confusion and a permanent loss of the unwanted memory. Thus, in hopeful fantasy, Bellamy foreshadowed the development of the theory and practice of modern electric convulsive ("shock") therapy.

Joseph Schiffman, "Edward Bellamy's Altruistic Man," *American Quarterly* 6, No. 3 (Fall 1954): 198–99

DAVID KETTERER   The narrative device of placing a representative of a bad old world amongst the new utopian world and chronicling the open-mouthed astonishment and somewhat slapstick action which results is another of the many clichés of the genre. Bellamy improves dramatically on this performance by concentrating on the psychological reaction of his protagonist, who describes himself successively as "a stranger from a strange age," "a stranded creature of an unknown sea," and, back in his own time, "a stranger in my own city." The reader is made to feel the alienating effects of the temporal dislocations which West undergoes and, thus, Bellamy gains a certain measure of sympathetic identification between West and the reader. Indeed, the emphasis which Bellamy places on a plausible protagonist is further evidence that he conceived *Looking Backward* not as a fantasy but as science fiction.

West's situation at the opening of the story is symbolic of the unhappy nature of his times. He is in love with and engaged to Edith Bartlett. Their marriage "only waited on the completion of the house which I was building for our occupancy." Labour problems, strikes in particular, delay the day of completion and, consequently, the wedding is yet to occur when West leaves the Boston of 1887. Symbolically translated, these events indicate that, in 1887, the economic and social situation prevents human fulfilment and happiness. Stranded in the year 2000, West falls in love with a girl also named Edith, who turns out to be the "great-granddaughter" of West's "lost

love, Edith Bartlett." This is the kind of genealogical coincidence with
which writers of time-travel science fiction have played around *ad nauseam*.
Henry James would appear to be indebted to Bellamy for the love interest
in his "look backward" in *The Sense of the Past*. James' protagonist is transported back in time where he meets the ancestor of his lost beloved. Bellamy
is interested in making the symbolic point that, in his utopia, the nineteenth-
century impediments which stood in the way of happiness do not apply.
We are given to understand at the conclusion of the novel that West does
achieve the dream which his surname represents and marries the second
Edith. The only "impediment" which comes between their engagement and
their marriage is again nineteenth-century disturbance, but this time only
in the form of a dream.

The dream mechanism on which the plot of the novel turns is itself of
metaphoric importance. It is a reflection of the nervous nature of the
times that West, in the nineteenth century, is "a confirmed sufferer from
insomnia." West claims, "I could not have slept in the city at all, with its
never ceasing nightly noises, if I had been obliged to use an upstairs chamber." Consequently, he has a sleeping chamber built under the foundations
of his house. The hierarchical arrangement between this "subterranean
room" and the "upper world" would appear to establish some Freudian
distinction between a subconscious world of wish-fulfilment and a conscious
reality. After two nights without sleep, West customarily called on Dr.
Pillsbury, a "Professor of Animal Magnetism," to put him in a trance. It is
a trance, however, from which he has to be awakened by "a reversal of the
mesmerizing process." However, one night in 1887 there is an accident and
the house burns down, leaving West's sleeping chamber undamaged but
hidden. Presumably West's Negro servant, who also lives in the house and
has been instructed to rouse West, dies in the "conflagration." West, between
mesmerists since Pillsbury has taken an appointment in a distant city, sleeps
on until he is discovered and awakened in the year 2000. The reader has
every reason to expect that West's subsequent experiences are a dream,
particularly given the architectural symbolism of the house with its "recess
[of mind?] in the foundation walls connecting with my chamber" and the
"magnetism" of Edith Leete's beauty. But the fire would appear to portend
that a genuine apocalypse of mind is in progress. West's subsequent grateful
awareness that he is "not still awaiting the end of the world in a living
tomb" confirms the metaphorical relationship between the Apocalypse and

his awakening revelation. Although no actual cause for the fire is specified, a clue is later provided by Dr. Leete as to the metaphorical cause:

> "It was the misfortune of your contemporaries that they had to cement their business fabric with a material which an accident might at any moment turn into an explosive. They were in the plight of a man building a house [this was West's situation] with dynamite for mortar, for credit can be compared with nothing else."

The logic of metaphor here implies that the barbaric economic system of the nineteenth century has resulted in a destructive and bloody revolution and that such an event preceded the world transformation which has taken place. Bellamy is strangely reticent about the transitional phase in the development of utopia but, on the occasions where the subject does arise, he attempts, by means of further metaphorical analogies, to give the impression that the process of transition was peaceable.

David Ketterer, "Utopian Fantasy as Millennial Motive and Science-Fictional Motif," *Studies in the Literary Imagination* 6, No. 2 (Fall 1973): 90–93

JEAN PFAELZER   Women in the year 2000 have incomes identical to those of men. They work in a separate branch of the Industrial Army and obey female generals and judges. Julian discovers that the highest governing council reserves one permanent seat for a woman, a seat which holds veto power on all matters relating to the female sex. The new society has centralized cooking and laundry, and most surprisingly, housework is paid. In the period when married women were not allowed to own property in their own names, Bellamy maintains that wives should "in no way be dependent on their husbands for economic security." After Frances Willard read *Looking Backward,* she wrote to Bellamy's publisher that "some of us think that Edward Bellamy must be Edwardina . . . i.e. we believe a big hearted, big brained woman wrote this book. Won't you please find out?" Nevertheless, Bellamy restricts women to "certain jobs because they are inferior in strength to men and further disqualified industrially in special ways," and he stresses that in utopia married women would be "allowed" to work.

Women in Bellamy's utopia exist to stimulate men: they are men's "main incentive to labour." Men permit "women to work because it makes them more attractive and fulfilling companions." Only women who have been both wives and mothers achieve high positions in the Industrial Army as "they alone fully represent their sex." Women, Bellamy announces, represent the "humanity of the new race." ⟨. . .⟩

Bellamy's image of women as selfless, pure, and maternal circumscribes the representation of equality in Looking Backward. Because women are more capable than men of sympathy and self-sacrifice, he calls it their "duty" to perpetuate the society's altruistic values. Looking Backward concludes with Julian kneeling at Edith's feet while she gathers flowers. He says, "Kneeling before her with my face in the dust I confessed with tears how little was my worth to breathe the air of this golden century, and how infinitely less to wear upon my breast its consummate flower. Fortunate is he who, with a case so desperate as mine, finds a judge so merciful."

Jean Pfaelzer, "A State of One's Own: Feminism as Ideology in American Utopias 1880–1915," *Extrapolation* 24, No. 4 (Winter 1983): 315–16

SYLVIA E. BOWMAN   Franklin Delano Roosevelt and his wife were acquainted with the books of Edward Bellamy. But Mrs. Roosevelt stated that, "while both my husband and I were familiar with Edward Bellamy's books and discussed them at various times in small groups of people, I really have very little knowledge of the effect that they had on other people." Although she stated that her husband was "always receptive to new ideas and loved to discuss them," she did not feel that Bellamy had had any effect upon him. Irving Flamm, a lawyer and the author of *An Economic Program for a Living Democracy* (1942), was impressed by the presence of *Looking Backward* in the "most conspicuous part of one of the bookcases in the library" of the White House when he toured it in 1933. Flamm, who had been "a Bellamy fan for some forty years after reading his two volumes" and who had distributed many copies of *Looking Backward*, said that seeing the book in the White House library had intrigued him about its possible influence upon Roosevelt because, in part, of "the caption of his own later book, *Looking Forward*" (1933).

Whatever the specific influence of Bellamy's ideas during the New Deal, the fact is that many of them, sponsored by so many Socialists and Bellamy-related organizations, were implemented; and some of Roosevelt's influential staff members were well acquainted with such proposals. Arthur Morgan,

Chairman of the Board of Directors of The Tennessee Valley Authority and a biographer of Edward Bellamy, was a believer in an "integrated social and economic order" that would be achieved as a result of "the democratic process of voluntary general agreement." According to Morgan, Adolf A. Berle, Jr., the assistant secretary of state and a respected member of the New Deal group, was the son of a man who had been an active member of the Boston Bellamy Club and was reared in a family in which *Looking Backward* was comparable to the family Bible. According to Berle, Jr., "It is unnecessary to say that any one who ever followed Bellamy could ever remain uninfluenced by his ideas."

    Sylvia E. Bowman, *Edward Bellamy* (Boston: Twayne, 1986), pp. 127–28

ROGER NEUSTADTER   In *Looking Backward* and its sequel *Equality* Bellamy insists that society cannot intelligently accept the practical benefits of the machine without accepting its moral and aesthetic imperatives. Bellamy presents the machine not only as an instrument for the production of goods but as a pedagogue. The significance of the machine in Bellamy's utopia is not limited to practical achievements—it becomes a model of efficiency and justice. Bellamy suggests that no part of the environment, no social conventions, can be taken for granted once the machine has shown how far order, system, and intelligence might prevail over the nature of things. For Bellamy the nature of the machine becomes a powerful metaphor for social and political organization.

    Bellamy calls the central organization of the new society the Industrial Army in which all citizens between the ages of twenty-one and forty-five have to serve. In describing the new social order Bellamy invokes the imagery of the machine. The main factor in modern production, Bellamy writes, "is the social organism, the machinery of associated labor" by which hundreds of millions of individuals provide for one another and complement one another's labors, "thereby making the productive and distributive systems of a nation and of the world one great machine." Thus, as the Industrial Army molds workers in cooperative virtue, it also forges them into a mighty economic and social machine. ⟨. . .⟩

    Bellamy clearly argues that a society of complex technology requires political centralization, a certain standardization of products, and the willingness of human beings to fit into the highly structured organization which results. All the production and distribution of the nation is carried out by a central administration under the supervision of experts. The system itself is mechanistic, requiring only supervision and management. Administrators in the Industrial Army, Dr. Leete assures West, need have no more than fair abilities: "The machine which they direct is indeed a vast one, but so logical in its principles and direct and simple in its workings, that it all but runs itself." Government also runs like an efficient autonomous machine. State government is superfluous, and Congress meets once every five years. The political system, like the economic system, requires only routine maintenance. ⟨. . .⟩

Technology also plays an important part in Bellamy's argument for economic equality. The four thousand dollars credit extended to individuals on a basis of absolute equality is attributable to the social cooperation reflected in technological progress rather than to individualistic efforts. Each person works only a few hours a day by virtue of the efficiency of machines. Bellamy's criticism aims at waste, haste, inefficiency, and injustice, not at the machine. He urges the substitution of the scientific methods of an organized and unified industrial system for the wasteful struggle of destructive competitive undertakings. Bellamy deploys the machine to redeem the nation's social, political, and economic organization from such a destructive system.

> Roger Neustadter, "Mechanization Takes Command: The Celebration of Technology in the Utopian Novels of Edward Bellamy, Chauncey Thomas, John Jacob Astor, and Charles Caryl," *Extrapolation* 29, No. 1 (Spring 1988): 24–26

W. WARREN WAGAR   In a minor profusion of short stories and novels written over the next fifteen years, Bellamy elaborated on the ideas broached in "The Religion of Solidarity." What emerges from a reading of these works of a utopographer's apprenticeship is the picture of a tormented soul, shy and insecure, who sought relief from his anxieties in fantasies of transformation and self-denial. ⟨. . .⟩

⟨. . .⟩ "The Blindman's World" (1886) is a tale of earth, seen from the point of view of Mars. Like every other intelligent species in the universe except for terrestrials, the Martians possess the faculty of foresight. Knowing their futures, they are spared all anxiety; but their powers of recollection are weakly developed, which shields them from the misery of painful memories and the ache of nostalgia. They live only for present and expected joys, pitying the "blind" folk of earth.

When the narrator asks his alien informant if it ever occurred to Martians to wish to alter the future, the Martian replies that no one but an earthling would ask such a question. "To foresee events was to foresee their logical necessity so clearly that to desire them different was as impossible as seriously to wish that two and two made five instead of four." Since all things great and small are woven together, "to draw out the smallest thread would unravel creation through all eternity." The narrator ends his story with the hope that some day mankind may also learn to live with its face to the future, no longer "doomed to walk backward, beholding only what has gone by, assured only of what is past and dead." As in *Dr. Heidenoff's Process*, individuality—which in real earthlings is preserved by memory and expectation alike—comes under attack, and Bellamy's blissful amnesiacs win release from the struggle for existence by submitting to a destiny they are excused from even wishing to change.

Having disposed of memory, in "To Whom This May Come" (1889) Bellamy went on to abolish privacy. Shipwrecked in the Indian Ocean, the narrator encounters a race of mind readers. These joyful telepaths know nothing of injustice or deception, or even the anxieties of courtship. Dispensing with names and titles, they are all one family. The narrator anticipates a great good time when the "mutual vision of minds" will be available to all peoples. In no way, he adds, will it "so enhance the blessedness of mankind as by rending the veil of self, and leaving no spot of darkness in the mind for lies to hide in. Then shall the soul no longer be a coal smoking among ashes, but a star in a crystal sphere."

W. Warren Wagar, "Dreams of Reason: Bellamy, Wells, and the Positive Utopia," *Looking Backward, 1988–1888: Essays on Edward Bellamy*, ed. Daphne Patai (Amherst: University of Massachusetts Press, 1988), pp. 111–12

Bibliography

Six to One: A Nantucket Idyl. 1878.

Dr. Heidenhoff's Process. 1880.

Miss Ludington's Sister: A Romance of Immortality. 1884.

Looking Backward, 2000–1887. 1888.

Plutocracy or Nationalism, Which? 1889.

Principles and Purposes of Nationalism. 1889.

State Management of the Liquor Traffic. c. 1892.

How to Employ the Unemployed in Mutual Maintenance. c. 1893.

Equality. 1897.

The Blindman's World and Other Stories. 1898.

The Duke of Stockbridge: A Romance of Shays' Rebellion. Ed. Francis Bellamy.
       1900.

Edward Bellamy Speaks Again! Articles—Public Addresses—Letters. 1937.

Talks on Nationalism. 1938.

The Religion of Solidarity. 1940.

Selected Writings on Religion and Society. Ed. Joseph Schiffman. 1955.

Positive Romance. 1970.

Edgar Rice Burroughs
1875–1950

EDGAR RICE BURROUGHS, best-selling writer of adventure, fantasy, and science fiction, was born in Chicago on September 1, 1875, the fourth of four children born to Charles Tyler Burroughs and Mary Eveline Zieger. During his sickly childhood Burroughs developed a love of classical mythology and showed an aptitude for Latin in school. In 1891 he left high school to work briefly on an Idaho ranch owned by his older brothers George and Harry. The experience improved his health and endowed him with a lifelong love of animals and the rugged outdoors.

Burroughs enrolled in the prestigious Phillips Academy in the fall of 1891 but the following year transferred to the Michigan Military Academy, from which he graduated in 1895. He embarked on a career in the military in 1896, but after ten disenchanting months at Fort Grant in the Arizona territory was discharged at his own request. In 1900 Burroughs married his former childhood sweetheart, Emma Hulbert, and for the next decade tried unsuccessfully to earn a living at a succession of jobs that included stationery store manager, gold prospector, railroad policeman, door-to-door salesman, and stenographer in the mail order department of Sears, Roebuck.

Financial necessity following failed efforts at self-employment and the birth of two children in 1908 and 1909 nurtured Burroughs's interest in writing for money. In 1911 he submitted his first novel for publication in the pulp fiction magazine *All-Story*, one of several all-fiction magazines published by the Frank A. Munsey Co. Published serially in 1912 as "Under the Moons of Mars" by "Norman Bean"—a stenographer's corruption of "Normal Bean," the pseudonym Burroughs had chosen to reassure readers that the imaginative tale was just the fantasy of a "normal being"—it recounted the adventures of John Carter, a former soldier miraculously transported to a vividly detailed Mars where he rises to a position of rank through his innate goodness and military prowess. Immensely popular with readers, Burroughs's novel inaugurated the scientific romance, a literary subgenre that melded elements of romance, adventure, and science fiction.

After failing to sell his second novel to either magazine or book publishers, Burroughs placed his third, *Tarzan of the Apes*, with *All-Story* in 1912. The story of an orphaned child of English nobility raised by apes in Africa, it yielded one of the most renowned heroes of twentieth-century popular fiction and provided Burroughs with a podium from which to espouse a subtle populist philosophy. The novel's tremendous success after serialization in newspapers around the country gave Burroughs the security he needed to work full-time as a writer.

Over the next thirty-eight years Burroughs wrote numerous other realistic, historical, western, science fiction, and fantasy stories, including seven books of adventures set in Pellucidar, a prehistoric world at the center of a hollow earth, and five set on the planet Venus. However, none were as popular as his Mars and Tarzan stories, with the result that the finance-conscious Burroughs returned to their lucrative worlds after every disappointing experiment, eventually producing eleven John Carter and twenty-four Tarzan books. Burroughs's success as a writer was a product not only of his prodigious output and fertile imagination but his sharp business sense. He diligently controlled serialization rights, formed his own publishing company to oversee preservation of his fiction in hardcover, and even incorporated himself as Edgar Rice Burroughs, Inc., in 1923.

Despite his lack of success at writing for the film industry, Burroughs moved his family to California in 1919, on land that would later be recognized as the town of Tarzana. Intensely patriotic, he joined the army reserves during World War I and served as a war correspondent during World War II, occasionally peppering his Tarzan novels with anti-German and anti-Japanese caricatures. His wife's drinking problems led to a divorce in 1934. Burroughs's marriage to Florence Dealholt in the following year also ended in divorce, in 1941. Burroughs was troubled by angina attacks in 1945 and later was diagnosed with arteriosclerosis. He died from complications of a heart attack on March 19, 1950.

▨ *Critical Extracts*

H. P. LOVECRAFT   In the present age of vulgar taste and sordid realism it is a relief to peruse a publication such as *The All-Story*, which has ever been and still remains under the influence of the imaginative school of Poe and Verne. ⟨. . .⟩

If, in fact, man is unable to create living beings out of inorganic matter, to hypnotize the beasts of the forests to do his will, to swing from tree to tree with the apes of the African jungle, to restore to life the mummified corpses of the Pharaohs and the Incas, or to explore the atmosphere of Venus and the deserts of Mars, permit us, at least, in fancy, to witness these miracles, and to satisfy that craving for the unknown, the weird, and the impossible which exists in every active human brain. ⟨. . .⟩

At or near the head of your list of writers Edgar Rice Burroughs undoubtedly stands. I have read very few recent novels by others wherein is displayed an equal ingenuity in plot, and verisimilitude in treatment. His only fault seems to be a tendency toward scientific inaccuracy and slight inconsistencies.

For example, in that admirable story, "Tarzan of the Apes," we meet *Sabor*, the tiger, far from his native India, and we behold the hero, before he has learned the relation between vocal sounds and written letters, writing out his name, *Tarzan, which he has known only from the lips of his hairy associates*, as well as the names of *Kerchak, Tantor, Numa,* and *Terkoz,* all of which he could not possibly have seen written.

Also, in "The Gods of Mars," Mr. Burroughs refers to the year of the red planet as having 687 *Martian* days. This is, of course, absurd, for while Mars revolves about the sun in 687 *terrestrial* days, its own day or period of rotation is almost forty minutes longer than ours, thus giving to Mars a year which contains but 668 2/3 *Martian* solar days. I note with regret that this error is repeated in "Warlord of Mars."

H. P. Lovecraft, Letter to the Editor of the *All-Story* (7 March 1914), *H. P. Lovecraft in the Argosy*, ed. S. T. Joshi (West Warwick, RI: Necronomicon Press, 1994), p. 27

EDGAR RICE BURROUGHS   I had a good reason for thinking I could sell what I wrote. I had gone thoroughly through some of the all-fiction magazines, and I made up my mind that if people were paid for writing rot such as I read I could write stories just as rotten. Although I had never written a story, I knew absolutely that I could write stories just as entertaining and probably a whole lot more so than any I chanced to read in those magazines.

I knew nothing about the technique of story writing, and now after eighteen years of writing, I still know nothing about the technique, although, with the publication of my new novel, *Tarzan and the Lost Empire*, there are thirty-one books on my list. I had never met an editor, or an author, or a publisher. I had no idea of how to submit a story or what I could expect in payment. Had I known anything about it at all I would never have thought of submitting half a novel, but that is what I did.

Thomas Newell Metcalf, who was then editor of the *All-Story Magazine*, published by Munsey, wrote me that he liked the first half of a story I had sent him, and if the second half was as good, he thought he might use it. Had he not given me this encouragement, I should never have finished the story and my writing career would have been at an end, since I was not writing because of any urge to write nor for any particular love of writing. I was writing because I had a wife and two babies, a combination which does not work well without money.

> Edgar Rice Burroughs, "How I Wrote the Tarzan Books," *New York World* (*Sunday World Magazine*), 27 October 1929, pp. 4, 23

FRITZ LEIBER   ⟨. . .⟩ many writers have been interested in and influenced by Theosophy, James Joyce and W. B. Yeats among them. Writers, quite properly seeking to escape the curse of compartmentalized knowledge, are forever attempting to think of everything at once and Theosophy, with its strongly synthetic spirit, does just that.

Volume II of *The Secret Doctrine* ⟨by Helena Blavatsky⟩, subtitled *Anthropogenesis*, deals with past, present, and future forms of intelligent life. According to the Theosophical phantasmagoria, there are seven "Root Races," each consisting of seven "Sub-Races." I find parallels between these and the races descended from the Barsoomian Tree of Life as described by Burroughs, especially in *The Gods of Mars*. ⟨. . .⟩

Parallels aside, the occult elements in Burroughs' books stand out sharply: instantaneous interplanetary travel by thought power; each planet having its characteristic ray (astrological inspirations indicated here) and airships held aloft by tanks (!) of these rays; Methuselah-size lifetimes of one thousand years, an occultist gimmick which also appealed to G. B. Shaw, whose *Back to Methuselah* gives a remarkably Theosophist picture of Earth's future; creation of phantom and living matter by thought power (*Thuvia, Maid of*

Mars); and addiction to simple living (nudism, etc.) and high thinking; and finally the oppression and persecution of wise free-thinkers by an evil priesthood.

This last point is worth dwelling on briefly. Anyone familiar with Rosicrucian advertisements know their thinly-veiled claims of persecution by organized religion, apparently chiefly the Roman Catholic Church ("The wisdom must die").

On Barsoom the evil priesthood is represented by the Holy Therns, whose diabolic activities sound very much like those of Rome as described by the wilder Protestant propagandists. False celibates, they riot in luxury in their secret Vatican City near Barsoom's south pole, indulging their sadistic lusts. Of course they are good swordsmen too—everybody had to double in steel in the Big Burroughs Space Show, even effetes, magicians, priests, and beautiful girls. And Phaidor, daughter of Matai Shang, father of Holy Therns, is right up there with Pope Joan in the Sex-Spiced-With-Blasphemy department.

In conclusion, it seems to me very plausible that Burroughs' writing in California in the early part of this century should have found background material in the cults flourishing right around him.

Fritz Leiber, "John Carter: Sword of Theosophy" (1959), *Fafhrd & Me* (Newark, NJ: Wildside Press, 1990), pp. 52–53

GORE VIDAL   There is something basic in the appeal of the 1914 Tarzan which makes me think that he can still hold his own as a daydream figure, despite the sophisticated challenge of his two contemporary competitors, Ian Fleming and Mickey Spillane. For most adults, Tarzan (and John Carter of Mars) can hardly compete with the conspicuous consumer consumption of James Bond or the sickly violence of Mike Hammer, but for children and adolescents, the old appeal continues. All of us need the idea of a world alternative to this one. From Plato's Republic to Opar to Bondland, at every level, the human imagination has tried to imagine something better for itself than the existing society. Man left Eden when we got up off all fours, endowing most of his descendants with nostalgia as well as chronic backache. In its naive way, the Tarzan legend returns us to that Eden where, free of clothes and the inhibitions of an oppressive society, a man can achieve in reverie his continuing need, which is, as William

Faulkner put it in his high Confederate style, to prevail as well as endure. The current fascination with L.S.D. and non-addictive drugs—not to mention alcoholism—is all part of a general sense of frustration and boredom. The individual's desire to dominate his environment is not a desirable trait in a society which every day grows more and more confining. Since there are few legitimate releases for the average man, he must take to daydreaming. James Bond, Mike Hammer and Tarzan are all dream-selves, and the aim of each is to establish personal primacy in a world which in reality diminishes the individual. Among adults, increasing popularity of these lively inferior fictions strikes me as a most significant (and unbearably sad) phenomenon.

Gore Vidal, "Tarzan Revisited," *Esquire* 50, No. 6 (December 1963): 264

SAM MOSKOWITZ   Those who have gained a stereotyped conception of Burroughs as a writer who conveys his plot line on a nonstop jetstream of action, moving his characters along so swiftly that readers cannot react to his flaws, are in great error.

The fascination of Burroughs rests in the careful delineation of the *setting* in which he has placed his characters and the sharpness with which he etches them, presenting their weaknesses as well as strengths, their eccentricities, philosophies, and environmental shapings. A character may be villainous in motivation, but nevertheless strikingly courageous. A hero may do a foolish or unbecoming deed through pride or vanity. Political expediency may turn enemies into allies and then into firm friends.

Under the Moons of Mars, unlike *Tarzan of the Apes*, is not a satiric and at times damning criticism of "civilized" man, but instead a brief for the family ties, post-Victorian social customs, and standards of morality of Burroughs' day. He shows what distortions can result from a more efficient and scientifically run social order. It was almost an anticipation of certain socialist and fascist governments.

There would be times in later years when he would be accused of borderline racism in his handling of African savages, but the message of *Under the Moons of Mars* that the outward form of a creature, no matter how bizarre, is not the measure of his value appears to anticipate and negate most such criticisms.

The readers of *Under the Moons of Mars* were getting marvelous escape into a never-never-land where no present-day elements could intrude. With no more training than the good fortune of being born with Earthly muscles, they were able to defeat alien giants and gain great respect and high position among a very civilized people. There was a noble and high-minded princess for the men to fall in love with and marry. Yet, all these elements of escapism, which Burroughs claims were at least in part derived from his own imaginings while tossing and turning from insomnia during financially taut years, are accomplished without stretching the moral standards of the people who indulge in them.

Perhaps most important, Edgar Rice Burroughs was a natural-born story-teller who lured the reader into the story and carried him effortlessly along as skillfully as almost any writer in English literature.

Sam Moskowitz, *Under the Moons of Mars: A History of "The Scientific Romance" in the Munsey Magazines, 1912–1920* (New York: Holt, Rinehart & Winston, 1970), pp. 297–98

PHILIP JOSÉ FARMER   Tarzan, though flesh and blood, woundable and killable, of certifiable and datable human ancestry, belongs to the heroes of old. He is like Melampus of Greek legend, who understood the language of the birds because a snake had licked his ears. Siegfried, or Sigurd, of the ancient Germanic legends, tasted the blood of the dragon he had slain, and he knew what the birds were saying. No claim, however, is made that Tarzan could speak with the birds. In fact, his biography has singularly few references to birds. Ska the vulture is most frequently mentioned, and he is no friend of Tarzan. The only other birds described are parrots, and these played villains.

Tarzan does not speak to birds for the simple reason that birds don't have language. Tarzan is legendary, but he also exists, and he is bound by the limitations of real existence. Thus, his communications are only with the higher, the greater brained, animals. And the higher the intelligence, the more the communication approaches the speech of man. The mangani were sentient, of course, and their language had strange, somewhat nonhuman sounds, due to the conformations of their oral cavities. But their language had a grammar. The gorillas, baboons, and other species of monkeys have no genuine linguistic ability, unlike the hominid mangani. It is true that Burroughs often interprets a dialog between Tarzan and the simians as if it were being conducted in proper English. But he makes it clear in more than one place that he is transmuting a simple system of signals into complex symbols for the reader's benefit.

> Philip José Farmer, *Tarzan Alive: A Definitive Biography of Lord Greystoke* (Garden City, NY: Doubleday, 1972), pp. 43–44

LESLIE A. FIEDLER   From the start, I believed it ⟨the Tarzan myth⟩ belonged to me, a small Jewish boy in Newark, N.J. appalled at the greyness of the urban world between the two Great Wars. It was a Green World I needed to dream of but not a pastoral or Arcadian one, which is to say, a world unremittingly green. No, it was a Darwinian world, one green in leaf, but red in fang and claw that the times and I demanded. And this Burroughs provided, aware somewhat that though, in his own heyday, the jurors at the Scopes Trial may have voted against evolution, the mass audience had decided otherwise. In the cities at least, Burroughs's Chicago, my Newark, no one could doubt the Struggle for Existence, the Survival of the Fittest, the bloody triumph of *homo sapiens* over the lesser beasts.

It is this triumph which Burroughs celebrates in the tale of Tarzan, making him the first Wild Man Saviour to have been suckled by a she-ape rather than a she-wolf. The latter had fostered mythic heroes from Romulus and Remus to the Mowgli of Kipling's *The Jungle Books;* but *On the Origin of Species* had persuaded Burroughs that apes are our closest kin. And the popular imagination had transformed them into our actual progenitors, twisting classical evolutionary theory just enough to suggest that our remotest ancestors have survived, and can be seen in the nearest zoo. Or better still, in their native habitat, the living past of "Africa." Taking his myth for fact, literal-minded readers are appalled by the mistakes Burroughs makes about the Dark Continent—especially about its fauna, or the languages spoken by its natives. But it is merely a convenient name for the absolute Elsewhere, where the pop Darwinian Jungle shelters Indian Tigers and African Lions side by side. And Burroughs relocated it, when he was so moved, in Sumatra, for instance, or the "Island of Uxmal," or the Center of the Earth: the imaginary womb of the Great Mother civilization has in fact sullied and raped.

Darwin alone, however, could not teach Burroughs to convert science to myth. This he learned from other tellers of tales, like Jack London and Kipling, for whom he has registered his admiration and gratitude. But a third great popular myth-maker, H. Rider Haggard, whom he does not mention, seems to me equally important for him. It was Haggard who first suggested the notion that in the preserved past of "Africa," a castaway from the present could reenact not only the victory of man over the beasts, but also the encounter of the male with the mystery of woman, the invention of eros.

> Leslie A. Fiedler, "Lord of the Absolute Elsewhere," *New York Times Book Review*, 9 June 1974, p. 8

IRWIN PORGES   Various theories have been advanced that Ed found his inspiration both for his stories of other planets and for the Tarzan idea in fictional works by well-known authors. He often insisted that in his adult years fiction held little interest for him, but had conceded that "as a boy and as a young man I read practically nothing else." The question of where he *might* have obtained his themes, especially for his earliest works, deserves examination.

In referring to an author whose novel features elements common to many stories of strange civilizations, Ed again stressed his reading habits: "I did read a part of Sir Arthur Conan Doyle's Lost World several years ago but never finished it for as a matter of fact I read practically no fiction although I remember that I was much impressed with the possibilities suggested by the story." Ed's "Under the Moons of Mars" (1911) predated *The Lost World* (1912) by one year; this very fact precluded any possibility of Ed's using Doyle's novel as a source. Moreover, any comparison of the two works reveals them as completely dissimilar. ⟨. . .⟩

On February 13, 1931, in a letter to the editor of *The Bristol Times*, Bristol, England, Ed replied to a statement accusing him of stealing his themes from the British writers Kipling, Wells, and Haggard. Ed tempered his reaction to the accusation by adding the phrase "unintentionally per-haps." After noting that "for some reason English reviewers have always been particularly unkind to me," Ed proceeded to a frank discussion of the authors: "To Mr. Kipling as to Mr. Haggard I owe a debt of gratitude for having stimulated my youthful imagination and this I gladly acknowledge, but Mr. Wells I have never read and consequently his stories of Mars could not have influenced me in any way."

> Irwin Porges, *Edgar Rice Burroughs: The Man Who Created Tarzan* (Provo, UT: Brigham Young University Press, 1975), pp. 128, 130

RICHARD LUPOFF   There is a mythic verity to the ⟨Martian⟩ stories, an aspect of utmost urgency and quite naive honesty, which gives the Martian cycle an appeal worlds beyond that of most stories of greater sophistication and control. These stories call out to the human psyche at a largely unconscious level, they call up the suppressed urges of the primitive man to take sword in hand and confront once and for all the vexatious world around him, they manipulate the most powerful of human archetypes.

A final assessment of the cycle finds it essentially an expression made with great honesty, or the strivings of a depressed and immature personality, to grow out of its infantile state and to achieve maturity and competence. As John Carter progresses from crawling infant to full manhood, so too does the personality of Edgar Rice Burroughs, with the Martian books providing a window upon Burroughs' psyche through which the reader observes this process.

Simultaneously the maturation of John Carter provides a mirror in which the reader sees his own struggle for maturity, responsibility and competence.

As the story ends with a renewal of John Carter's growth upon still another world, so the series suggests to the reader that the attainment of maturity is not the completion of the life-process, but the initiation of a new kind of growth and enlightenment.

Burroughs meant only to entertain. At least, he claimed as much. He achieved more than he set out to do.

> Richard Lupoff, *Barsoom: Edgar Rice Burroughs and the Martian Vision* (Baltimore: Mirage Press, 1976), pp. 154–55

BRIAN W. ALDISS   ERB's influence on magazine sf was extensive—greater than Wells's and less benevolent, greater than Lovecraft's and less disastrous. Since a whole central part of sf became more intellectual and questioning, the Burroughs syndrome has broken out anew into s-&-s, as its devotees call Sword-and-Sorcery—another urban escape route which bears the name Burroughs over its main exit. Better to have Burroughs than his imitators, no doubt.

He possessed a barbaric imagination. The gross simplification of having Julian and Orthis survive through generations would sink anything approaching Literature. But it serves for Myth, besides according well with

ERB's hazy notions of reincarnation and heredity. Such idiocies he often turns into strengths.

His remorseless worlds, with their grotesque cultures, their war-obsessed warriors, their steel-muscled heroes, and their women ever cowering before obnoxious intentions, do touch on a genuine lode of feeling. ERB was a railroad cop and an assistant in Sears Roebuck before making good with the first Barsoom novel in 1912. How common his brutal fantasies are to all cops, store assistants, and other respectable citizens, has been proved by the realities we have soldiered through since that date.

Brian W. Aldiss, "Burroughs: Less Lucid Than Lucian," This World and Nearer Ones: Essays Exploring the Familiar (London: Weidenfeld & Nicolson, 1979), pp. 199–200

ERLING B. HOLTSMARK   From the start of his writing career Burroughs was taken with the old idea that a counterworld existed at the center of our own earth. Although he certainly did not invent the notion, he worked with it in a series of "inner-world" novels beginning with *At the Earth's Core* in 1913 ⟨. . .⟩

A curious paradox emerges from a consideration of the conceptual underpinning of this novel. As an anti-world, Burroughs treats it in many ways as a prism through which are refracted institutions and practices on earth, to the detriment of the latter. Thus, where earth has water, Pellucidar has land, and vice versa, and this topographical antithesis parallels more interesting cultural antitheses. This world has developed along different evolutionary lines, and where earth holds reptiles in lowest esteem, in Pellucidar they are the ruling race. These Mahars, as they are called, indulge in practices that from the earthman's perspective are repugnant, but in fact are no different from what earthmen do vis-à-vis other living things that they, earthmen, consider inferior to themselves. And since mankind has progressed only to a Stone Age level in Pellucidar and are deemed of an inferior status by the Mahars, their treatment (which includes vivisection by Mahar scientists) by the Mahars is quite logical. ⟨. . .⟩

The narrative aspects of *At the Earth's Core* are pure Burroughs. Innes, the hero, falls in love with the primitive Dian the Beautiful, and sets off on a long quest in search of her after an abduction. On the way he makes friends with local primitives, fights gorillalike savages and a host of paleontological monsters, endures capture and makes escapes, and is finally reunited and married with Dian. The amatory element in the story is spiced up with the usual triangular complications (e.g., Jubal the Ugly and Hooja the Sly One), and Dian herself proves to be of royal blood among the tribe of Amoz, over whom her brother Dacor the Strong rules. The story moves at a swift pace, but is predictable; its general shape was to be recast on numerous occasions in subsequent stories featuring Tarzan, John Carter, Carson Napier, and others. In 1913 it was still fresh, but readers coming to it after the major works will find little of novelty.

Erling B. Holtsmark, *Edgar Rice Burroughs* (Boston: Twayne, 1986), pp. 76–78

BENJAMIN S. LAWSON   Burroughs furnished a ready escape from and predictable formulas in uncertain and stressful times. In so doing, he was able to establish, or at least popularize, major genres of "lowbrow" literature. "Burroughs turned the entire direction of science fiction from prophecy and sociology to romantic adventure, made the major market for such work the all-fiction pulp magazines, and became *the* major influence on the field through to 1934" ⟨Sam Moskowitz⟩. Soon to follow were the all-science fiction magazines of Hugo Gernsback and others. ⟨. . .⟩

In Burroughs's novels "a retreat to the primitive" and the simple, a "flight from urban culture and rational thought," comparable to Gaugin's, logically results from the threat of a congeries of forces at work early in the century: industrialization, the growth of big business and labor, urbanization, immigration, and imperialism. The American population had increased from about forty million to over ninety million between 1870 and 1910. Many new Americans—over a million a year, mainly new immigrants, during the peak years from 1900 to 1914—constituted a largely urban, cheap labor force that became the subject of both settlement-house reform and nativist attack (the midwestern evangelist Billy Sunday invaded American cities in 1912 to take on the devil on Satan's own immoral, foreign, liberal, clearly non-Protestant grounds). Industrial and technological change, the immigrant and his unfamiliar tenement world were strange to many Americans. Perhaps Brian Aldiss is exaggerating only a little in his conclusion that "the important thing for ERB and his devotees is a loathing of urban culture . . . and a mystical obsession with land, purity of blood, courage, leadership, and rape," and a preference for "women dragged away by their hair, sentries being killed barehanded, endless blood-letting, and inferior races breeding like rabbits." Ironically, Burroughs could cash in on these fantasies only in a modern American capitalist society.

In this spirit, John Carter's voyage is "a nostalgia trip to the past," to a Mars organized into tribal units, clans, or feudal monarchies. Violence is a way of life, and Carter achieves his purposes—usually the rescuing of Dejah Thoris—by killing hundreds of Martians. In *The Warlord of Mars,* he recalls fighting with his friend "through long, hot Martian days, as together we hewed down our enemies until the pile of corpses about us rose higher than a tall man's head." Only the physically fittest survive on an atavistic Mars "where bloody strife is the first and greatest consideration of individuals, nations, and races" (*A Princess of Mars*). The very flora and fauna of the planet are threatening, and Carter frequently credits his success to instincts over which his conscious mind has lost control. This reliance upon warfare as an answer to problems, this callous fascination with maiming described in the interminable and numerous battle scenes, makes the Mars series a sort of pornography of violence.

> Benjamin S. Lawson, "The Time and Place of Edgar Rice Burroughs's Early Martian Trilogy," *Extrapolation* 27, No. 3 (Fall 1986): 210–11

BRIAN STABLEFORD   *Tarzan of the Apes* is a curious celebration of Rousseauesque ideas about the nobility of the savage and the idea that a fundamentally virtuous human nature is routinely spoiled and perverted by cultural artifice. As a parable of the power of innocence, it has a considerable appeal to those individuals who feel most acutely the manifold constraints and petty injustices of life in civilized society. Many of those most afflicted by such stress are children, but anyone can identify with Tarzan who has felt the weariness of conformity with social norms and the frustrations of confrontation with cultural complexity. Tarzan is, however, more than just a mighty barbarian licensed by circumstance to do all the things we are physically and circumstantially prevented from doing: he has a *wholeness* which we have not. He has the heart of a lion and the mind of an aristocrat, *and the two are not in conflict.* In him, emotion and intellect, appetite and self-control, *id* and *superego,* are in perfect harmony. If he is out of place in high society, that is only because high society is not worthy of him: he is at home in the jungle not because he is bestial but because he is strong enough to subject the jungle to his ennobling influence, in becoming its rightful and acknowledged king.

The most lyrical passages in the Tarzan books describe the moments when Tarzan comes home to the jungle after a time in the civilized world, and celebrates his release. There is a similar critical moment in *The Son of Tarzan*, when Tarzan's son—who has been brought up to be properly civilized—is forced by circumstance to discover his true self in that same jungle. This is the ultimate liberation which the Tarzan books offer their readers: not simply the joy of casting off all the shackles of civilization, but the promise that when that is done, *you will find yourself at home*. Perhaps Tarzan's jungle is a perverse Utopia, but it is a Utopia nevertheless. It is an unpeaceful Garden of Eden where the lion will never lie down with the lamb, nor can he ever be expected to. It is a paradise for the adventurous, who would be bored to tears in Heaven. Many adults deem this a childish idea, and it is perfectly understandable that no one but a child is likely to be sufficiently unselfconscious to confess that his idea of the good life involves the freedom to slaughter human and animal villains on a massive scale; but if we were honest, there would probably be few among us who could claim to be entirely unafflicted by fantasies of doing violence—often extreme and ingenious violence—to those who annoy and frustrate us in the thousand trivial ways which everyday life permits and necessitates.

Brian Stableford, "Yesterday's Bestsellers, 5: Edgar Rice Burroughs and Tarzan of the Apes," Interzone No. 51 (September–October 1991): 50–51

⊠ *Bibliography*

Tarzan of the Apes. 1914.
The Return of Tarzan. 1915.
The Beasts of Tarzan. 1916.
The Son of Tarzan. 1917.
A Princess of Mars. 1917.
The Gods of Mars. 1918.
Tarzan and the Jewels of Opar. 1918.
The Warlord of Mars. 1919.
Jungle Tales of Tarzan. 1919.
Thuvia, Maid of Mars. 1920.

Tarzan the Untamed. 1920.

Tarzan the Terrible. 1921.

The Mucker. 1921, 1922 (as *The Mucker* and *The Man without a Soul*; 2 vols.).

The Chessmen of Mars. 1922.

At the Earth's Core. 1922.

Pellucidar: A Sequel to At the Earth's Core. 1923.

Tarzan and the Golden Lion. 1923.

The Girl from Hollywood. 1923.

The Land That Time Forgot. 1924.

Tarzan and the Ant Men. 1924.

The Eternal Lover. 1925.

The Bandit of Hell's Bend. 1925.

The Cave Girl. 1925.

The Moon Maid. 1926.

The Mad King. 1926.

The Tarzan Twins. 1927.

The Outlaw of Tarn. 1927.

The War Chief. 1927.

The Master Mind of Mars: Being a Tale of Weird and Wonderful Happenings on the Red Planet. 1928.

Tarzan, Lord of the Jungle. 1928.

The Monster Men. 1929.

Tarzan and the Lost Empire. 1929.

Tarzan at the Earth's Core. 1930.

Tanar of Pellucidar. 1930.

A Fighting Man of Mars. 1931.

Tarzan the Invincible. 1931.

Tarzan Triumphant. 1932.

Jungle Girl. 1932.

Tarzan and the City of Gold. 1933.

Apache Devil. 1933.

Tarzan and the Lion Man. 1934.

Pirates of Venus. 1934.

Tarzan and the Leopard Men. 1935.

Lost on Venus. 1935.

Swords of Mars. 1936.

Tarzan and the Tarzan Twins, with Jad-Bal-Ja, the Golden Lion. 1936.

Tarzan's Quest. 1936.

Back to the Stone Age. 1937.

The Oakdale Affair; The Rider. 1937.

Tarzan and the Forbidden City. 1938.

The Lad and the Lion. 1938.

Carson of Venus. 1939.

Official Guide to the Tarzan Clans of America. 1939.

Tarzan the Magnificent. 1939.

Synthetic Men of Mars. 1940.

The Deputy Sheriff of Comanche County. 1940.

Land of Terror. 1944.

Escape on Venus. 1946.

Tarzan and "The Foreign Legion." 1947.

Llana of Gathol. 1948.

Beyond Thirty. 1955, 1963 (as *The Lost Continent*).

The Man-Eater. 1955.

Savage Pellucidar. 1963.

Beyond the Farthest Star. 1964.

Tales of Three Planets. 1964.

Tarzan and the Madman. 1964.

Tarzan and the Castaways. 1964.

John Carter of Mars. 1964.

The Girl from Farris's. 1965.

The Efficiency Expert. 1966.

I Am a Barbarian. 1967.

The Wizard of Venus. 1970.

Pirate Blood. 1970.

Sir Arthur Conan Doyle
1859–1930

ARTHUR CONAN DOYLE was born on May 22, 1859, in Edinburgh. He was educated at Hodder and Stonyhurst academies and the University of Edinburgh, where he studied medicine. In 1880–81 he traveled to the Arctic and to West Africa as a ship's surgeon. He began a medical practice the next year at Southsea. In 1885 he married Louise Hawkins; they had two children.

Doyle had begun writing while in medical school in the 1870s but took to it in earnest during the early years of his medical practice, when he had few patients. In 1891 he was able to abandon medicine for full-time writing because of the popularity of his Sherlock Holmes tales. In 1894 Doyle made an extensive lecture tour of the United States, and he also visited Switzerland and Egypt in an attempt to relieve his wife's tuberculosis. He attempted to enlist for combat duty in the Boer War in 1899 but was rejected because of his age; he instead served as a medical officer and also wrote several books about the conflict. In 1902, largely in recognition of his services in defending England's role in the war, he was knighted.

The Sherlock Holmes saga had begun in 1887 with the short novel *A Study in Scarlet* in *Beeton's Christmas Annual* (published as a book the following year) and attained immediate popularity. Many subsequent tales were published in the *Strand* and were eventually collected in five volumes of short stories (*The Adventures of Sherlock Holmes*, 1892; *The Memoirs of Sherlock Holmes*, 1894; *The Return of Sherlock Holmes*, 1905; *His Last Bow*, 1917; *The Case-Book of Sherlock Holmes*, 1927) and three additional novels (*The Sign of Four*, 1890; *The Hound of the Baskervilles*, 1902; *The Valley of Fear*, 1915). Doyle, having wearied of Holmes, had killed him off in the final story of the *Memoirs*, but public outrage forced him to bring Holmes back to life for further adventures. As Poe had done with "The Mystery of Marie Rogêt," Doyle employed the ratiocinative methods he attributed to his detective in solving two real cases—those of George Edalji and Oscar Slater, both of which he wrote up in articles and books.

Doyle both became a significant forerunner of science fiction and achieved popularity with a series of works involving an eccentric scientist, Professor Challenger: the short novels *The Lost World* (1912), *The Poison Belt* (1913), and *The Land of Mist* (1926), and some short stories. The first of these is perhaps the most notable, as Challenger goes to South America and comes upon still-living dinosaurs in the depths of the jungle. In 1925 *The Lost World* was made into a highly successful silent film noted for its use of special effects. *The Maracot Deep* (1929) can also qualify as science fiction in its account of a trip to the ocean floor.

Doyle, however, considered his most serious work to be his historical novels, beginning with *Micah Clarke* (1889) and continuing with *The White Company* (1891), *Sir Nigel* (1906), and others. Doyle conducted scrupulous historical research in the writing of these novels. He wrote many short stories of sport, medicine, the supernatural (including the celebrated "Lot No. 249"), and adventure.

Louise Doyle, who had been an invalid during the last decade of her life, died in 1906. Doyle had since 1897 maintained a platonic relationship with Jean Leckie, and he married her in 1907; they had three children. Early in World War I Doyle was sent by the government to Italy on a mission, and throughout the war he wrote a history of the conflict, ultimately published in six volumes.

The horrors of the war turned Doyle from an agnostic into a spiritualist, and he began vigorously preaching the cause on tours throughout the world. He joined the Society for Psychical Research, established the Psychic Book-shop in London, and held séances in the homes of various illustrious people. He persisted in this interest in spite of the considerable amount of ridicule he suffered as a result of it. Sir Arthur Conan Doyle died on July 7, 1930.

▦ *Critical Extracts*

ARTHUR BARTLETT MAURICE   In *The Poison Belt*, as in *The Lost World* of a year or so ago, Sir Arthur Conan Doyle has found expression in the singular personality of Professor George Edward Challenger. The name itself is diagnostic. From the beginning the huge beard of the strange violent scientist bristles, and the hoarse bellowing voice booms out. These last two stories have been less telling of tales than the illumination of a character in which the author seems to find particular delight. Yet this character is too artificial, too much builded up of complexities, to be entirely convincing. In the Doyle portrait gallery he is hardly worthy of a place with Sherlock Holmes, with the Brigadier Gerard, with Sir Nigel Loring, or with the delightful Sir Charles Tregellis. His proper place is behind the counterfeit presentment of the well-meaning but monotonous Dr. Watson. That he is even there is due to the fact that his creator under all conditions is an accomplished literary workman. In less practiced and dexterous hands Challenger would be a rank absurdity. Another point. There was a suggestion of the character in an earlier tale by Conan Doyle. In many ways Challenger is a reincarnation of that singular evil genius who haunted the pages of the *Stark-Munro Letters*.

The story of *The Poison Belt* is entertaining but inconsequential. ⟨. . .⟩ It all depends whether the tale is of a kind that appeals to the reader. If it does he is assured of an authorship which, despite the amazing extent of its popularity, has never received its full meed of serious consideration.

Arthur Bartlett Maurice, [Review of *The Poison Belt*], *Bookman* (New York) 38, No. 3 (November 1913): 299–300

JOHN LAMOND   *The Lost World* is an example of Sir Arthur's creative genius in a field that until his time had not been explored. Swift, in his *Gulliver's Travels*, certainly discovered countries that existed only in his imagination and created characters and situations that had an ironical resemblance to the political conditions of his time, and which therefore gave to his tales a lively interest for his contemporaries which escapes the modern reader. Still, even by the modern reader, Gulliver's adventures are followed with zest. In *The Lost World* there is no effort to parallel existing political conditions. It is an attempt to reconstruct the world of prehistoric times, when the dinosaur and the pterodactyl were the dominant animals, and when man, if he lived at all, must have occupied a very subordinate position. "The Lost World" existed somewhere in South America on an elevated plateau at a considerable distance from one of the affluents of the Amazon, and certainly remote from the ordinary routes of the modern traveller.

It was a Professor Challenger who maintained against all opponents that this "Lost World" existed, and it was to prove the existence of this world that an expedition was undertaken in which various characters took part, and who again figure in one of Conan Doyle's later psychic books, *The Land of Mist*. This Professor Challenger was one of his favourite characters, and in his private conversation he often alluded to him. The simple truth is that there was a good part of Professor Challenger in Conan Doyle himself when in one of his iconoclastic moods. Not that he ever gave way to the extravagances that are depicted on the part of his hero, but rather it was the masterful personality of Challenger that was reflected in himself when Challenger was ready to face the world in defence of truth, and when he would brook no opposition to the promulgation of his beliefs. The description of the land of the pterodactyl is a *tour de force* on the part of the author, in which his creative imagination had full scope, and becomes so realistic that the reader for the time being is actually living in that extraordinary country with its ceaseless adventures and hair-breadth escapes. The book is an example of Conan Doyle's masterful handling of an entirely new subject, and an indication of what he might have continued to produce in literary form had not other interests monopolised his energies.

John Lamond, *Arthur Conan Doyle: A Memoir* (London: John Murray, 1931), pp. 110–12

SAM MOSKOWITZ   A. Conan Doyle was determined to build for himself a reputation in science fiction as great as the one that caused him to be canonized by detective story lovers. When *The Lost World* appeared it seemed that it was almost within his ability to accomplish that feat. Though the basic idea ⟨. . .⟩ was unabashedly inspired by Verne's *A Journey to the Center of the Earth*, the superior elements of characterization, humor, and pace that Doyle added to the idea set it distinctly apart. ⟨. . .⟩

Superb characterization, coupled with fine humor and good science, lifted *The Lost World* above the level of the average adventure story. As a result, the novel was an instant success and new editions began to multiply. The following year, 1913, *The Poison Belt*, "being an account of another amazing adventure of Professor Challenger," began in *The Strand* for April.

This novel has always been overshadowed by the fame of *The Lost World*, but it is outstanding in its own right. For this story, Doyle borrowed again from Edgar Allan Poe, enlarging on the idea presented in "The Conversation of Eiros and Charmion": the atmosphere of the earth is "poisoned" by a change resulting from conditions in outer space. In this novel, Challenger, foreseeing catastrophe, gathers his wife and the three companions of his previous adventure in an airtight room in his home. There, sustained by containers of oxygen, they watch the entire world come to a catastrophic stop. The penetrating British humor stands up even across the gulf of the years. As they prepare for the hour of doom, Challenger turns to his manservant, and says, quite calmly, "I'm expecting the end of the world today, Austin."

"Yes, sir," the servant replies. "What time, sir?"

Doyle strikes a telling blow at the theory of the survival of the fittest when he permits the only person in all London apparently still alive to be an asthmatic old woman, who thought she was having an attack when the character of the atmosphere began to change and fed herself oxygen out of a container she kept at her bedside for emergencies.

The philosophical description of the world's extermination provided by Doyle is worth repeating. Speaking through Challenger's lips he says:

> You will conceive a bunch of grapes which are covered by some
> infinitesimal but noxious bacillus. The gardener passes it through
> a disinfecting medium. It may be that he desires his grapes to be
> cleaner. It may be that he needs space to breed some fresh
> bacillus less noxious than the last. He dips it into the poison and
> they are gone. Our gardener is, in my opinion, about to dip the
> solar system, and the human bacillus, the little mortal vibrio
> which twisted and wiggled upon the outer rind of the earth, will
> in an instant be sterilized and out of existence.

The Lost World and The Poison Belt provided evidence that Doyle had it in him to be one of the greatest science fiction writers of all time.

Sam Moskowitz, "Arthur Conan Doyle: A Study in Science Fiction," *Explorers of the Infinite: Shapers of Science Fiction* (Cleveland: World Publishing Co., 1963), pp. 165–68

JOHN DICKSON CARR   When he was still plain Dr. Conan Doyle, a struggling young physician at Portsmouth on the south coast of England, he wrote his first venture into science fiction for the *Cornhill Magazine* during the early 1880's. A short story called "Habakkuk Jephson's

Statement," it dealt with what still remains one of the great sea mysteries: the problem of the derelict ship *Mary Celeste*, found drifting with not a soul aboard and few clews as to what fate could have overtaken her crew. ⟨...⟩

Several times in later years Conan Doyle returned to the short story of science fiction. One such tale, if this can be credited, is a comedy of the electric chair at a time when electricity constituted a new means of execution. A mining town in the American Old West, determined on being progressive, sets up an electric chair as a deterrent to evildoers.

But when they try it out on a notorious bad man who deserves death ten times over ("Touch her off!" roars the desperado, sitting down), something goes wrong. They jolt the victim with too much electricity; far from killing him according to plan, they succeed only in curing his rheumatism and making him all but deathless. The execution, to the joy of all humane people, must be indefinitely postponed; and so ends "The Los Amigos Fiasco."

With "The Horror of the Heights," a grim and grisly affair, Conan Doyle envisaged perils which might lurk in the upper air; and, though today we travel such sky lanes without a tremor of fear, the author's extrapolation was valid at the time he wrote it. In "Danger!" he warned of the German submarine menace before this menace became a terrible reality during World War I.

But it was with his novels, and with a set of characters as engaging as Dumas's musketeers, that he took his rightful place in the hierarchy of the scientific romance. ⟨...⟩

As his inspiration for Sherlock Holmes had been one of his professors at Edinburgh University—Joseph Bell, the surgeon—so as his model for the protagonist of *The Lost World* he chose another Edinburgh teacher—Professor Rutherford, the zoologist, a stunted Hercules with a booming voice and a black beard like an Assyrian bull. ⟨...⟩

His creator was really fond of Challenger, the explosive one; he enjoyed Challenger more than any character he had ever created. He would imitate Challenger for the edification of family and friends. He had himself photographed as Challenger, decked out with false beard and adhesive eyebrows. In his Challenger get-up, acting to the top of his bent, he once called on his brother-in-law, Willie Hornung, and precipitated family trouble when Willie penetrated his disguise.

John Dickson Carr, "Introduction," *The Maracot Deep* by Sir Arthur Conan Doyle (New York: Modern Promotions, [1965]), pp. 8–11

CHARLES HIGHAM   The book ⟨*The Lost World*⟩ is a masterpiece of imaginative fiction, reminiscent of Jules Verne but not suffering from the comparison. After the funny and grotesque opening, the arrival at the Amazon basin is wonderfully described. When the travelers enter the jungle, we are reminded of the journeys of Darwin:

> During the hot hours of the day only the full drone of insects, like
> the beat of a distant surf, filled the air, while nothing moved amid
> the solemn vistas of stupendous trunks, fading away into the
> darkness which held us.

The vault of interlacing leaves, the emerald river, the black-velvet chittering monkeys and green-eyed pumas, the brilliantly colored wings of birds—the vision of the wilderness brings out the poet in Conan Doyle, while the long, dreamlike, thrusting journey to the mysterious lost plateau excites the adventurer in him.

Gradually, the romantic image of forest and stream changes into a nightmare; we move from Hudson and Rousseau to Dante and Doré as we see the rookery of pterodactyls, with their red eyes and flapping spined wings, their yellow eggs and disgusting fetid odor. The tortured cry of an iguanodon echoes through the forest; ape men dart among the trees; a huge toadlike face stares through the leaves; and the night has the flat, static terror of a drug-induced hallucination:

> I stood and glared with starting eyes down the moonlit path
> which lay behind me. All was quiet as in a dream landscape.
> Silver clearings and the black patches of the bushes—nothing else
> could I see. Then, from out of the silence, imminent and
> threatening, there came once more that low throaty croaking. . . .

The story is humanized by the fantastic bitter humor of the explorers, scoring points off each other as though in a London club; and the climax at the Queen's Hall reaches extraordinary heights of comedy and terror. As Professor Challenger delivers his lecture, he presents a mysterious box:

> "Come then, pretty, pretty!" [he said] in a coaxing voice.
>   An instant later, with a scratching, rattling sound, a most
> horrible and loathsome creature appeared from below and perched
> itself upon the side of the case. Even the unexpected fall of the
> Duke of Durham into the orchestra, which occurred at that
> moment, could not distract the petrified attention of the vast
> audience.

The Duke of Durham's mishap is, of course, the master touch; the incongruous note of farce makes the apparition of the monster all the more unsettling. As the pterodactyl flaps around the hall, with its putrid odor and its hump-backed, shawled look, it is like a devil returned from the black past to terrorize London. Later, it appears before a sentry like a demon flying across the moon. The crowd outside, stretched from the Langham Hotel to Oxford Circus, recovers from its panic to cheer the explorers in triumph. But there is a twist in the tail, typical of Conan Doyle's sardonic wit. Malone had been impelled to accompany the expedition largely because a certain challenging young woman wanted to see him prove himself as a hero and man of adventure. He rushes off to her house in Streatham to claim her, as a knight would claim his lady, and is horrified to discover she is married to a mediocre solicitor's clerk who has never been anywhere.

Charles Higham, *The Adventures of Conan Doyle* (New York: W. W. Norton, 1976), pp. 235–36

RONALD PEARSALL   *The Poison Belt* was Doyle's second novel of the 'what would happen if . . .?' type and was one of many to reflect a mood of apprehension arising from the probability of European war. The threat was cosmic rather than localized, as with William le Queux's novel, serialized in the *Daily Mail*, dealing with the 'horrid and thrilling invasion' of London by the Germans. With *The Lost World*, Doyle had in mind a mixed readership of children and adults, very clear from his dedication:

> I have wrought my simple plan,
> If I bring one hour of joy,
> To the boy who's half a man
> Or the man who's half a boy.

Presumably *The Poison Belt* had the same audience in mind. The world passes through a noxious gas, and all living things die. The first symptoms are personality disorders, with men and women acting out of character, and Challenger, by means of spectrum analysis, anticipates the disaster; he and his friends hole up in an airtight room in his house, supplied with oxygen. Eventually the oxygen runs out, and, philosophically, they unseal the room to meet their death. But the poison belt has passed on, leaving the planet clear. They motor to London through scenes of disaster, meeting one old lady who has oxygen to keep her alive, but otherwise everyone is dead.

Intensely depressed, they return to Challenger's home in the country, but suddenly a carthorse begins to move, golfers continue golfing, children continue playing, and the chauffeur rubs his eyes and carries on hosing the car, oblivious of the time that has elapsed. Death was a form of catalepsy.

This theme has furnished material for innumerable science-fiction stories and films. Doyle was at his best when describing the scenes of disaster, fires burning, trains crashing, and he succeeds in evoking the claustrophobic feeling of the airtight room, with the occupants aware that their oxygen supply is running out. One of the most interesting episodes concerns the quartet's facing of death, and for the first time in his novels Doyle's inner preoccupation with life after death comes to the fore as propaganda. The mouthpiece is Challenger, and for the purpose he goes into a dreamy monotone that is decidedly out of character: 'Nature may build a beautiful door and hang it with many a gauzy and shimmering curtain to make an entrance to the new life for our wandering souls.' He addresses the sceptical Summerlee, claiming that he was 'too great a thing to end in mere physical constituents, a packet of salts and three bucketfuls of water'. In case the reader has failed to get the message, Challenger returns to it soon afterwards:

> As to the body, we do not mourn over the parings of our nails
> nor the cut locks of our hair, though they were once part of
> ourselves. Neither does a one-legged man yearn sentimentally over
> his missing member. The physical body has rather been a source
> of pain and fatigue to us. It is the constant index of our
> limitations. Why then should we worry about its detachment from
> our psychical selves?

Ronald Pearsall, *Conan Doyle: A Biographical Solution* (New York: St. Martin's Press, 1977), pp. 132–34

JAMES L. CAMPBELL   Published in 1929, a year before Doyle's death, *The Maracot Deep* is based on two literary themes, the wonderful journey and the wonderful discovery. Shaped in part by the Atlantis myth and by Doyle's doctrine of the accretion of matter and decline of spirit, it is a pale remake of *The Lost World*. Instead of the discovery of a lost civilization on a plateau in the Amazon basin, the story describes the discovery of a lost civilization at the bottom of the Atlantic. The three

principal characters are patterned on the Challenger characters, but less
well defined. Dr. Maracot resembles Challenger; Cyrus Headley is an Ameri-
canized blend of Malone and Summerlee; and Bill Scanlan, with his American working-class slang evocative of the novels of John Dos Passos or James
T. Farrell, is a proletarian Lord John Roxton. ⟨. . .⟩

The focus of the novel is the ancient Atlantean civilization, rather than
the culture of its modern descendants. Here the moral failure that caused
ancient Atlantis to decline before the catastrophe is most important. Such
information is given to the Maracot group by a telepathic cinema. The
historical narrative projected via telepathy—more specifically, the moral
and ethical values in the story of the catastrophe—shapes the novel, giving
it power and meaning. As ancient Atlantis becomes a great world power
and as its superior technology and materialistic sciences make it the first
nation among many, a spiritual and moral decline sets in that greatly under-
mines the quality of its civilization. Despite attempts to reform the society
and reverse its moral decline, nothing can avert the coming disaster. As
Doyle's narrator says, with his eye fixed on twentieth-century civilization,
Atlantis is an example of what can happen to a state when its intellect
outruns its soul. That is what destroyed Atlantean civilization, and it may
yet be the ruin of our own.

James L. Campbell, "Sir Arthur Conan Doyle," *Science Fiction Writers*, ed. E. F.
Bleiler (New York: Charles Scribner's Sons, 1982), p. 49

DANA MARTIN BATORY   Of the five adventures constituting
the Challenger Chronicles ⟨"When the World Screamed"⟩ is the strangest
and most erotic.

The seminal idea can be traced back to French astronomer Camille
Flammarion (1842–1925), who put forward one of the first schemes of
digging a shaft deep into the Earth for scientific purposes. He sketched out
his proposal in an article, "A Hole through the Earth," in the September
1909 issue of the *Strand Magazine*.

Professor Challenger, after long conversation, has concluded that "the
world upon which we live is itself a living organism, endowed . . . with a
circulation, a respiration, and a nervous system of its own . . . It is quite
unaware of this fungus growth of vegetation and evolution of tiny animalcules
which has collected upon it during its travels round the sun as barnacles

gather upon the ancient vessel. That is the present state of affairs, and that is what I propose to alter."

But Doyle's story is far more than just a simple tale of science: it's also a lascivious account of one man's search for the ultimate in copulation.

The Professor's plan is to dig "by every known species of drill, borer, crusher, and explosive" to the Earth's highly sensitive inner membrane and then to plunge a drill into it.

"But it is essential," says Peerless Jones, expert artesian well engineer, "that you should let me know what soil the drill is to penetrate. Sand, or clay, or chalk, would each need different treatment."

"Let us say jelly," answers Challenger. "Yes, we will for the present suppose that you have to sink your drill into jelly." Scholar, ex-sailor, and man-of-the-world, Doyle was well aware that "jelly" was contemporary slang for a buxom, good-looking girl. ⟨. . .⟩

The tale reverberates with psychosexual overtones and connotations that would later be called Freudian. Professor Challenger, through Jones, the peerless surrogate lover, with no consideration or compassion toward his partner's feelings, has surpassed every man's libidinous dream of coition. Pain, violence, force are the images that come to the forefront.

These elements of the story, I hasten to add, do not reflect Doyle's personal behavior, but rather served as a catharsis—an elimination of some complex (or hang-up, as we would say) by bringing it to consciousness and giving it expression.

Dana Martin Batory, "The Climax of 'When the World Screamed,' " *Riverside Quarterly* 8, No. 2 (March 1988): 124, 127–28

▦ *Bibliography*

A Study in Scarlet. 1888.

The Mystery of Cloomber. 1889.

Micah Clarke. 1889.

Mysteries and Adventures ⟨*The Gully of Bluemansdyke and Other Stories*⟩. 1889, 1893 (as *My Friend the Murderer and Other Mysteries and Adventures*).

The Captain of the Polestar and Other Tales ⟨*The Great Keinplatz Experiment and Other Stories*⟩. 1890.

The Firm of Girdlestone: A Romance of the Unromantic. 1890.

The Sign of Four. 1890.

The White Company. 1891. 3 vols.

The Doings of Raffles Haw. 1892.

The Adventures of Sherlock Holmes. 1892.

The Great Shadow. 1892.

The Refugees: A Tale of Two Continents. 1893. 3 vols.

The Great Shadow and Beyond the City. 1893.

Jane Annie; or, The Good Conduct Prize (with J. M. Barrie). 1893.

The Memoirs of Sherlock Holmes. 1894.

An Actor's Duel and The Winning Shot. 1894.

Round the Red Lamp: Being Facts and Fancies of Medical Life. 1894.

The Parasite. 1894.

The Stark Munro Letters. 1895.

The Exploits of Brigadier Gerard. 1896.

Rodney Stone. 1896.

Uncle Bernac: A Memory of the Empire. 1897.

The Tragedy of Korosko ⟨A Desert Drama⟩. 1898.

Songs of Action. 1898.

A Duet with an Occasional Chorus. 1899.

The Green Flag and Other Stories of War and Sport. 1900.

The Great Boer War. 1900, 1901, 1902.

The Immortal Memory. 1901.

The War in South Africa: Its Cause and Conflict. 1902.

The Hound of the Baskervilles: Another Adventure of Sherlock Holmes. 1902.

Works (Author's Edition). 1903. 13 vols.

The Adventures of Gerard. 1903.

A Duet (A Duologue). 1903.

The Return of Sherlock Holmes. 1905.

The Fiscal Question: Treated in a Series of Three Speeches. 1905.

An Incursion into Diplomacy. 1906.

Sir Nigel. 1906.

The Croxley Master: A Great Tale of the Prize Ring. 1907.

Waterloo. 1907.

The Story of George Edalji. 1907.

Through the Magic Door. 1907.

Round the Fire Stories. 1908.

The Crime of the Congo. 1909.

Divorce Law Reform: An Essay. 1909.

Songs of the Road. 1911.

Why He Is Now in Favour of Home Rule. 1911.

The Last Galley: Impressions and Tales. 1911.

The Case of Oscar Slater. 1912.

The Speckled Band: An Adventure of Sherlock Holmes. 1912.

The Lost World. 1912.

The Poison Belt. 1913.

The Adventure of the Dying Detective. 1913.

Divorce and the Church (with Lord Hugh Cecil). 1913.

Civilian National Reserve. 1914.

Great Britain and the Next War. 1914.

To Arms! 1914.

The World War Conspiracy: Germany's Long Drawn Plot against England. 1914.

In Quest of Truth (with H. Stansbury). 1914.

The German War. 1914.

Western Wanderings. 1915.

The Valley of Fear. 1915.

The Outlook on the War. 1915.

An Appreciation of Sir John French. 1916.

A Petition to the Prime Minister on Behalf of Roger Casement. 1916.

A Visit to Three Fronts: June 1916. 1916.

The British Campaign in France and Flanders. 1916–20 (6 vols.), 1928 (as *The British Campaigns in Europe 1914–1918*).

Supremacy of the British Soldier. 1917.

His Last Bow: Some Reminiscences of Sherlock Holmes. 1917.

The New Revelation. 1918.

Danger! and Other Stories. 1918.

The Vital Message. 1919.

The Guards Came Through and Other Poems. 1919.

Our Reply to the Cleric. 1920.

"The Truth of Spiritualism" (with Joseph McCabe). 1920.

Spiritualism and Rationalism: With a Drastic Examination of Mr. Joseph M'Cabe. 1920.

The Wanderings of a Spiritualist. 1921.

D. D. Home: His Life and Mission by Mrs. Douglas Home (editor). 1921.

[*Sherlock Holmes* (with William Gillette). 1922.]

The Poems: Collected Edition. 1922.

Tales of the Ring and Camp. 1922.

Tales of Pirates and Blue Water. 1922.

Tales of Terror and Mystery. 1922.

Tales of Twilight and the Unseen. 1922.

Tales of Adventure and Medical Life. 1922.

Tales of Long Ago. 1922.

The Coming of the Fairies. 1922.

Spiritualism—Some Straight Questions and Direct Answers. 1922.

The Case for Spirit Photography (with others). 1922.

Three of Them: A Reminiscence. 1923.

Our American Adventure. 1923.

Our Second American Adventure. 1924.

Memories and Adventures. 1924.

The Spiritualists' Reader (editor). 1924.

The Mystery of Joan of Arc by Léon Denis (translator). 1924.

The Early Christian Church and Modern Spiritualism. 1925.

Psychic Experiences. 1925.

The Land of Mist. 1926.

The History of Spiritualism. 1926. 2 vols.

Pheneas Speaks: Direct Spirit Communications in the Family Circle. 1927.

The Case-Book of Sherlock Holmes. 1927.

Spiritualism. c. 1927.

What Does Spiritualism Actually Teach and Stand For? 1928.

A Word of Warning. 1928.

Sherlock Holmes: The Complete Short Stories. 1928.

An Open Letter to Those of My Generation. 1929.

Our African Winter. 1929.

The Roman Catholic Church: A Rejoinder. 1929.

The Maracot Deep and Other Stories. 1929.

The Conan Doyle Stories. 1929.

Sherlock Holmes: The Complete Long Stories. 1929.

The Edge of the Unknown. 1930.

Works (Crowborough Edition). 1930. 24 vols.

The Conan Doyle Historical Romances. 1931–32. 2 vols.

The Field Bazaar. 1934.

The Professor Challenger Stories. 1952.

The Complete Napoleonic Stories. 1956.

The Crown Diamond: An Evening with Sherlock Holmes. 1958.

Great Stories. Ed. John Dickson Carr. 1959.

Strange Studies from Life: Containing Three Hitherto Uncollected Tales. Ed. Peter Ruber. 1963.

The Annotated Sherlock Holmes. Ed. William S. Baring-Gould. 1967. 2 vols.

My Life with Sherlock Holmes: Conversations in Baker Street. Ed. J. R. Hamilton. 1968.

The Complete Adventures and Memoirs of Sherlock Holmes: A Facsimile of the Original Strand Magazine *Stories 1891–1893*. 1975.

The Hound of the Baskervilles: A Facsimile of the Adventure as It Was First Published in the Strand Magazine, *London*. 1975.

The Return of Sherlock Holmes: A Facsimile of the Adventure as It Was First Published in the Strand Magazine, *London*. 1975.

Sherlock Holmes: The Published Apocrypha (with others). Ed. Jack Tracy. 1980.

Best Science Fiction. Ed. Charles G. Waugh and Martin H. Greenberg. 1981.

Uncollected Stories. Ed. John Michael Gibson and Richard Lancelyn Green. 1982.

Essays on Photography. Ed. John Michael Gibson and Richard Lancelyn Green. 1982.

The Uncollected Sherlock Holmes. Ed. Richard Lancelyn Green. 1983.

Letters to the Press. Ed. John Michael Gibson and Richard Lancelyn Green. 1986.

Aldous Huxley
1894–1963

ALDOUS LEONARD HUXLEY was born on July 6, 1894, in Godalming, Surrey. He came from a family of distinguished scientists and writers: his grandfather was Thomas Henry Huxley, the great proponent of evolution, and his brother was Julian Sorrell Huxley, who became a leading biologist. Aldous attended the Hillside School in Godalming and then entered Eton in 1908, but he was forced to leave in 1910 when he developed a serious eye disease that left him temporarily blind. In 1913 he partially regained his sight and entered Balliol College, Oxford.

Around 1915 Huxley became associated with a circle of writers and intellectuals who gathered at Lady Ottoline Morell's home, Garsington Manor House, near Oxford; here he met T. S. Eliot, Bertrand Russell, Osbert Sitwell, and other figures. After working briefly in the War Office, Huxley graduated from Balliol in 1918 and the next year began teaching at Eton. He was, however, not a success there and decided to become a journalist. Moving to London with his wife Maria Nys, a Belgian refugee whom he had met at Garsington and married in 1919, Huxley wrote articles and reviews for the *Athenaeum* under the pseudonym Autolycus.

Huxley's first two volumes were collections of poetry, but it was his early novels—*Crome Yellow* (1921), *Antic Hay* (1923), and *Those Barren Leaves* (1925)—that brought him to prominence. By 1925 he had also published three volumes of short stories and two volumes of essays. In 1923 Huxley and his wife and son moved to Europe, where they traveled widely in France, Spain, and Italy. A journey around the world in 1925–26 led to the travel book *Jesting Pilate* (1926), just as a later trip to Central America produced *Beyond the Mexique Bay* (1934). *Point Counter Point* (1928) was hailed as a landmark in its incorporation of musical devices into the novel form. Huxley developed a friendship with D. H. Lawrence, and from 1926 until Lawrence's death in 1930 Huxley spent much time looking after him; in 1932 he edited Lawrence's letters.

In 1930 Huxley purchased a small house in Sanary, in southern France. It was here that he wrote one of his most celebrated volumes, *Brave New World* (1932), a negative utopia or "dystopia" that depicted a nightmarish vision of the future in which science and technology are used to suppress human freedom.

Huxley became increasingly concerned about the state of civilization as Europe lurched toward war in the later 1930s: he openly espoused pacifism and (in part through the influence of his friend Gerald Heard) grew increasingly interested in mysticism and Eastern philosophy. These tendencies were augmented when he moved to southern California in 1937. With Heard and Christopher Isherwood, Huxley formed the Vedanta Society of Southern California, and his philosophy was embodied in such volumes as *The Perennial Philosophy* (1945) and *Heaven and Hell* (1956).

During World War II Huxley worked as a scenarist in Hollywood, writing the screenplays for such notable films as *Pride and Prejudice* (1941) and *Jane Eyre* (1944). This experience led directly to Huxley's second futuristic novel, *Ape and Essence* (1948), a misanthropic portrait of a postholocaust society written in the form of a screenplay.

In California Huxley associated with Buddhist and Hindu groups, and in the 1950s he experimented with hallucinogenic drugs such as LSD and mescalin, which he wrote about in *The Doors of Perception* (1954). *Brave New World Revisited* (1958), a brief treatise that discusses some of the implications of his earlier novel, continues to be very pessimistic about the future of society, particularly in the matters of overpopulation and the threat of totalitarianism. But in *Island* (1962)—the manuscript of which Huxley managed to save when a brush fire destroyed his home and many of his papers in 1961—he presents a positive utopia in which spirituality is developed in conjunction with technology.

Late in life Huxley received many honors, including an award from the American Academy of Letters in 1959 and election as a Companion of Literature of the British Royal Society of Literature in 1962. His wife died in 1955, and the next year he married Laura Archera, a concert violinist. Aldous Huxley died of cancer of the tongue on November 22, 1963, the same day as John F. Kennedy and C. S. Lewis.

▣ *Critical Extracts*

HENRY HAZLITT   Mr. Huxley has portrayed here ⟨in *Brave New World*⟩ a Utopia that obviously he would wish to avoid. It is set ostensibly in the far future, the year of Our Ford, 632. One has not read very far, however, before one perceives that this is not really Mr. Huxley's idea of what the future will be like, but a projection of some contemporary ideals. So far as progress in invention is concerned, there is very little in this Utopia, outside of the biological sphere at least, that does not seem realizable within the next twenty years—though people do go to the "feelies." Economically, the ideals that prevail are those usually associated with Henry Ford—mass production and particularly mass consumption. ⟨. . .⟩ The official religion is Fordianity: people under stress of emotion say "Ford forbid!" or "Ford's in his flivver; all's well with the world," and make the sign of the T. *My Life and Work* has replaced the Bible, and all old books are forbidden to circulate because they suggest the past and history is bunk. Moreover, reading wastes time that should be given to consumption. ⟨. . .⟩

What is wrong with this Utopia? Mr. Huxley attempts to tell us by the device of introducing a "savage," brought up under other ideals on an Indian reservation, and having read that author unknown to the Model T Utopia, Shakespeare. In the admittedly violent and often irrational reactions of the "savage" we have the indictment of this civilization. Not only is there no place in it for love, for romance, for fidelity, for parental affection; there is no suffering in it, and hence absolutely no need of nobility and heroism. In such a society the tragedies of Shakespeare become not merely irrelevant, but literally meaningless. This Model T civilization is distinguished by supreme stability, comfort, and happiness, but these things can be purchased only at a price, and the price is a high one. Not merely art and religion are brought to a standstill, but science itself, lest it make discoveries that would be socially disturbing. Even one of the ten World Controllers is led to suspect the truth, though of course forbidding the publication, of a theory holding that the purpose of life is not the maintenance of well-being, but "some intensification and refining of consciousness, some enlargement of knowledge."

Brave New World is successful as a novel and as a satire; but one need not accept all its apparent implications. A little suffering, a little irrationality, a little division and chaos, are perhaps necessary ingredients of an ideal state, but there has probably never been a time when the world has not had an oversupply of them. Only when we have reduced them enormously will Mr. Huxley's central problem become a real problem.

Henry Hazlitt, "What's Wrong with Utopia?," *Nation*, 17 February 1932, pp. 204, 206

ALDOUS HUXLEY   A really efficient totalitarian state would be one in which the all-powerful executive of political bosses and their army of managers control a population of slaves who do not have to be coerced, because they love their servitude. ⟨. . .⟩ The love of servitude cannot be established except as the result of a deep, personal revolution in human minds and bodies. To bring about that revolution we require, among others, the following discoveries and inventions. First, a greatly improved technique of suggestion—through infant conditioning and, later, with the aid of drugs, such as scopolamine. Second, a fully developed science of human differences, enabling government managers to assign any given individual to his or her proper place in the social and economic hierarchy. (Round pegs in square holes tend to have dangerous thoughts about the social system and to infect others with their discontents.) Third (since reality, however utopian, is something from which people feel the need of taking pretty frequent holidays), a substitute for alcohol and the other narcotics, something at once less harmful and more pleasure-giving than gin or heroin. And fourth (but this would be a long-term project, which it would take generations of totalitarian control to bring to a successful conclusion) a foolproof system of eugenics, designed to standardize the human product and so to facilitate the task of the managers. In *Brave New World* this standardization of the human product has been pushed to fantastic, though not perhaps impossible, extremes. Technologically and ideologically we are still a long way from bottled babies and Bokanovsky groups of semi-morons. But by A.F. 600, who knows what may not be happening? Meanwhile the other characteristic features of that happier and more stable world—the equivalents of soma and hypnopaedia and the scientific caste system—are probably not more than three or four generations away. Nor does the sexual promiscuity of *Brave New World* seem so very distant. There are already certain American cities in which the number of divorces is equal to the number of marriages. In a few years, no doubt, marriage licenses will be sold like dog licenses, good for a period of twelve months, with no law against changing dogs or keeping more than one animal at a time. As political and economic freedom diminishes, sexual freedom tends compensatingly to increase. And the dictator (unless he needs cannon fodder and families with which to colonize empty or conquered territories) will do well to encourage that freedom. In conjunction with the freedom to daydream under the influence of dope and movies and the radio, it will help to reconcile his subjects to the servitude which is their fate.

> Aldous Huxley, "Foreword," *Brave New World* (New York: Harper & Brothers, 1946), pp. xvi–xix

GEORGE ORWELL   The first thing anyone would notice about ⟨E. I. Zamyatin's⟩ *We* is the fact—never pointed out, I believe—that Aldous Huxley's *Brave New World* must be partly derived from it. Both books deal with the rebellion of the primitive human spirit against a rationalised, mechanised, painless world, and both stories are supposed to take place about six hundred years hence. The atmosphere of the two books is similar, and it is roughly speaking the same kind of society that is being described, though Huxley's book shows less political awareness and is more influenced by recent biological and psychological theories. ⟨. . .⟩

⟨. . .⟩ In Huxley's book the problem of "human nature" is in a sense solved, because it assumes that by pre-natal treatment, drugs and hypnotic suggestion the human organism can be specialised in any way that is desired. A first-rate scientific worker is as easily produced as an Epsilon semi-moron, and in either case the vestiges of primitive instincts, such as maternal feeling or the desire for liberty, are easily dealt with. At the same time no clear reason is given why society should be stratified in the elaborate way that is described. The aim is not economic exploitation, but the desire to bully and dominate does not seem to be a motive either. There is no power hunger, no sadism, no hardness of any kind. Those at the top have no strong motive for staying at the top, and though everyone is happy in a vacuous way, life has become so pointless that it is difficult to believe that such a society could endure.

> George Orwell, [Review of *We* by E. I. Zamyatin] (1946), *Collected Essays, Journalism and Letters*, ed. Sonia Orwell and Ian Angus (New York: Harcourt, Brace & World, 1968), Vol. 4, pp. 72–73

PETER E. FIRCHOW   That the United States is the present model for Huxley's vision of the future ⟨in *Brave New World*⟩ emerges even more clearly from an essay entitled, "The Outlook for American Culture, Some Reflections in a Machine Age," published in 1927. Huxley begins this essay with the observation that "speculating on the American future, we are speculating on the future of civilized man." According to Huxley, one of the most ominous portents of the American Way of Life is that it embraces a large class of people who "do not want to be cultured, are not interested in the higher life. For these people existence on the lower, animal levels is perfectly satisfactory. Given food, drink, the company of their fellows, sexual enjoyment, and plenty of noisy distractions from without, they are happy." Furthermore, in America and in the rest of the technologically advanced world, "all the resources of science are applied in order that imbecility may flourish and vulgarity cover the whole earth." The resources of science are so applied because quantity rather than quality is profitable for the capitalists involved: "The higher the degree of standardization in popular literature and art, the greater the profit for the manufacturer." All this mechanical and intellectual standardization, however, leads to the exaltation of the standardized man. It is this development which Huxley views with most concern: "This tendency to raise the ordinary, worldly man to the level of the extraordinary and disinterested one seems to me entirely deplorable. The next step will be to exalt him above the extraordinary man, who will be condemned and persecuted on principle because he is not ordinary—for not to be ordinary will be regarded as a crime. In this reversal of the old values I see a real danger, a menace to all desirable progress."

Brave New World is the fictional extension of Huxley's earlier views on the nature of American "culture"; it is a portrait of the Joy City spread over the whole globe. And as Huxley was to remark with considerable alarm some three decades later in his *Brave New World Revisited*, it is a portrait which is beginning to seem more and more as if it were drawn from the life. In the only too near future, in Huxley's view, it may prove difficult not to revisit the brave new world.

Peter E. Firchow, "The Satire of Huxley's *Brave New World*," *Modern Fiction Studies* 12, No. 4 (Winter 1966–67): 455–56

GEORGE WOODCOCK   The mood of ⟨*Brave New World Revisited*⟩, most of whose material originally appeared as a special supplement to *News-*

day, is one of urgent warning. *Brave New World* itself looked with a dispassionate eye on a future that might take place centuries ahead. But by 1958 Huxley sees the situation completely changed; conditions unforeseen in 1931 have immensely accelerated the tendency towards universal totalitarianism.

The main danger is the biological one—the drastic lowering of the death rate in the poorer countries, which has brought a rise in population that proceeds by geometric rather than arithmetic progression. Rising population means in turn that any increase in agricultural productivity is cancelled before it can have beneficial effects; the resultant situation of permanent biological crisis encourages the other great enemy to human freedom, over-organization, already too far advanced in the industrial nations.

As a result of these pressures, Huxley sees the possibility of a totalitarian world in twenty years' time, which brings one to 1978, six years before Orwell's doomsday. And, while he admits that in 1948 the brutal world of *1984* 'seemed dreadfully convincing', Huxley in 1958 believes that because of recent developments in psychological techniques a world like that portrayed in *Brave New World* is after all more likely. For persuasion is more effective than force, and rulers now have in their hands all the basic techniques for the creation of a foolproof system of mental conditioning. Moreover, while in the Thirties when he wrote *Brave New World* men were acutely concerned for their liberties, in 1958 'even the desire for this freedom seems to be on the wane'. What Huxley did not take into account was the volatilization of opinion that came with the appearance of television and the civil rights campaigns of the early 1960's, which between them resulted in an apparent thaw of the conformity rampant in the McCarthy era. Whether in the long run this will make any difference is another question. The young of today seem just as suggestible in their own way as those of the 1950's, and their vaunted counter-culture appears on examination to be merely a counter-conformity. Huxley's placing of *Brave New World* in time may, like Orwell's, be pessimistic, but unless the political crises caused throughout the world by demographic changes are quickly solved there seems no alternative to a totalitarian world that will mean the end to civilization as we have known it in the western world since the Renaissance; the great civilization of China has already succumbed, and ours shows every sign of following.

George Woodcock, *Dawn and the Darkest Hour: A Study of Aldous Huxley* (London: Faber & Faber, 1972), pp. 271–72

WILLIAM M. MATTER   The examination of Huxley's three utopian novels against a background of the utopian tradition allows one to see more clearly those themes that influenced Huxley most. He shows the reader that the ends many utopists have sought, and not the means they employ to achieve these ends, are at fault. After reading *Brave New World*, one might assume that Huxley feels that conditioning infants is always wrong. Upon perusing *Island*, however, one becomes aware that it is only the end toward which conditioning is directed in *Brave New World* that Huxley resents. In *Island*, conditioning for love and not for fear is endorsed. Similarly, after reading Huxley's depiction of the liberal sex practices of the brave new world and the "heat" period of 2108, one might conclude that the author is puritanical with respect to sex. But in *Island* each child is instructed in the yoga of love and is permitted at an early age to have sexual experiences. Again, it is the end toward which sex is directed in *Brave New World* and *Ape and Essence* that Huxley deplores. Meaningful sexual relationships, especially those involving a yoga of love, are applauded; only shallow, unthinking adventures in sex are condemned. The worst of the East and the West is discussed in *Ape and Essence*, but Huxley is strongly in favor of a meeting of the best aspects of the East and West. In *Brave New World* artificial insemination and sperm banks lead to production-line people; in *Island* the same devices of science, employed for humane goals, improve the race. *Ape and Essence* and *Brave New World* are attacks upon man's use of technology. In *Island* science serves man; it does not control him. Similarly, *soma* is evil because it is used for escape; but *moksha*-medicine reveals reality.

William M. Matter, "The Utopian Tradition and Aldous Huxley," *Science-Fiction Studies* 2, No. 2 (July 1975): 149

C. S. FERNS   In *Brave New World* any form of sexual behaviour *other* than promiscuity is socially unacceptable, and by making promiscuity respectable, Huxley deprives it of its aura of daring and excitement, thereby exposing its emptiness as a way of life. At the same time convention, once it is seen to uphold values to which it is normally opposed, no longer appears to be some kind of absolute standard, but merely a reflection of the unthinking assumptions of the day. The appalling inanity of the conversation in the helicopter between Henry and Lenina, where both complacently parrot the sentiments they have been conditioned into accepting, or the triteness of the synthetic folk wisdom enshrined in the proverbs everyone uses ('a gramme is better than a damn', 'one cubic centimetre cures ten gloomy sentiments'), stand out because of the unfamiliarity of the underlying assumptions, but the real target is clearly the fatuity of the popular beliefs of Huxley's own day. Few readers are likely to be free of their own unthinking assumptions—assumptions which are not thought about because of their very familiarity: it is the *unfamiliarity* of the endlessly reiterated sentiments in *Brave New World* that highlights the extent to which people's beliefs are unthinking and conditioned. It would be hard for any reader to ignore the relevance to the present world of high technology, mass communications, and advertising of the depiction of a society where everyone's opinions are acquired during their sleep.

Huxley similarly exploits incongruities for satiric effect by linking technology and religion. By making the deity ('Our Ford') a motor manufacturer, Huxley satirizes the way in which technological and scientific progress is worshipped as an end in itself: in the society of the future the salient qualities of the machine—efficiency and productivity—have become the cardinal virtues of mankind. At the same time, religion is exposed as mere escapist ritual; the pomp and dignity normally associated with religious ceremonies are deflated by the ludicrous rites of Ford-worship, solemnized by such officials as the Arch Community-Songster of Canterbury.

Incongruity, too, is at the root of Huxley's portrayal of the relations between Lenina and the Savage, in which both the irresponsible hedonism of the former and the romantic illusions of the latter are ridiculed. The Savage's intense emotions, dressed up in grand Shakespearian language, are rendered farcical by the object of his love. For an object is precisely what Lenina is, the product of conditioning rather than a person in her own right. Yet by her very vacuousness she helps to expose what a great deal of romantic love is all about—the projection into someone else of a private fantasy, rather than a genuine attempt to *know* them. Lenina shows up this element of projection so clearly because she is, so to speak, a blank screen. On the other hand, ridiculous though the Savage is made to look, the fact that he has real emotions at all, however mis-directed, highlights the blandness and shallowness of the relations which the citizens of Brave New World accept as normal.

    C. S. Ferns, *Aldous Huxley: Novelist* (London: Athlone Press, 1980), pp. 141–42

ROBERT S. BAKER   Throughout the twenties Huxley repeatedly expressed his misgivings concerning not only the methodological principles underlying the study of the past but the actual course taken by modern British and European history. By 1928 he had become increasingly aware of the threat posed by the two principal variants of modern totalitarianism, Italian fascism and Russian communism. While neither as overtly political nor as sensitive to contemporary developments in Europe as *Eyeless in Gaza* or *After Many a Summer Dies the Swan*, *Brave New World* is an implicit condemnation of collectivist absolutism, despite the fact that in Huxley's dystopia, coercion is exercised in an ingratiatingly mild and benevolent form. The inhabitants of the World State are condemned to a life of discreetly stimulated apathy, and as Huxley argued in a letter to George Orwell, he firmly believed that his gently paternalistic form of despotism was much more likely to evolve out of current historical conditions than the systematically violent alternative envisaged in *Nineteen Eighty-four*. ⟨. . .⟩

   In *Brave New World* Huxley attempted to envisage a very distant development of the society depicted in *Antic Hay* and *Point Counter Point*. The liberal "Utopia" of tolerable humaneness and partial freedom described in *The Olive Tree* was rejected in favor of a more likely alternative, a collectivist dystopia. Occupying neither the "crest" nor the "trough" of the wave, Mustapha Mond's World State is a massive socioeconomic improvisation marking the termination of history, an apocalyptic ushering-in of a society so authoritarian and immobile that historical process has been halted, rather like a river frozen in its bed. As an attempt to dam up the forces of history, such a society is founded on fear and revulsion, specifically a dread of those libidinal and sadomasochistic urges and violent attitudes of socially emblematic characters like Maurice Spandrell, Lucy Tantamount, Everard Webley, and Illidge of *Point Counter Point*. Throughout the period 1928 to 1939, Huxley's letters and essays illustrate his belief that he could detect social processes at work that seemed vaguely and only conjecturally lawlike in their pervasive effect and apparent inevitability. This intractably "Euclidean" set of conditions he associated with social fragmentation, increasingly irrational behavior, moral "decadence," and a kind of social death-wish.

   Robert S. Baker, *The Dark Historical Page: Social Satire and Historicism in the Novels of Aldous Huxley* (Madison: University of Wisconsin Press, 1982), pp. 136, 138

DAVID LEON HIGDON   One of the first British authors to
respond to the new nuclear age was Aldous Huxley in *Ape and Essence* (1948).
Early in 1948, Huxley wrote Fairfield Osborn, author of *Our Plundered Planet*,
that: "The great question now is: will the public and those in authority pay
any attention to what you say, or will the politicians go on with their lunatic
games ... ignoring the fact that the world they are squabbling over will
shortly cease to exist in its old familiar form, but will be transformed, unless
they mobilize all available intelligence and ... good will, into one huge
dust bowl." He did not add that he was only weeks away from completing
his own sardonic and savage vision of this dust bowl of the year 2108 in
which clothing is secured by exhuming corpses, where human bones are
transformed into tools, and where 80 percent of all live births result in
deformed infants. It is a world bereft of human affection, human joy, and
human companionship, for these have been replaced by hunger, fear, and
cruelty. Civilization has been replaced by a puritanical blood worship of
Belial. A new Dark Age has descended upon mankind. Though it is first
an attack on the technology Huxley had made his target since *Brave New
World* (1932), the narrator of *Ape and Essence* generalizes the attack further:

> Progress is the midwife of Force. Doubly the midwife, for the fact
> of technological progress provides people with the instruments of
> ever more indiscriminate destruction, while the myth of political
> and moral progress serves as the excuse for using these means to
> the very limit.

In the novel and its reviews, we glimpse a confrontation between British
pessimism, reserved distrust of technology as solution, and seasoned, tested
assumptions concerning human nature and American optimism, faith in
technology, and naïveté concerning human nature typical of this period.
One reviewer oddly claimed that "perhaps the Huxley name will carry this
to a certain market but for the average normal reader, this form of satire
at its most extreme may well prove disastrous," or as Paul Brians succinctly
characterized the difference: "Let the effete English weep over the impending
doom of humanity ... American grit and know-how will cope with even
the worst disaster." *Catholic World* accused Huxley of letting "his imagination
run in a riotous extreme, giving us pictures grotesque and horrible, and not
always decent," adding as a further warning to its readers that "the motif
of sex is repeatedly and obscenely stressed." Most reviewers simply dismissed
Huxley as a soured man who had fallen out of love with humanity. *Time*

stated that "he simply can't stand the world any more, not even enough to pillory it," and the *New York Tribune Weekly Book Review*, calling *Ape and Essence* a "rather sterile fantasy," marvelled at Huxley's "grand disgust with all of us alive today." As we have recently seen, at times people prefer to hear good news even when there is little or none. No wonder then that American reviewers failed to see that Huxley held out a slight hope in allowing his main characters to escape this world, that the United States government would soon give us "Duck and Cover" programs, and that John Campbell, the influential editor of *Astounding*, would shortly inform contributors that "we have specified to our authors that the 'atomic doom' stories are not wanted."

> David Leon Higdon, " 'Into the Vast Unknown': Directions in the Post-Holocaust Novel," *War and Peace: Perspectives in the Nuclear Age*, ed. Ulrich Goebel and Otto Nelson (Lubbock: Texas Tech University Press, 1988), pp. 118–19

GORMAN BEAUCHAMP   The door to enlightenment in Pala ⟨in *Island*⟩ is entered with the imaginary drug—apparently a sort of LSD-manqué—called *moksha*-medicine, "the reality revealer, the truth-and-beauty pill." *Moksha* is a Sanskrit word meaning liberation, and through the agency of the drug, which is made from toadstools, the Palanese adept is "liberated from his bondage to the ego." Liberation is, in the later writing of Huxley, a key concept, suggestive of the whole epistemology of mysticism that opens the mind to new levels of awareness. One of Farnaby's cicerones explains, "Just how the *moksha*-medicine produces those unusual stimuli we haven't yet found out," but it "does something to the silent areas of the brain which opens some kind of neurological sluice and allows a larger volume of Mind with a large 'M' to flow into your mind with a small 'm.' " The skeptical Farnaby protests that such experiences are merely subjective with "no reference to any external fact except a toadstool." He is answered by Dr. McPhail, grandson of the original Palanese McPhail, and the island's chief minister and guru:

> Even if it doesn't refer to anything outside itself, it's still the most important thing that ever happened to you. . . . And if you give the experience a chance, if you are prepared to go along with it, the results are incomparably . . . therapeutic and transforming. So maybe the whole thing does happen inside one's skull. Maybe it *is*

> private and there's no unitive knowledge of anything but one's
> own physiology. Who cares? The fact remains that the experience
> can open one's eyes and make one blessed and transform one's
> whole life.

It is, Dr. McPhail concludes, "much more real than what you call reality."

The liberating or reality-heightening property of *moksha* places it at the farthest pharmacological and political remove from the other imaginary drug that Huxley made famous in *Brave New World*, soma. Soma's effect is, of course, not psychedelic but sedative—providing "a holiday from reality," rather than a heightening of reality. The purpose of saturating the Brave New World with a sedative is social control: any potential frustration can be defused with a few grams of soma. Playing on the negative associations that attach to "drugging" people, *Brave New World*—like later dystopias such as Anthony Burgess' *A Clockwork Orange* or Ira Levin's *This Perfect Day*—depicts the practice satirically, as one means of condemning the obsession with manipulating not merely the actions but the thoughts of its citizens that characterizes many, perhaps most, utopias. ⟨. . .⟩

The climax of *Island* comes with Farnaby's own experience with the *moksha*-medicine, an event towards which the argument of the novel inevitably leads. What will transpire—we are continually encouraged to wonder—when the man who cannot take yes for an answer pops the truth and beauty pill, as, of course, he must? The results, however, are hardly unexpected: "the dreadful miracle of creation had been reversed. From a preternaturally wretched and delinquent self he had been unmade into pure mind, mind in its natural state, limitless, undifferentiated, luminously blissful, knowledgelessly understanding." But to assert this miraculous transformation is one thing, to dramatize it persuasively is another. The problem with the depiction inheres, in large part, in the nature of the mystical experience itself, the distinctive hallmark of which, notes William James, is its ineffability. "The subject of it immediately says that it defies expression, that no adequate report of its contents can be given in words. It follows from this that its quality must be directly experienced; it cannot be imparted or transferred to others. . . . Mystical truth exists for the individual who has the transport, but for no one else." The logical consequence would seem to be silence on the mystic's part: about the ineffable, Wittgenstein advised, say nothing. Of those mystics (if any) who adhere to this advice, who remain silent, we know, of course, nothing. Those we know, did not, of course, remain silent, but rehearsed their experiences repeatedly, even compulsively. The mystic is not one to hide his enlightenment under a bushel.

Gorman Beauchamp, "*Island*: Aldous Huxley's Psychedelic Utopia," *Utopian Studies* 1, No. 1 (1990): 64, 67

Bibliography

The Burning Wheel. 1916.

Oxford Poetry 1916 (editor; with W. R. Childe and T. W. Earp). 1916.

Jonah. 1917.

The Defeat of Youth and Other Poems. 1918.

Limbo. 1920.

Leda. 1920.

Crome Yellow. 1921.

A Virgin Heart by Remy de Gourmont (translator). 1921.

Mortal Coils. 1922.

On the Margin: Notes and Essays. 1923.

Antic Hay. 1923.

The Discovery by Frances Sheridan (adapter). 1924.

Little Mexican and Other Stories ⟨*Young Archimedes and Other Stories*⟩. 1924.

Those Barren Leaves. 1925.

Along the Road: Notes and Essays of a Tourist. 1925.

Selected Poems. 1925.

Two or Three Graces and Other Stories. 1926.

Jesting Pilate: The Diary of a Journey. 1926.

Essays New and Old. 1926.

Proper Studies. 1927.

Point Counter Point. 1928.

Arabia Infelix and Other Poems. 1929.

Holy Face and Other Essays. 1929.

Do What You Will: Essays. 1929.

Brief Candles. 1930.

Vulgarity in Literature: Digressions from a Theme. 1930.

Apennine. 1930.

Music at Night and Other Essays. 1931.

The World of Light. 1931.

The Cicadas and Other Poems. 1931.

Brave New World. 1932.

The Letters of D. H. Lawrence (editor). 1932.

Texts and Pretexts: An Anthology with Commentaries. 1932.

Rotunda: A Selection from the Works of Aldous Huxley. 1932.

T. H. Huxley as a Man of Letters. 1932.

Retrospect: An Omnibus of Aldous Huxley's Books. 1933.

Beyond the Mexique Bay. 1934.

1936 . . . Peace? 1936.

Eyeless in Gaza. 1936.

The Olive Tree and Other Essays. 1936.

What Are You Going to Do about It? The Case for Constructive Peace. 1936.

Ends and Means: An Enquiry into the Nature of Ideals and into the Methods for Their Realization. 1937.

Stories, Essays, and Poems. 1937.

An Encyclopedia of Pacifism (editor). 1937.

The Elder Peter Bruegel, 1528(?)–1569 (with Jean Videpoche). 1938.

The Most Agreeable Vice. 1938.

The Gioconda Smile. 1938.

After Many a Summer ⟨*After Many a Summer Dies the Swan*⟩. 1939.

Words and Their Meanings. 1940.

Grey Eminence: A Study in Religion and Politics. 1941.

The Art of Seeing. 1942.

Time Must Have a Stop. 1944.

Twice Seven: Fourteen Selected Stories. 1944.

The Perennial Philosophy. 1945.

Science, Liberty, and Peace. 1946.

Verses and a Comedy. 1946.

The World of Aldous Huxley: An Omnibus of His Fiction and Non-Fiction over Three Decades. Ed. Charles J. Rolo. 1947.

Ape and Essence. 1948.

The Gioconda Smile (drama). 1948.

Prisons: With the "Carceri" Etchings by G. B. Piranesi. 1949.

Food and People (with Sir John Russell). 1949.

Themes and Variations. 1950.

The Devils of Loudun. 1952.

Joyce, the Artificer: Two Studies of Joyce's Method (with Stuart Gilbert). 1952.

A Day in Windsor (with J. A. Kings). 1953.

The Doors of Perception. 1954.

The French of Paris. 1954.

The Genius and the Goddess. 1955.

Adonis and the Alphabet and Other Essays ⟨*Tomorrow and Tomorrow and Tomorrow and Other Essays*⟩. 1956.

Heaven and Hell. 1956.

L'Après-midi d'un faune by Stéphane Mallarmé (translator). 1956.

Collected Short Stories. 1957.

Tyranny over the Mind: A Shocking New Look at Today's World. 1958.

Brave New World Revisited. 1958.

Collected Essays. 1959.

On Art and Artists: Literature—Painting—Architecture—Music. Ed. Morris Philipson. 1960.

Selected Essays. Ed. Harold Raymond. 1961.

Island. 1962.

Literature and Science. 1963.

The Politics of Ecology: The Question of Survival. 1963.

The Crows of Pearblossom. 1967.

New-Fashioned Christmas. 1968.

Letters. Ed. Grover Smith. 1969.

America and the Future: An Essay. 1970.

Collected Poetry. Ed. Donald Watt. 1971.

Moksha: Writings on Psychedelics and the Visionary Experience (1931–1963). Ed. Michael Horowitz and Cynthia Palmer. 1977.

The Human Situation: Lectures at Santa Barbara 1959. Ed. Piero Ferrucci. 1977.

Between the Wars: Essays and Letters. Ed. David Bradshaw. 1994.

C. S. Lewis
1898–1963

CLIVE STAPLES LEWIS was born in Belfast, Ireland, on November 29, 1898. After the death of his mother in 1908 he saw little of his father and spent several miserable years at private schools in England. A private tutor prepared him for Oxford, but he joined the English army and went to France in November 1917. He was wounded at the Battle of Arras in 1918 and returned to England, the next year resuming his studies at University College, Oxford. He received his B.A. in 1922, taught philosophy for one term (1924–25) at University College, then spent the next thirty years as a tutor in English at Magdalen College, Oxford.

As a teenager Lewis had discarded the conventional Anglican religion of his parents and became for a time an atheist; but gradually he began converting to Christianity. His early religious struggles are poignantly etched in his autobiography, *Surprised by Joy* (1955). His conversion was complete by 1931, and after publishing a book of poems, *Spirits in Bondage* (1919), and a novel, *Dymer* (1926), under the pseudonym Clive Hamilton, Lewis began his prolific career as a Christian apologist, literary scholar, and fiction writer.

Of his Christian writings, *The Pilgrim's Regress* (1933) and *The Screwtape Letters* (1942) are the best known. A series of radio broadcasts was collected as *Mere Christianity* (1952). *The Allegory of Love* (1936) was Lewis's first significant work of literary criticism, and he went on to write several other distinguished volumes, including *A Preface to* Paradise Lost (1942) and *English Literature in the Sixteenth Century, Excluding Drama* (1954), the latter for the prestigious Oxford History of English Literature series.

Around 1937 Lewis formed a loose group of friends called the Inklings to discuss literature and theology and to read their works in progress. This group included Lewis's longtime friend Owen Barfield, J. R. R. Tolkien (whom Lewis had first met in 1926), and later Charles Williams, who came to Oxford in 1939. A number of Lewis's works were developed from discussions with the Inklings.

Lewis's main contribution to science fiction rests in his trilogy of novels involving space travel, *Out of the Silent Planet* (1938), *Perelandra* (1943), and *That Hideous Strength* (1945). Some of his short stories also approach science fiction, especially those posthumously collected in *The Dark Tower and Other Stories* (1977), the title story of which is an unfinished novelette about time travel. Lewis has gained great renown as the author of a seven-volume series of fantasy novels for children, beginning with *The Lion, the Witch, and the Wardrobe* (1950) and concluding with *The Last Battle* (1956). Both this series and the science fiction trilogy have been criticized as being excessively heavy-handed in their religious symbolism. Lewis also retold the myth of Cupid and Psyche in *Till We Have Faces* (1956).

In 1948 Lewis began corresponding with an American writer, Helen Joy Davidman Gresham. He met her for the first time in 1952, and in 1956, two years after her divorce from her estranged husband, he married her. She died in 1960, causing Lewis to write the anguished autobiography, *A Grief Observed* (1961). C. S. Lewis, who left Oxford in 1954 after nearly forty years there to become Professor of Medieval and Renaissance Literature at Magdalene College, Cambridge, died on November 22, 1963, on the same day as John F. Kennedy and Aldous Huxley.

Critical Extracts

VICTOR M. HAMM   Milton wrote the epics of *Paradise Lost* and *Paradise Regained*. Mr. C. S. Lewis has essayed the epic of Paradise Retained. Not our Paradise, the human. That has been lost for good. But *a* Paradise. Where? By a bold stroke of what one can only call the mythopoeic imagination Mr. Lewis places the Paradise of his story on another planet: Venus we call it; in the language of the universe, which Lewis has given the name "Old Solar," it is known as "Perelandra."

The novel *Perelandra* is at once an escape and an apocalypse. It is an escape to another planet. It is an apocalypse of Paradise without a Fall. ⟨...⟩

⟨...⟩ One facet of Lewis's genius ⟨...⟩ is his sheer imaginative power. But even the most imaginative art is derivative in its materials. It uses the stuff of popular legend. It draws on the philosophies and myths of all time.

But it weaves anew. Thus the Time Machine of Wells, the Martians of the same writer's *War of the Worlds,* Jules Verne's earlier rocket-ship, the "She" of Rider Haggard's exotic romance, the speculations of Plato and the Neo-Platonists, of the Kabbala and the Rosicrucians, the myths of Greece and the Orient, even ⟨. . .⟩ the Tarzan books, have contributed to Mr. Lewis's fable. Shelley's myths, especially in *Prometheus Unbound,* the gods of Keats's *Hyperion,* Blake's heroic drawings and prophetic figures, the vivid symbols of Dante's vision, enter the creation as well, not as crude material, but as assimilated flesh and blood of the imagination.

The reader is quite lifted out of this world by the prismatic splendor of Ransom's descriptions of the Perelandrian sea and sky, of the tastes and sounds and odors of that new world. It is much more concrete than Shelley's dream-worlds. In sensuousness it resembles rather Keats, in thaumaturgic power the *Prophetic Books* of Blake; in precision and sharpness of outline the world of Dante's imagination. ⟨. . .⟩

To some this sheer imaginative power will alone be enough to rank the novel among the great works of invention, and I have no desire to underrate the enchantment it wields. But beyond all this, the form that vivifies and organizes Mr. Lewis's art is his Christian faith which has given him the power to see as in a dream the incorporation of a futurable, the reality of a possibility. Perhaps only the shattering cataclysm of the present war which in England for five years blacked and blotted out the bourgeois, agnostic life of the world we were used to, could have precipitated the detachment that Lewis's vision achieves.

Victor M. Hamm, "Mr. Lewis in Perelandra," *Thought* No. 77 (June 1945): 271, 273–74, 276

C. S. LEWIS   I turn at last to that sub-species ⟨of science fiction⟩ in which alone I myself am greatly interested. It is best approached by reminding ourselves of a fact which every writer on the subject whom I have read completely ignores. Far the best of the American magazines bears the significant title *Fantasy and Science Fiction.* In it (as also in many other publications of the same type) you will find not only stories about space-travel but stories about gods, ghosts, ghouls, demons, fairies, monsters, etc. This gives us our clue. The last sub-species of science fiction represents simply an imaginative impulse as old as the human race working under the special conditions of our own time. It is not difficult to see why those who wish to visit strange regions in search of such beauty, awe, or terror as the actual world does not supply have increasingly been driven to other planets or other stars. It is the result of increasing geographical knowledge. The less known the real world is, the more plausibly your marvels can be located near at hand. As the area of knowledge spreads, you need to go further afield: like a man moving his house further and further out into the country as the new building estates catch him up. ⟨. . .⟩

In this kind of story the pseudo-scientific apparatus is to be taken simply as a 'machine' in the sense which that word bore for the Neo-Classical critics. The most superficial apperance of plausibility—the merest sop to our critical intellect—will do. I am inclined to think that frankly supernatural methods are best. I took a hero once to Mars in a space-ship, but when I knew better I had angels convey him to Venus. Nor need the strange worlds, when we get there, be at all strictly tied to scientific probabilities. It is their wonder, or beauty, or suggestiveness that matter. When I myself put canals on Mars I believe I already knew that better telescopes had dissipated that old optical delusion. The point was that they were part of the Martian myth as it already existed in the common mind.

The defence and analysis of this kind are, accordingly, no different from those of fantastic or mythopoeic literature in general. But here sub-species and sub-sub-species break out in baffling multitude. The impossible—or things so immensely improbable that they have, imaginatively, the same status as the impossible—can be used in literature for many different purposes.

C. S. Lewis, "On Science Fiction" (1955), *Of Other Worlds: Essays and Stories*, ed. Walter Hooper (1966; rpt. New York: Harcourt, Brace & World, 1967), pp. 67–69

MARK R. HILLEGAS   The adventures which began with Ransom's journey to Malacandra culminate in *That Hideous Strength*, the most anti-utopian volume in the trilogy and the one in which ⟨H. G.⟩ Wells appears in person as Horace Jules, the figurehead director of the National Institute for Co-ordinated Experiments. In *That Hideous Strength* the dark spirits of earth inspire evil men, those who actually lead the N.I.C.E., to work to turn the world into a nightmare society where behavior is scientifically manipulated. The N.I.C.E. is a fictional embodiment of Lewis's fears about a new science of man which are set forth more directly in his little book, *The Abolition of Man* (1943). In that book Lewis argued that the traditional system of values will inevitably be destroyed by such a science of human nature—that when man has seen through human nature there will be nothing to guide him except the lowest kind of animal impulses. And then, in this moral vacuum, the world will consist of the great mass of men— the conditioned—snug and unknowing under the rule of the behavioral scientists, the conditioners. It is this situation which the N.I.C.E.—backed by the powers of Thulcandra—tries to create on earth. ⟨. . .⟩

But fortunately the realization of this utopia is prevented. The opposition to the N.I.C.E. is headed by Ransom and a little company of Christians, supported by the Oyarsa of each planet, the great *eldila* ("spirits" or "angels" would be our closest approximation) of the solar system who can now enter the sphere of earth because Weston and Devine have destroyed the barrier that had previously kept Thulcandra quarantined. Ransom, who turns out to be Mr. Fisher-King as well as the current Pendragon of Logres (King of Arthur's realm, which continues to exist in secrecy), is also assisted by a clairvoyant young woman, by a bear, and by the Arthurian Merlin, who has awakened from his centuries-long trance to play a crucial role at this crisis in history. In its use of Arthurian myth to provide meaning, *That Hideous Strength* can, of course, be profitably studied in connection with T. S. Eliot's *Waste Land* and such poems by Charles Williams as *The Figure of Arthur* and *Taliessin Through Logres*.

Mark R. Hillegas, The Future as Nightmare: The Fantasies of C. S. Lewis, J. R. R. Tolkien, and Charles Williams (New York: Oxford University Press, 1967), pp. 136–38

RUDOLF B. SCHMERL   A different problem, at least to a non-Christian reader, is presented by, for instance, the C. S. Lewis trilogy, *Out of the Silent Planet, Perelandra,* and *That Hideous Strength*. The reality to which the three novels are related is Christian metaphysics. Like others of Lewis's books, the trilogy is belligerently affirmative; that is, his purpose is not to satirize but to proselytize. Orwell's deliberately distorted horror can be interpreted as necessary exaggeration, and the reader who has a rosier crystal ball can at least extend a certain esthetic tolerance to *1984*. He has not been told to save his soul, merely that the future will very probably not allow him to have any. But the Lewis trilogy, no matter how much of it is simply suspense and entertainment, is unflinchingly didactic, and it is of obvious significance that Lewis's Christ figure, Dr. Ransom, wins no final victory over the forces of darkness. The reader who is incapable of belief in Christianity can well inquire whether a religion whose truth is far from evident to him can provide a more legitimate framework for responsible fantasy than can pseudo-scientific speculation about the ultimate destiny of humanity.

> Rudolf B. Schmerl, "Fantasy as Technique," *Virginia Quarterly Review* 43, No. 4 (Autumn 1967): 653

KATHRYN HUME   Lewis' craftsmanship deserves more recognition. Each book is notable for its own particular virtues. *Out of the Silent Planet* is unrivaled among the three for its symbolic landscapes. I mentioned earlier the hedge, but there are yet more significant details in that one scene alone: the geography of The Rise is further elaborated:

> The drive branched into two a little way ahead of him—the righthand path leading in a gentle sweep to the front door, while the left ran straight ahead, doubtless to the back premises of the house. He noticed that this path was churned up into deep ruts—now full of water—as if it were used to carrying a traffic of heavy lorries. The other, on which he now began to approach the house, was overgrown with moss.

The broad, straight, much-traveled road runs to the space ship, violator of deep heaven, even as its iconographic counterparts lead to Hell or, in Spenser's equivalent in the Forest of Error, to the monster Error. It is literally as well as symbolically "sinister." Moss on the path to the *right* is as clear a sign as cobwebs across a door that no one has been using it. The mossy path would have been trodden bare had there been normal social intercourse and proper relations with the neighbors. Another tour-de-force of a different sort is Ransom's translation of Weston's philosophic manifesto into the language of Solar honesty.

Though Malacandrian scenery is well described, that of Perelandra is the second book's most memorable feature. Lewis' ability to command color, sensations, and emotions and the fertility of his inventions as well as of his invented land are all to be praised. Here, too, scenes and situations have iconographic or symbolic overtones. The predominant colors, for example, are yellow and green, those of youth ⟨. . .⟩ In a fashion suitable to so young a land, many of the situations Ransom finds himself in are suggestive of birth. *That Hideous Strength* excels in depicting the wheelings and dealings of petty political maneuver. Lewis is as varied in his talents as he is steadfast in his religious purposes. This specialization of effect, of course, helps him to avoid repeating himself, as does also his juggling of structures and locale, but we should not be misled by such deliberate differentiation into thinking of the three as simply three disjunct novels.

Little has been made of these works as romances, but the romance form is demonstrably of central significance to Lewis' basic purposes. For him, the acceptance of society normal to much of comedy is morally impossible, and comedy's use of corrective laughter insufficient to the evils he confronts. Given the Christian premises of his thought, significant tragedy is equally out of the question. Romance of the sort delineated in this essay, however, is by definition concerned with a hero's struggles against evil and his alliance with higher spiritual powers. These are precisely Lewis' concerns; all his didacticism aims at these two ends. The romance form is, therefore, the proper vehicle for his enterprise, and its characteristic tripartite structure would naturally suggest the suitability of three novels to the author wishing to extend and develop to logical conclusions the problems set up in *Out of the Silent Planet*. Though he may not have had sequels in mind when writing the first novel (1938), the timing of the second two (1943, 1945) suggests that they were conceived of together. And indeed, Ransom's fate at the end of *Perelandra* demands some account of how this demi-god could bear the imperfections of earth after living in paradise. The romance form gives Lewis tools ready-made to meet such demands.

> Kathryn Hume, "C. S. Lewis' Trilogy: A Cosmic Romance," *Modern Fiction Studies* 20, No. 4 (Winter 1974–75): 516–17

DABNEY ADAMS HART   The first two stories in Lewis's space trilogy are based on his concept of different models of truth in other worlds. In *Out of the Silent Planet*, the human traveler learns that the Malacandrians had no idea that there was intelligent life in his world. Ransom's first encounter with a *hross* (something like a penguin, an otter, a seal, and a stoat), a talking nonhuman creature, was an experience "which completely altered his state of mind." Lewis's description of "the first tingling intercourse of two different, but rational, species," which is climaxed by the offer and acceptance of a shell cup of wine, illustrates memorably the interaction of new models and changeless realities. An even more striking version of this concept is the model of unfallen innocence in *Perelandra*, where Ransom, on the planet that we call Venus, meets a Green Lady whose home is a Floating Island. For her the prohibition essential to the theme is that she may not stay overnight on the Fixed Land. The familiar imagery of firm foundations is not easy to abandon, but the twofold meaning is not ambiguous. In this novel, as in the Narnia stories, Lewis meant that man cannot rely on stability, permanence, or any kind of natural security—his only security is in faith and obedience. But the images are not intended as allegory. Lewis created different worlds with different systems of time and space as well as different models of relationship with the Creator.

Dabney Adams Hart, *Through the Open Door: A New Look at C. S. Lewis* (University: University of Alabama Press, 1984), pp. 131–32

JOE R. CHRISTOPHER   In "A Reply to Professor Haldane," Lewis comments that the science in *Out of the Silent Planet* is not intended to be perfectly accurate. He used canals on Mars, for example, because they were part of the popular picture of that planet, not because they were still believed in by scientists in 1938. Lewis also notes that, although he has to be a physicist for plot purposes (to have developed the spaceship), Weston talks little but biological, or "metabiological," theory. ⟨. . .⟩ In short, the science in *Out of the Silent Planet* is often used with a romancer's hand, not a realist's.

Most explicators today spend much time on the Christian background implicit in the book, but few of the early reviewers noticed it—which suggests it is more thoroughly background than most of today's writers acknowledge. In theological terms Lewis is describing an unfallen, sinless world under the direction of an angelic Intelligence. The *eldila*, visible only with difficulty, are angels. In the case of the *eldil* who comes walking across water to Ransom during the *hnakra* hunt (chap. 13), the *eldil* functions as a traditional angelic messenger (with the added touch of echoing Christ's walking on water). Lewis also, however, provides a "scientific" explanation of *eldila* as beings existing at the energy level of light, and thus finding different things solid and infirm than do humans and Malacandrians (chap.

15). In one passage, a *hross* explains that Maleldil the Young (i.e., Christ) made and rules the world, and lives with the Old One (i.e., God the Father) (chap. 11). But non-Christians, who do not tend to think of God the Son outside of his earthly incarnation, would probably miss the reference—and it is appropriate that a Malacandrian would not know of the Incarnation. The word *Maleldil* is misleading, because many readers, meeting it for the first time, probably associate *mal-* with evil. (Actually, Lewis seems to have derived the word from Anglo-Saxon, *mal* [an agreement, a judgment] or *mael* [a sign] + *ealdor* [lord]; hence, Lord of the Sign, Lord of Judgment, or Lord of the Agreement/Covenant.) Of these Christian motifs, probably the angels (with the "War in Heaven" explanation for Earth being the "silent planet") are the most obvious; but none of the material is didactic in any direct way.

Indeed, if one wants a classification for *Out of the Silent Planet* besides "science-fiction romance," the term is *not* "Christian didacticism" but "religious Utopia." (Many of the early Utopian works were also religious in orientation—as were many of the early Utopian communities in America.) One critic ⟨Angele Botros Samaan⟩ has suggested that Lewis belongs to a reaction against H. G. Wells's Utopian works, such as *A Modern Utopia* (1905) and *Men Like Gods* (1923); another ⟨Dabney Adams Hart⟩, that the three types of Malacandrians—the *pfifltriggi, hrossa,* and *séroni* (or *sorns*)—parallel the three classes in Plato's *Republic*—the workers, guardians (in Lewis, just a group that emphasizes physical bravery), and philosophers. In this light, it is fitting that Oyarsa, in answering Weston's beliefs, does *not* say, "Thus saith the Lord," but instead replies in terms of natural law: he refers to the laws that all *hnau* (intelligent beings) know, including the love of kindred, and says that Weston substituted that one lesser moral law for all the others (chap. 20). In short, Lewis's emphasis on the fallen nature of mankind in this book serves as foil to establish the Platonic-and-pre-Christian religious (or natural law) Utopia of Malacandra.

Joe R. Christopher, *C. S. Lewis* (Boston: Twayne, 1987), pp. 92–94

DAVID HOLBROOK   At the beginning of *That Hideous Strength,* the "I" of the book reflects, "But when alone—really alone—everyone is a child: or no one? Youth and age touch only the surface of our lives." *That Hideous Strength* is yet another attempt to solve the timeless existential problems of the tormented child, who cannot find his world. Lewis is also haunted by that dread that "the real universe might be simply silly." As for oneself, there is often the dread that, "suppose one were a thing, a thing designed and invented by someone else and valued for qualities quite different from what one had decided to regard as one's true self." However deeply hidden, Lewis seems to have had fundamentally schizoid insecurity about what was his true self, and a deep uncertainty about what was real.

So again, examined phenomenologically, everything happens in terms of externalized "split-offs." In *That Hideous Strength* the hideous strength itself, the tower, is such a split-off subject, a huge penis with a shadow six miles long. Against it have to be sent split-off aggressive entities. The climax of the story is the moment when these frightening entities meet. When (one might say) all the oral-aggressive dynamics of the dissatisfied infant engage with the salty taste, pash, crunch, and blood of the combined parents, who are (in any case) engaged in a dangerous (if not fatal) mutual eating. The great bad-male-doing penis is destroyed; but there is no gain in understanding.

So, the victory at the end of *That Hideous Strength* is not a victory of human conscience, or courage, or devotion, against hubristic arrogance. It is a victory of irrational wish-fulfillment—of magic—against "science" (but a science that is heavily caricatured and misrepresented as being possessed by the devil).

What is endorsed here is mumbo-jumbo—the deliberate cultivation of irrationality and superstition. Even if we take them as symbols, what do Merlin's dogs, elephants, and snakes in *That Hideous Strength* represent? In what sense, against hubristic "science," does one seek to invoke beasts that will mutilate and kill "bad" scientists who are badly wrong in their philosophies and cause social havoc? These might be brought under examination by reasonable discourse (as over genetic engineering, or germ warfare, or experiments on mental patients, animals, or human embryos). It does no good to any cause to convey to readers that it could somehow be in God's purpose or human interests for them to be eaten by ghostly wild animals, in an orgiastic act of revenge, justified by the allegation that they are serving "bent angels."

In the face of the mechanism and materialism of our age and its blindness, Lewis invokes an entity parallel to the "Big Dog," Aslan, in Narnia—omnipresent phantoms which can solve human problems by magic manipulation. This childish solution is no answer to the spiritual problems of our time, or those posed by the moral failures of the scientific era.

David Holbrook, *The Skeleton in the Wardrobe: C. S. Lewis's Fantasies: A Phenomenological Study* (Lewisburg, PA: Bucknell University Press, 1991), pp. 231–32

DAVID C. DOWNING   Besides complaints about flat characters in the trilogy, reviewers and critics have often echoed ⟨J. B. S.⟩ Haldane in commenting on what seems to be Lewis's habitual aversion for science and scientists. In his "Reply to Professor Haldane," Lewis disagrees that the main targets of his satire in the trilogy are scientists. He notes that the one real scientist in *That Hideous Strength* is murdered because he wants to leave N.I.C.E. once he has discovered that its work is not really about science. Rather Lewis identifies his real targets as "scientism" and collectivism. Scientism, according to Lewis, is the quasi-religious hope of using technology to perpetuate the species on other worlds and to grope toward godhood. Lewis found this philosophy articulated less often by actual scientists than by scientific popularizers like Wells and Stapledon. Lewis concludes his reply by saying he intended the trilogy as a cautionary tale against totalitarians who use "scientific planning" as their catchphrase to attract popular support. He says that the underlying theme of *That Hideous Strength* is not, as Haldane claims, "that scientific planning will certainly lead to hell," but rather the converse that "under modern conditions any effective invitation to hell will certainly appear in the guise of scientific planning—as Hitler's regime in fact did." It is not the sciences themselves, according to Lewis, that pose the danger but those who would use the prestige of science and the power of the state to impose an "ideological oligarchy." These are the views expressed more fully in *The Abolition of Man*.

Lewis's self-defense is partly convincing on this point. Indeed, most of the degenerate characters at N.I.C.E. are managers and technocrats, not research scientists. And Lewis does show a trained scientist as a part of the company at St. Anne's (though he is the least attractive member of the group—partly because of his overbearing, no-nonsense scientific manner). But there does seem to be an excessively sweeping condemnation of technology in the trilogy. In *Out of the Silent Planet* Ransom is embarrassed to report to the hrossa of all the "wars and industrialisms" that have plagued earth, as if the two are twin curses. In *Perelandra*, space travel is treated as a breaking of Maleldil's quarantine, a spreading of earth's corruption to other worlds. Indeed, when Lewis heard rumors of actual plans for space travel, he commented acerbically, "I begin to be afraid that the villains will really contaminate the moon." In *That Hideous Strength* modern technology seems to be almost totally in the hands of those leading a vast global conspiracy to rob humans of their personhood. ⟨. . .⟩

Lewis's antagonism to science, however, has often been overstated. Philip Deasy, for example, called the trilogy "a total and unrelenting attack on science." Bruce R. Reichenbach offers a more measured and careful critique, noting that Lewis's chief concerns were the reduction of everything, even values, to the mathematical and the mechanical; the rapid development of technology without regard for long-term effects; the idea of "progress" as automatic and morally imperative; the banality of mass culture; and the brutality of much scientific research on animals. All in all, Reichenbach's is the most sensible and balanced study of Lewis's attitudes toward science and technology and one that shows Lewis's opinions to be prescient more often than they were simply crotchety. Indeed, Lewis's concerns about exploitation of the environment for short-term economic goals and about the needless suffering of animals used in scientific research anticipate widespread public awareness of these issues by almost a half-century.

> David C. Downing, "The Achievement of C. S. Lewis: Assessing the Trilogy," *Planets in Peril* (Amherst: University of Massachusetts Press, 1992), pp. 144–46

❖ *Bibliography*

Spirits in Bondage: A Cycle of Lyrics. 1919.

Dymer. 1926.

The Pilgrim's Regress: An Allegorical Apology for Christianity, Reason and Romanticism. 1933.

The Allegory of Love: A Study in Medieval Tradition. 1936.

Out of the Silent Planet. 1938.

The Personal Heresy: A Controversy (with E. M. W. Tillyard). 1939.

Rehabilitations and Other Essays. 1939.

The Problem of Pain. 1940.

The Weight of Glory. 1942.

The Screwtape Letters. 1942, 1961 (with *Screwtape Proposes a Toast*).

A *Preface to* Paradise Lost. 1942.

Broadcast Talks ⟨*The Case for Christianity*⟩. 1942.

The Abolition of Man; or, Reflections on Education with Special Reference to the Teaching of English in the Upper Forms of Schools. 1943.

Christian Behaviour: A Further Series of Broadcast Talks. 1943.

Perelandra. 1943.

Beyond Personality: The Christian Idea of God. 1944.

The Great Divorce: A Dream. 1945.

That Hideous Strength: A Modern Fairy-Tale for Grown-Ups. 1945.

George MacDonald: An Anthology (editor). 1946.

Essays Presented to Charles Williams (editor). 1947.

Miracles: A Preliminary Study. 1947.

Vivisection. c. 1947.

Autumn. 1948.

Transposition and Other Addresses. 1949.

The Lion, the Witch, and the Wardrobe: A Story for Children. 1950.

The Literary Impact of the Authorised Version. 1950.

Prince Caspian: The Return to Narnia. 1951.

The Voyage of the Dawn Treader. 1952.

Mere Christianity. 1952.

The Silver Chair. 1953.

English Literature in the Sixteenth Century, Excluding Drama. 1954.

The Horse and His Boy. 1954.

De Descriptione Temporum: An Inaugural Lecture. 1955.

The Magician's Nephew. 1955.

Surprised by Joy: The Shape of My Early Life. 1955.

The Last Battle. 1956.

Till We Have Faces: A Myth Retold. 1956.

Reflections on the Psalms. 1958.

The Four Loves. 1960.

The World's Last Night and Other Essays. 1960.

Studies in Words. 1960.

An Experiment in Criticism. 1961.

A Grief Observed. 1961.

They Asked for a Paper: Papers and Addresses. 1962.

Beyond the Bright Blur. 1963.

Letters to Malcolm, Chiefly on Prayer. 1964.

The Discarded Image: An Introduction to Medieval and Renaissance Literature. 1964.

Poems. Ed. Walter Hooper. 1964.

Screwtape Proposes a Toast and Other Pieces. 1965.

Of Other Worlds: Essays and Stories. Ed. Walter Hooper. 1966.

Studies in Medieval and Renaissance Literature. Ed. Walter Hooper. 1966.

Letters. Ed. W. H. Lewis. 1966, 1988 (ed. Walter Hooper).

Spenser's Images of Life. Ed. Alastair Fowler. 1967.

Christian Reflections. Ed. Walter Hooper. 1967.

Letters to an American Lady. Ed. Clyde S. Kilby. 1967.

Mark vs. Tristram: Correspondence between C. S. Lewis and Owen Barfield. Ed. Walter Hooper. 1967.

A Mind Awake: An Anthology of C. S. Lewis. Ed. Clyde S. Kilby. 1968.

Narrative Poems. Ed. Walter Hooper. 1969.

Selected Literary Essays. Ed. Walter Hooper. 1969.

God in the Dock: Essays on Theology and Ethics. Ed. Walter Hooper. 1970.

The Humanitarian Theory of Punishment. 1972.

The Dark Tower and Other Stories. Ed. Walter Hooper. 1977.

They Stand Together: The Letters of C. S. Lewis to Arthur Greeves 1914–1963. Ed. Walter Hooper. 1979.

A Cretaceous Perambulator (with Owen Barfield). Ed. Walter Hooper. 1983.

Boxen: The Imaginary World of the Young C. S. Lewis. Ed. Walter Hooper. 1985.

Letters to Children. Ed. Lyle W. Dorsett and Marjorie Lamp Mead. 1985.

The Latin Letters of C. S. Lewis to Don Giovanni Calabria of Verona and to Members of His Congregation 1947–1961. Ed. Martin Moynihan. 1987.

The Essential C. S. Lewis. Ed. Lyle W. Dorsett. 1988.

All My Road Before Me: The Diary of C. S. Lewis 1922–1927. Ed. Walter Hooper. 1991.

Jack London
1876–1916

JACK LONDON was born in San Francisco on January 12, 1876, the only child of a spiritualist, Flora Wellman; his mother claimed that Jack's father was an itinerant astrologer, William Henry Chaney. Wellman married John London, a widower and father of two, in September 1876. John London gave his name to his wife's child, and it was not until his college days that Jack learned the truth about his birth. As a child Jack was ignored by his mother and was all but raised by his stepsister Eliza. His stepfather was a devoted family man but often could not work because of injuries suffered during the Civil War.

London completed grammar school in Oakland and then began working eighteen-hour days at a cannery. Frustrated with the low pay and poor working conditions, he bought a small sloop named the *Razzle-Dazzle* and began pirating the commercial oyster beds. Known as "the Prince of the Oyster Beds," he briefly joined the California Fish Patrol after being caught by the government. In 1893 he signed on with the *Sophia Sutherland* and set sail for Asia. After his return he wrote "Story of a Typhoon off the Coast of Japan," which won him first prize and $25 in a San Francisco newspaper contest. In 1894 he set out with Kelly's Army, a group of militant unemployed workers determined to march to Washington. Eventually the group disbanded somewhere in the Midwest and London was arrested in Buffalo on charges of vagrancy. He described the wanderings of a tramp in *The Road* (1907). After serving his thirty-day sentence he decided to return to Oakland to finish his education. During his year as a nineteen-year-old student at Oakland High School he joined the Socialist Labor party. In 1896 he passed the difficult entrance exam for the University of California and began his studies at Berkeley that fall. He lasted only one semester; this time he was off to the Klondike in search of gold.

His adventures in the tundra provided the impetus for his first successful works of fiction. Although he returned to California prematurely because of an attack of scurvy, he had seen enough in one year to write about the wilderness at length. By 1900 his stories were being published in national magazines. His famous *The Call of the Wild* (1903) and *The Sea-Wolf* (1904) both sold well. During a visit to England he collected material about life in London's East End. These reflections on the ravages of industrialism were published in *The People of the Abyss* (1903). In 1904 he traveled to Asia to cover the Russo-Japanese War for the Hearst newspapers. His articles were tinged by ardent Anglo-Saxon bias, which today would be described as white supremacism. London ran for mayor of Oakland on the Socialist ticket in 1905. That same year he married Charmian Kittredge after divorcing Bessie Maddern, his wife of five years, and purchased a 130-acre ranch near Glen Ellen, California. Although he never had the son he longed for, he fathered two daughters by his first wife; a daughter by his second wife died in infancy.

From 1900 onward London was a full-time writer, although he continued his very wide travels: he visited Hawaii, Tahiti, Samoa, the Fiji Islands, and other locales in the Pacific on a boat trip in 1907–08; after being hospitalized in Sydney, Australia, in 1909, he returned to California via Ecuador, Panama, and New Orleans; in 1912 he sailed around Cape Horn. In 1913 he reported on the Mexican Revolution for *Collier's*. Throughout his final years, in spite of his doctors' warnings, he continued to drink heavily and consume his regular diet of raw meat and raw fish. He died on November 22, 1916.

A significant proportion of London's prolific literary work can be considered within the realm of science fiction. Among his novels, *Before Adam* (1906) tells of a man who establishes a mental link with a prehistoric ancestor; *The Iron Heel* (1907) is a dystopian novel containing premonitions of fascism; *The Scarlet Plague* (1915) deals with a germ that wipes out almost the entire population of the earth; and *The Star Rover* (1915) involves a man who, by astral projection, relives the lives of many individuals in the recent and distant past. Many of London's short stories are also science-fictional.

◈ *Critical Extracts*

JACK LONDON   I am hard at work (and 1/8 done) on a new novel—a long one, to be called *The Iron Heel*. It is a socialistic-capitalistic novel. The Iron Heel is the oligarchy of the master capitalists. The period covered is between 1912 and 1932—the twenty years that begin with the Peasant Revolt & the Chicago Commune, and that culminated in the Second Revolt in 1932.

But know that this Second Revolt was a failure, and that the Iron Heel ruled three centuries longer. Then came the new era of the Brotherhood of Man, and it was in the fourth century B.O.M. that the manuscript was discovered & published—seven centuries after it was written. Of course, there is a foreword written by a historian. Also, the book is copiously annotated by said historian, & you can imagine, with his seven centuries of perspective, the delicious slings he takes at the irrational and anarchic organization & management of society of to-day.

I'm having the time of my life writing the story.

> Jack London, Letter to Cloudesley Johns (12 September 1906), *The Letters of Jack London*, ed. Earle Labor, Robert C. Leitz III, and I. Milo Shepard (Stanford: Stanford University Press, 1988), Vol. 2, p. 605

JACK LONDON   I wrote *Before Adam* as a reply to the *Story of Ab* ⟨by Stanley Waterloo⟩, because I considered the latter unscientific. Mr. Waterloo crowded the social evolution of a thousand generations into one generation. The whole point of *Before Adam*, on the other hand, is to demonstrate the excessive slowness of social evolution in the primitive world. Also, I tried to reproduce the primitive world in an artistic form, which same Mr. Waterloo did not do. His whole story is full of meat, and interesting; yet, through the use of an awkward form, Mr. Waterloo failed to create the convincing illusion that is proper to any work of fiction.

> Jack London, Letter to B. W. Babcock (3 December 1906), *The Letters of Jack London*, ed. Earle Labor, Robert C. Leitz III, and I. Milo Shepard (Stanford: Stanford University Press, 1988), Vol. 2, p. 644

ANATOLE FRANCE   The Iron Heel is the powerful name by which Jack London designates Plutocracy. The book bearing this title was published in 1907, and describes the struggle that one day will break forth between Plutocracy and the people, should the Fates in their fury allow it.

Alas! Jack London had that particular genius which perceives what is hidden from the common herd and possessed a special knowledge enabling him to anticipate the future. He foresaw the general trend of events which are now taking place. The awesome drama which he invites us to witness in *The Iron Heel* has not yet become reality though, and we do not know when and where the prophecy of this American disciple of Marx will be fulfilled. ⟨. . .⟩

But one day the struggle between Labour and Capital will flare up again. Then we shall see days of unutterable horror such as those forecast by Jack London in his descriptions of the uprisings of San Francisco and Chicago. However, there is no reason to believe that at that time, be it sooner or later, socialism will again be crushed beneath the Iron Heel and drowned in its own blood.

In 1907 Jack London was accused of being a frightful pessimist. Even sincere socialists blamed him for casting terror within the ranks of the party. They were wrong; those who have the rare and precious gift of foreseeing the future have a duty to reveal their forebodings of danger. I remember hearing the great Jaurès say on several occasions that "the power of the classes against whom we have to struggle is not sufficiently recognized among us. They are strong and they are said to be virtuous; their priests have abandoned the ethics of the Church to embrace those of the factory; and when they are threatened society will with one accord hasten to defend them." He was right as London is right to hold before our eyes the prophetic mirror in which are reflected our faults and our imprudences.

Anatole France, "Preface" (tr. Jacqueline Tavernier-Courbin), *Le Talon de fer* ⟨*The Iron Heel*⟩ by Jack London (1923), *Critical Essays on Jack London*, ed. Jacqueline Tavernier-Courbin (Boston: G. K. Hall, 1983), pp. 35–36

LEON TROTSKY   The book ⟨*The Iron Heel*⟩ produced upon me— I speak without exaggeration—a deep impression. Not because of its artistic qualities: the form of the novel here represents only an armor for social analysis and prognosis. The author is intentionally sparing in his use of artistic means. He is himself interested not so much in the individual fate of his heroes as in the fate of mankind. By this, however, I don't want at all to belittle the artistic value of the work, especially in its last chapters beginning with the Chicago commune. The pictures of civil war develop in powerful frescoes. Nevertheless, this is not the main feature. The book surprised me with the audacity and independence of its historical foresight.

The world workers' movement at the end of the last and the beginning of the present century stood under the sign of reformism. The perspective of peaceful and uninterrupted world progress, of the prosperity of democracy and social reforms, seemed to be assured once and for all. The first Russian Revolution, it is true, revived the radical flank of the German social democracy and gave for a certain time dynamic force to anarcho-syndicalism in France. *The Iron Heel* bears the undoubted imprint of the year 1905. But at the time when this remarkable book appeared, the domination of counter-revolution was already consolidating itself in Russia. In the world arena the defeat of the Russian proletariat gave to reformism the possibility not only of regaining its temporarily lost positions but also of subjecting to itself completely the organized workers' movement. It is sufficient to recall that precisely in the following seven years (1907–14) the international social democracy ripened definitely for its base and shameful role during the World War.

Jack London not only absorbed creatively the impetus given by the first Russian Revolution but also courageously thought over again in its light the fate of capitalist society as a whole. Precisely those problems which the official socialism of this time considered to be definitely buried: the growth of wealth and power at one pole, of misery and destitution at the other pole; the accumulation of social bitterness and hatred; the unalterable preparation of bloody cataclysms—all those questions Jack London felt with an intrepidity which forces one to ask himself again and again with astonishment: when was this written? Really before the war?

> Leon Trotsky, "Jack London's *The Iron Heel*" (1937), *Leon Trotsky on Literature and Art*, ed. Paul N. Siegel (New York: Pathfinder Press, 1970), pp. 221–22

GEORGE ORWELL   London had been deeply influenced by the theory of the Survival of the Fittest. His book, *Before Adam*—an inaccurate but very readable story of prehistory, in which ape-man and early and late Palaeolithic men are all shown as existing simultaneously—is an attempt to popularise Darwin. Although Darwin's main thesis has not been shaken, there has been, during the past twenty or thirty years, a change in the interpretation put upon it by the average thinking man. In the late nineteenth century Darwinism was used as a justification for *laissez-faire* capitalism, for power politics and for the exploiting of subject peoples. Life was a free-for-all in which the fact of survival was proof of fitness to survive: this was a comforting thought for successful businessmen, and it also led naturally, though not very logically, to the notion of "superior" and "inferior" races. In our day we are less willing to apply biology to politics, partly because we have watched the Nazis do just that thing, with great thoroughness and with horrible results. But when London was writing, a crude version of Darwinism was widespread and must have been difficult to escape. He himself was even capable at times of succumbing to racial mysticism. He toyed for a while with a race theory similar to that of the Nazis, and throughout his work the cult of the "nordic" is fairly well marked. It ties up on the one hand with his admiration for prize-fighters, and on the other with his anthropomorphic view of animals: for there seems to be good reason for thinking that an exaggerated love of animals generally goes with a rather brutal attitude towards human beings. London was a Socialist with the instincts of a buccaneer and the education of a nineteenth-century materialist. In general the background of his stories is not industrial, nor even civilized. Most of them take place—and much of his own life was lived—on ranches or South Sea islands, in ships, in prison or in the wastes of the Arctic: places where a man is either alone and dependent on his own strength and cunning, or where life is naturally patriarchal.

> George Orwell, "Introduction to *Love of Life and Other Stories* by Jack London" (1946), *Collected Essays, Journalism and Letters of George Orwell*, ed. Sonia Orwell and Ian Angus (New York: Harcourt, Brace & World, 1968), Vol. 4, pp. 27–28

FREDERIC COPLE JAHER   In 1915, London brought out another novel, *The Scarlet Plague*, which foretold a dim future for America. A corrupt coterie has enslaved the workers in a caste system so rigid that they communicate with their rulers only through intermediaries. In 2012, "the year Morgan the fifth was appointed President of the United States by the Board of Magnates," a great plague destroys civilization. Despite London's atheism, this holocaust has an Old Testament tone of evil and retribution. Reminiscent of biblical vengeance, the plague is a visitation of justice upon a wicked land. After describing the carnage and brutality accompanying the old order's death throes, London paints an equally ugly picture of what emerges. Culture and discipline have been destroyed and

the population decimated by plague. Survivors return to a natural stage
where the strongest and most savage dominate. Former underdogs now lord
it over effete aristocratic remnants. Savagery so permeates the new age that
speech is barely distinguishable from animal sounds. ⟨. . .⟩

His portrayal of a destiny of unmitigated misery for society reveals the
deep depression of London's last years. Even in an earlier work, "A Curious
Fragment," in which he depicts a society with no hope of immediate deliverance, there is a promise of final salvation. The narrator of that tale comes
to educate the workers with stories of sacrifices their brothers have made
for freedom. His mission is to prepare the oppressed for their eventual
emancipation. But there is no hope in *The Scarlet Plague*. At least order
and culture are maintained by the rulers in *The Iron Heel* and "A Curious
Fragment," but when the rabble triumphs in *The Scarlet Plague*, civilization
is destroyed. London's old themes of life and vigor had been transmuted
into despair and death. The return to nature once viewed as revivifying
now is claimed to brutalize man. Socialist utopia, so much a part of orthodox
Marxism and hovering at the end of London's earlier cataclysmic tales, had
disappeared into the dead end of historical cycles. Perhaps Jack London no
longer foresaw a final deliverance because of socialism's decline, but more
likely the reason was something far deeper and more personal. He predicted
doom after his expectations had been constantly disappointed. Wealth and
prestige once won meant little to him and real power eluded him. Life
seemed a vicious swindle and Jack dreamed of revenge. In retribution for
his own frustrations he demanded society's destruction. Visions of catastrophe and the figures involved as agents served as vicarious grasps of power.
Forecasting disaster, however, was as much a gesture of self-rejection as of
self-assertion. Phantasy compensated for failure in the real world, and he
dreamed of holocaust to make victory impossible. The aging adventurer,
conscious of his own waning powers, was descending into the despondency
of his final years. He saw no hope for the world because he could find no
hope for himself.

> Frederic Cople Jaher, "Jack London: 'The Stone the Builders Rejected,' " *Doubters
> and Dissenters: Cataclysmic Thought in America 1885–1918* (New York: Free Press of
> Glencoe, 1964), pp. 208–10

RICHARD GID POWERS   London's science fiction novels and
the rest of his science fiction short stories derive from two scientific theories

he relied upon to give order to his life and to make sense out of nature and society. These two theories were the doctrines of evolutionary racism and of revolutionary socialism.

It may seem bewildering today that so intelligent a man as London could have been committed to theories as totally opposed as these. It certainly was puzzling to London's socialist friends whose reproaches once drove London to shout at them in exasperation: "What the devil! I am first of all a white man and only then a socialist!" But in the late nineteenth century the two great intellectual syntheses were Darwin's and Marx's, and attempts to combine them into one overarching *summa* were not unusual. For instance, Etienne Lantier, Emile Zola's hero in *Germinal,* was ridiculed for attempting just such an intellectual integration. But if it was not rare to find these two intellectual traditions in combination, still London's accep-tance of the racist and revolutionary varieties of each was peculiar.

All of London's science fiction stories show at least some trace of his interest in evolutionary racism and revolutionary socialism. Nevertheless it is possible to discuss each story as having a more direct dependence on either one theory or the other. His evolutionary racism produced two science fiction novels, *Before Adam* (1906), and *The Star Rover* (1915), and six of the stories in this edition: "A Relic of the Pliocene," "The Strength of the Strong," "The Scarlet Plague," "When the World Was Young," "The Unparalleled Invasion" and "The Red One." London's socialism led to the third science fiction novel, *The Iron Heel* (1907), as well as "The Minions of Midas," "The Dream of Debs," "Goliah" and "A Curious Fragment."

Richard Gid Powers, "Introduction," *The Science Fiction of Jack London,* ed. Richard Gid Powers (Boston: Gregg Press, 1975), pp. xiii–xiv

FRANCIS LACASSIN   There is no doubt that *The Star Rover* can be read on several levels.

In the most easily accessible sense, the novel is an adventure story, and the adventures themselves, with no respect for chronology, spread through the ages from the dawn of mankind up to the twentieth century. Here we have the fantastic exploits of one man—the narrator—who recovers the memory of his previous incarnations thanks to a phenomenon he calls "the little death," a sort of state of being in which time and distance cease to exist. This allows the narrator to relive, in the space of a few weeks, entire lives he has known in other places and other centuries.

The phenomenon in question is brought about at will by means of self-hypnosis intended, in the first place, to render the narrator oblivious to the sufferings inflicted on him in the cell of the American prison where he is being held. What happens in fact is that his guards immobilize him in a straitjacket and then deprive him of food for weeks on end.

The cruel and abnormal world of the penitentiary is described in each of the sequences dealing with the present. Thus the telling of a strange adventure merges into a novel of protest whose vehemence is worthy of *The Iron Heel*. But if this was how Jack London liked to see his work, it was not an interpretation to find favor with his readers.

Few people caught the meaning of the book at yet a third level, where London tries to demonstrate the superiority of mind over matter. Only the spirit is free: neither the prison of the flesh nor the walls of a cell can subjugate it. Only the spirit survives: whereas matter suffers and dies, the spirit glides over the centuries, passing from one reincarnation to another. A man is the sum total of the experience he has acquired during the migrations of his spirit, and not the result of successive adaptations of his material being to its environment.

The hero's capacity for disembodiment and his journeyings in defiance of all logic and reason, as well as his imprisonment laced with rough handling, have all been taken for so many decorative motifs intended to add heightened color to the adventure story. Or else they have been seen as additives used simply to bolster the element of strangeness and mystery. Even today, *The Star Rover* is looked upon as a novel of extraordinary adventures. It may be granted greater novelty than is usual in this type of work, but it is seen nevertheless as a book in which the wholehearted indignation typical of Jack London has once more colored his imagination.

How many readers have in fact understood that the adventure story is merely a means of illustrating an argument, merely the story line of a moral fable? Certainly Jack London has not always been properly understood in such works as *Martin Eden*, *Burning Daylight*, and *The Sea-Wolf*, which were intended to combat individualism, but were interpreted, on the contrary, as exalting it. Moreover, *The Star Rover* is no more a true novel of the fantastic than *The Sea-Wolf* is really a novel of the sea. Remaining loyal to his concept of the novel in general, Jack London wanted to make *The Star Rover* what in fact it is and what a careful reading reveals it to be: an instrument for use in the fight against social injustice. But for the first time he adds a message of hope.

> Francis Lacassin, "On the Roads of the Night: A Search for the Origins of *The Star Rover*" (1976), tr. Margaret Stanley, *Critical Essays on Jack London*, ed. Jacqueline Tavernier-Courbin (Boston: G. K. Hall, 1983), pp. 181–82

CHARLES N. WATSON, JR.   By thus tying the immediate action ⟨of *The Iron Heel*⟩ to larger myths of cosmic process and purpose, London is following Zola's *Germinal*, where violent class conflict is set against the cyclical processes of nature: germination, growth, and fruition. Though London had read *Germinal* years earlier, a nearer influence may have been Frank Norris's *The Octopus* (1901), itself strongly influenced by *Germinal*. Despite his reservations about the "inordinate realism" of minute detail, London praised and quoted at length from the "broad canvas" and heightened rhetoric of Norris's description of the colossal power of the railroad and the primordial energy of the wheat. Thus, even more than in *The Sea-Wolf*, he directs *The Iron Heel* toward the large effects of the abstract forces of virtue and villainy, which are thrown into violent conflict in the Armageddon of class warfare. When Avis finds among the socialists nothing but "unselfishness and high idealism," or when Ernest speaks in the stylized platitudes of heroic romance ("To-morrow the Cause will rise again, strong with wisdom and discipline"), we are meant to accept these violations of verisimilitude as appropriate to a didactic fable.

Whether such allowances can in fact be made, however, is a question that will be answered differently by different readers. We can thank recent Marxist criticism for a clearer appreciation of the function of the double point of view and for a proper insistence that *The Iron Heel* cannot be judged solely by the criteria of the realistic novel. Yet these corrections do not dispose of the two inescapable flaws: the unconvincing characterization of Avis, and the absence of the hero at the climax. Ernest's martyrdom, which should have come at the height of the Chicago cataclysm, is instead displaced into the hazy future, where its impact is drastically diminished. Bluntly, if we are to take Ernest seriously, we need to see him die.

With subtler art, with more careful novelistic construction, London might have turned a "minor revolutionary classic" ⟨Walter B. Rideout⟩ into a major one. Even the most sensitive of the Marxist critics descend at times to special pleading in their defense of a novel that London seems to have written too much out of his heart, too little out of his head. That disproportion is no doubt responsible for the most successful scenes, which depict a society's capacity for vindictive violence and injustice. Unfortunately, it is responsible also for the crippling flaws.

> Charles N. Watson, Jr., "Revolution and Romance: *The Iron Heel*," *The Novels of Jack London: A Reappraisal* (Madison: University of Wisconsin Press, 1983), pp. 121–22

GORMAN BEAUCHAMP   "Basically the story is a cry of despair," writes Billy Collins in a perceptive essay on "The Red One." "Although London allows Bassett and the reader to hope for an evolution to a higher stage of human perfection, there is no present hope for happiness left on earth. Bassett, as a representative of man's highest point of evolution, proves himself a brutal killer and perverter and user of human love. His end, with his head smoking in a witch doctor's fire, is appropriate." London's long-held belief in the essential savagery of man, in the persistence of the brute beneath even the most civilized veneer, may be said to receive its final expression here. The story has much in common with Conrad's *Heart of Darkness* and may, as Collins thinks, be directly indebted to it. Bassett, like Kurtz, discovers "The horror! The horror!" in the heart of man. Yet London, like his protagonist a dying man, offers a glimpse—shadowy, indecipherable, but immensely portentous—of something beyond the horror of human history that might redeem man if he could but grasp its Medusa-like Truth. Bassett dies, however, at the moment of his epiphany: what he saw in that moment we do not know. But in that moment London seemed to invest his final hope.

Though "The Red One" lacks the renown among readers of science fiction that it deserves, knowledgeable London critics concur that, as Richard G. Powers puts it, "it is both his finest science fiction story and one of his best efforts in any genre." Dale Walker calls it an extraordinary fantasy "of shuddering impact." Though by no means flawless—the tortuously baroque style can prove annoying—"The Red One" is a minor masterpiece of science fiction, more teasingly ambiguous yet more compelling than anything else that London ever wrote in this form. Here his art soars infinitely far above

his wonted Naturalistic theories and achieves an imaginative purity of vision all too rare in his other work. The tale is a fitting coda to London's career.
Gorman Beauchamp, *Jack London* (San Bernadino, CA: Borgo Press, 1984), p. 85

JAMES LUNDQUIST   *Before Adam* begins with the narrator's complaint about being tormented by "a procession of nightmares" in his childhood, and goes on to tell of a recurrent dream he has of himself as the pre-human Big-Tooth, who lives in the mid-Pleistocene Age. His tribe, known as the Folk, are the "missing link" between the Tree People and homo sapiens, the Fire People. Like the heroes of many London stories, Big-Tooth and his friend Lop-Ear run away on a journey toward maturity that takes them to the "high backbone of earth" and down into a valley of riches, the streams "packed thick with salmon" and the grasslands incredibly fertile. The pilgrimage is circular, in a sense, and Big-Tooth eventually rejoins the Folk and takes the Swift One as his mate. When attacked by the Fire People, Big-Tooth and the Swift One must flee into a swamp, but they live to raise a family. London does not trace the descent of man, but the narrator says: "One thing only is certain, and that is that Big-Tooth did stamp into the cerebral constitution of one of his progeny all the impressions of his life, and stamped them in so indelibly that the hosts of intervening generations have failed to obliterate them."

The novel ends with what seems to be a statement of literal belief in primal memory, but London covered for himself by pointing out that most of the time he slept "like a babe" and that the book offered proof of several theories he had regarding human prehistory. London argued, in a letter to a fellow socialist who had asked about the book's purpose, that *Before Adam* had been written to show the slow development of primitive man. London pointed out that the novel demonstrates how the process of biological evolution resulted in "mistakes and lost off-shoots," and that in a single generation the most likely device his prehistoric characters could have invented was the use of gourds to carry water and berries. This may be so, and London certainly did write to correct some of the errors of other writers in the "caveman" stories that were popular at the time, but it is the romance of the "unknown ages" that carries the story and makes it one of the most readable of London's minor works. "As a half-grown boy, I reveled in the book, opening as it did vast vistas of the human past with which I was unfamiliar," Loren Eiseley testifies. "Reading it today as a professional anthropologist, I find that none of that old thrill has departed. . . . The great swamp that is the scene of Big-Tooth's final flight, that waste which caused my flesh to creep even as a boy, I as a man now mentally perceive as a symbol of man's long journey, harried by his own ferocity from age to age."

James Lundquist, *Jack London: Adventures, Ideas, and Fiction* (New York: Ungar, 1987), pp. 168–69

▧ *Bibliography*

The Son of the Wolf: Tales of the Far North. 1900.

The God of His Fathers and Other Stories. 1901.

Children of the Frost. 1902.

The Cruise of the Dazzler. 1902.

A Daughter of the Snows. 1902.

The Kempton-Wace Letters (with Anna Strumsky). 1903.

The Call of the Wild. 1903.

The People of the Abyss. 1903.

The Faith of Men and Other Stories. 1904.

The Sea-Wolf. 1904.

War of the Classes. 1905.

Jack London: A Sketch of His Life and Work. 1905.

The Game. 1905.

Tales of the Fish Patrol. 1905.

Moon-Face and Other Stories. 1906.

White Fang. 1906.

Scorn of Women. 1906.

What Life Means to Me. 1906.

The Apostate. 1906.

Before Adam. 1906.

Love of Life and Other Stories. 1907.

The Road. 1907.

The Iron Heel. 1907.

Martin Eden. 1909.

Revolution. 1909.

The Dream of Debs: A Story of Industrial Revolt. 1909.

Lost Face. 1910.

Revolution and Other Essays. 1910.

Burning Daylight. 1910.

Theft. 1910.

When God Laughs and Other Stories. 1911.

Adventure. 1911.

The Cruise of the Snark. 1911.

South Sea Tales. 1911.

The House of Pride and Other Tales of Hawaii. 1912.

A Son of the Sun. 1912.

Smoke Bellow. 1912.

The Night-Born, and Also the Madness of John Horned, When the World Was Young, The Benefit of the Doubt, Winged Blackmail, Bunches of Knuckles, War, Under the Deck Awnings, To Kill a Man, The Mexican. 1913.

The Abysmal Brute. 1913.

Jack London by Himself. 1913.

John Barleycorn. 1913.

The Valley of the Moon. 1913.

The Strength of the Strong. 1914.

The Mutiny of the Elsinore. 1914.

The Scarlet Plague. 1915.

The Jacket. 1915.

The Star Rover. 1915.

The Resignation of Jack London. 1916.

The Acorn Planter: A California Forest Play. 1916.

The Little Lady of the Big House. 1916.

The Turtles of Tasman. 1916.

The Human Drift. 1917.

Jerry of the Islands. 1917.

Michael, Brother of Jerry. 1917.

The Red One. 1918.

Hearts of Three. 1918.

On the Makaloa Mat. 1919.

Works (Sonoma Edition). 1919. 27 vols.

Dutch Courage and Other Stories. 1922.

Essays of Revolt. Ed. Leonard D. Abbott. 1926.

Works (Fitzroy Edition). Ed. I. O. Evans. 1962–68. 18 vols.

The Assassination Bureau, Ltd. (with Robert L. Fish). 1963.

The Bodley Head London. Ed. Arthur Calder-Marshall. 1963–66. 4 vols.

Letters from Jack London, Containing an Unpublished Correspondence between London and Sinclair Lewis. Ed. King Hendricks and Irving Shepard. 1965.

Daughters of the Rich. Ed. James E. Sisson. 1971.

Goliah: A Utopian Essay. 1973.

The Science Fiction of Jack London. Ed. Richard Gid Powers. 1975.

Curious Fragments: Jack London's Tales of Fantasy Fiction. Ed. Dale L. Walker. 1975.

Jack London on the Road: The Tramp Diary and Other Hobo Writings. Ed. Richard W. Etulain. 1979.

No Mentor But Myself: A Collection of Articles, Essays, Reviews, and Letters on Writing and Writers. Ed. Dale L. Walker. 1979.

Articles and Stories in The Ægis. Ed. James Sisson III. 1980.

Novels and Stories. 1982.

Novels and Social Writings. 1982.

A Klondike Trilogy: Three Uncollected Short Stories. Ed. Earle Labor. 1983.

Dearest Greek: Jack and Charmian London's Presentation Inscriptions to George Sterling. Ed. Stanley Wertheim and Sal Noto. 1983.

With a Heart Full of Love: Jack London's Presentation Inscriptions to the Women in His Life. Ed. Sal Noto. 1986.

Letters. Ed. Earle Labor, Robert C. Leitz III, and I. Milo Shepard. 1988. 3 vols.

Complete Short Stories. Ed. Earle Labor, Robert C. Leitz III, and I. Milo Shepard. 1993. 3 vols.

Science Fiction Stories. Ed. James Bankes. 1993.

The Portable Jack London. Ed. Earle Labor. 1994.

⧈ ⧈ ⧈

H. P. Lovecraft
1890–1937

HOWARD PHILLIPS LOVECRAFT was born on August 20, 1890, in Providence, Rhode Island. When he was three his father, a traveling salesman, suffered a seizure and spent the rest of his life in an insane asylum, dying of syphilis in 1898. The boy's upbringing was left to his overprotective mother, his two aunts, and his grandfather, Whipple Phillips, a wealthy industrialist. A precocious boy, Lovecraft was reading at two, writing poems and stories at seven, and learning Latin and Greek at eight.

The family's fortunes suffered a reversal in 1904 at the death of Whipple Phillips, and Lovecraft and his mother were forced to move into smaller quarters in Providence. Distressed at the loss of his birthplace, the young Lovecraft briefly pondered suicide but then plunged himself into intellectual pursuits. His formal education was sporadic because of his chronic ill health, and in 1908 he suffered an apparent nervous breakdown that forced him to leave Hope Street High School without a diploma. The next five years were spent in virtual hermitry, as Lovecraft continued to amass an impressive self-education in literature, science, and philosophy.

In 1914 Lovecraft joined the amateur journalism movement, plunging into the literary and political activities of the United Amateur Press Association and, later, the National Amateur Press Association. He produced thirteen issues of his own journal, *The Conservative* (1915–23), filling it with poems, essays, and commentary. Gradually, at the urging of friends, Lovecraft recommended the writing of horror tales: "The Tomb" (1917) is the first story of his mature period.

For years Lovecraft had no thought of publishing his work professionally. In 1923, however, he was urged to contribute to the fledgling pulp magazine *Weird Tales*. Over the next fifteen years, the bulk of his fiction appeared in the pages of that magazine; in 1924 he was even asked to be its editor, but he refused. Lovecraft's genteel upbringing rendered him persistently diffident about commercially marketing his writing, and several attempts by book publishers to issue his work came to nothing.

Lovecraft's mother died in 1921; two months later he met Sonia Haft Greene, a Ukrainian Jew several years his senior. In 1924 they married, and Lovecraft moved into Sonia's apartment in Brooklyn. Their marriage, however, was not a success: Lovecraft was unable to find regular work, a hat shop owned by Sonia went out of business, and later her health gave way; she was forced to take a job in the Midwest, leaving Lovecraft alone in a city he had come to loathe for its noise, overcrowding, and "foreigners." He wrote few stories during this period, but did the bulk of work on his study "Supernatural Horror in Literature" (first published in an amateur magazine, the *Recluse*, in 1927).

In April 1926 Lovecraft returned to Providence, essentially ending the marriage, and proceeded to write his greatest work—tales such as "The Call of Cthulhu" (1926), "The Colour out of Space" (1927), "The Whisperer in Darkness" (1930), "The Shadow over Innsmouth" (1931), *At the Mountains of Madness* (1931), and "The Shadow out of Time" (1934–35). Several of these stories appeared in such early science fiction pulp magazines as *Amazing Stories* and *Astounding Stories*, and much of his work can be thought to be science-fictional in its discarding of pure supernaturalism, its propounding of scientific justifications of weird phenomena, its accounts of invasions of Earth from extraterrestrial entities, and its conjectures on the future political and social development of the human race.

During the last ten years of his life Lovecraft traveled widely on various antiquarian expeditions and became a stunningly voluminous letter writer, corresponding with fantasists such as August Derleth, Donald Wandrei, Clark Ashton Smith, Robert E. Howard, Frank Belknap Long, Robert Bloch, James Blish, and many others. Although a towering figure in the realms of amateur journalism and pulp fiction, Lovecraft had only one small book, *The Shadow over Innsmouth* (1936), issued by a small press before his death of intestinal cancer on March 15, 1937.

After his death Lovecraft's friends set about rescuing his work from oblivion. Derleth and Wandrei founded the firm of Arkham House for the express purpose of publishing his work in hardcover; their first volume, *The Outsider and Others* (1939), is a landmark. Lovecraft's work has subsequently appeared in many hardcover and paperback editions and has been translated into more than a dozen languages. His *Selected Letters* appeared in five volumes between 1965 and 1976, and his collected fiction was republished in a corrected text under the editorship of S. T. Joshi between 1984 and 1989. His *Miscellaneous Writings* was published in 1994.

▨ *Critical Extracts*

H. P. LOVECRAFT   Despite the current flood of stories dealing with other worlds and universes, and with intrepid flights to and from them through cosmic space, it is probably no exaggeration to say that not more than a half-dozen of these things, including the novels of H. G. Wells, have even the slightest shadow of a claim to artistic seriousness or literary rank. Insincerity, conventionality, triteness, artificiality, false emotion, and puerile extravagance reign triumphant throughout this overcrowded genre, so that none but its rarest products can possibly claim a truly adult status. And the spectacle of such persistent hollowness has led many to ask whether, indeed, any fabric of real literature can ever grow out of the given subject matter.

The present commentator does not believe that the idea of space-travel and other worlds is inherently unsuited to literary use. It is, rather, his opinion that the omnipresent cheapening and misuse of that idea is the result of a widespread misconception; a misconception which extends to other departments of weird and science fiction as well. This fallacy is the notion that any account of impossible, improbable, or inconceivable phenomena can be successfully presented as a commonplace narrative of objective acts and conventional emotions in the ordinary tone and manner of popular romance. Such a presentation will often "get by" with immature readers, but it will never approach even remotely the field of aesthetic merit.

Inconceivable events and conditions form a class apart from all other story elements, and cannot be made convincing by any mere process of casual narration. They have the handicap of incredibility to overcome; and this can be accomplished only through a careful realism in every *other* phase of the story, plus a gradual atmospheric or emotional building-up of the utmost subtlety. The emphasis, too, must be kept right—hovering always over *the wonder of the central abnormality itself*. It must be remembered that any violation of what we know as natural law is *in itself* a far more tremendous thing than any other event or feeling which could possibly affect a human being. Therefore in a story dealing with such a thing we cannot expect to create any sense of life or illusion of reality if we treat the wonder casually and have the characters moving about under ordinary motivations. The characters, though they must be natural, should be subordinated to the central marvel around which they are grouped. The true "hero" of a marvel tale is not any human being, but simply *a set of phenomena*.

H. P. Lovecraft, "Some Notes on Interplanetary Fiction," *Californian* 3, No. 3 (Winter 1935): 39

CLEVELAND C. SOPER   ⟨. . .⟩ why in the name of science-fiction did you ever print such a story as *At the Mountains of Madness* by Lovecraft? Are you in such dire straits that you *must* print this kind of drivel? In the first place, this story does not belong in *Astounding Stories,* for there is no science in it at all. You even recommend it with the expression that it was a fine word picture, and for that I will never forgive you.

If such stories as this—of two people scaring themselves half to death by looking at the carvings in some ancient ruins, and being chased by something that even the author can't describe, and full of mutterings about nameless horrors, such as the windowless solids with five dimensions, Yog-Sothoth, etc.—are what is to constitute the future yarns of *Astounding Stories,* then heaven help the course of science-fiction. I know that it is your policy to print more of the whimsy type of science-fiction than of the type having science as a base but, at least, you don't have to wish this bunk on us.

    Cleveland C. Soper, Letter to the Editor, *Astounding Stories* 17, No. 4 (June 1936): 159

FRITZ LEIBER   Beginning with "The Call of Cthulhu" and "The Colour out of Space," speculative science played a larger part in Lovecraft's fiction: hibernating races and travel through space, hyperspace, and time. That those two tales were written very soon after *Amazing Stories* was founded in 1926 and the second published in that magazine is at least suggestive.

Amazing Stories began with reprints of Wells and Verne, giving hopes of at least a moderately high literary level—hopes largely dashed, which may account for Lovecraft's veering away from that market after his first sale.

In more than half his subsequent fiction, however, monsters raised by black magic and thwarted by white are replaced by extraterrestrial or even extracosmical beings who sojourned on earth in the past and may secretly reside among us today. The *Necronomicon* largely ceases to be used for its spells of exorcism, but remains a sourcebook on the habits and history of these more realistic monsters. ⟨. . .⟩

But during the very Gernsback era he detested, Lovecraft made his own contribution to speculative fiction ⟨. . .⟩

These contributions were largely in the direction of paying proper attention to cosmology, astronomy, and geology and to impressing on the reader the vast size and duration of the cosmos. Lovecraft's extraterrestrials were never stock humanoid figures (such as the appealing yet ridiculous oviparous princesses of Burroughs' Mars), but beings with a wholly nonhuman morphology and biology, and with languages, architectures, industries, and cultures wholly their own.

Lovecraft did his best to get writers to stop using obvious English roots in devising the names of earth-aliens—"Tarko," say, or "Akor"—and instead try to imagine nonhuman sounds and then render them phonetically. While some of his biological creations are masterful feats of imagination: the appearance of a specimen of the Old Ones, as described by Lake in *At the Mountains of Madness*, is chillingly real—if the reader will make the effort to visualise the being as described in dry scientific language. If Lovecraft had been able and willing to put such a being *into action* in one of his tales, he would doubtless have won many new readers. But for reasons in part aesthetic he never took this step. Perhaps he was tempted to and his hesitation fully to abandon supernatural horror for less restrictive speculative fiction was one of the reasons for his creative slow-down during his last years.

Certainly Lovecraft helped lead the way toward greater realism in subsequent speculative fiction.

It must be admitted, however, that Lovecraft devoted very little attention to novel inventions, to scientific speculations for their own sake, and to extrapolations from present-day society into the future—aside from a general conviction that human affairs would get worse, at least from the viewpoint of a lover of traditions and of social stability. After all, his chief artistic interest was in creating backgrounds for horror stories; graveyards and homely ghosts were losing interest, while cosmic outsideness was gaining, and in one way he simply followed this trend—to the point of seeing both *At the Mountains of Madness* and "The Shadow out of Time" published in *Astounding Stories*.

Fritz Leiber, "Through Hyperspace with Brown Jenkin: Lovecraft's Contribution to Speculative Fiction" (1966), *H. P. Lovecraft: Four Decades of Criticism*, ed. S. T. Joshi (Athens: Ohio University Press, 1980), pp. 140, 142–43

MAURICE LÉVY   Lovecraft was decidedly fascinated with the sciences that allowed the investigation of the earliest stretches of time. His scholars are ethnologists, folklorists, and geologists. In *At the Mountains of*

Madness the narrator organizes a scientific expedition to the Antarctic (the author owed this to Poe) whose goal is the study of deep-buried rock. In the course of these researches the scientists one day encounter, in the debris of primitive shellfish and fragments of divers bones of archaic mammals, the monstrous fossils of organisms several thousand million years old. In the Lovecraftian universe there is manifestly an "edge of time" as well as an "edge of the world," and the author, close to vertigo, ill resists the attraction of this new gulf.

In attaining this anterior period in history, Lovecraft was as always aided by antique homes and cities, whose architectural structures guide the imagination in its dynamic descent. The depths of space they define, around the vertical axis of their spiral staircase, are an adequate materialization of the shadows out of time that seem to have hypnotized the author. Here again the exploration of a mythic past coincides with the descent of two survivors of the expedition along subterranean tunnels and helicoidal inclined planes, in the ruins of the ancient city that still remain on the deserted and inaccessible expanse of the malefic Plateau of Leng. The frescoes they admire as they plunge into the nighted gulf record the history of those who once lived there, thus creating a type of inverse chronology. The metamorphosis of the universe at the heart of geological cycles and the stages of the fabulous existence of the Old Ones unravel thus *backward* before our eyes.

The descent into the entrails of the earth corresponds to a voyage in time. For then, at the bottom of the abyss and at the end of their quest, the adventurers encounter a . . . shoggoth, still living, a plastic and globulous entity, which by suction decapitates the last descendants of a prestigious race. The whole tale aims once more at this reactivation of a latent horror, which lies, always menacing, beyond space and time, at the heart of the world. "It is absolutely necessary, for the peace and safety of mankind, that some of earth's dark, dead corners and unplumbed depths be let alone; lest sleeping abnormalities wake to resurgent life, and blasphemously surviving nightmares squirm and splash out of their black lairs to newer and wider conquests."

It is within the framework of these remarks on the images of the deep—characteristic, we think, of his writing—that it is useful to read Lovecraft's pseudo-science fiction tales. There is sometimes a tendency to class some of his tales ("The Colour out of Space," for example, or "The Whisperer in Darkness") as among the masterpieces of that other and similar genre. This assimilation, however, can seem wrong if we consider that interstellar space is perceived by our author less as the exciting place of future adventures than as a type of reversed abysm, another depth at the other extremity of the vertical axis of the imagination, an "anti-gulf" from which new horrors come, always associated with the origins of the universe and not with its final ends. Lovecraft belongs to that class of dreamers for whom the deep is *also* above.

> Maurice Lévy, *Lovecraft: A Study in the Fantastic* (1972), tr. S. T. Joshi (Detroit: Wayne State University Press, 1988), pp. 69–70

KENNETH STERLING   I lived in Providence for a year. During the academic year, excepting Christmas and spring recesses, the Science Club met weekly. That meant I had a schedule of one scientist a week—all, with two exceptions, from the Brown University faculty—and every time I walked up College Hill toward the Brown campus I visited Lovecraft for several hours. The total number of hours I conversed with him was huge. ⟨. . .⟩

⟨. . .⟩ If one theme dominated my conversations with Lovecraft it was the interplanetary one.

"About rockets," he wrote to me later (November 20, 1935)—"certainly I realise that the major experiments involve really serious research. They can probably get higher up in the stratosphere than anything else ever can, and it is surely fitting that all their possibilities be investigated. But I trust that repeated accidents will cause experimenters to take additional precautions—excluding spectators when anything problematical or of unusual magnitude is attempted. The *newness* of all this business is quite bewildering to an old man—when I was young the rocket principle was never heard of in connexion with locomotion, so that in writing my ponderous essay 'Can the Moon Be Reached by Man?' in 1906 I enumerated only three possible motive powers—shooting from a cannon, screen to cut off gravity (if such be ever discovered), and some future manipulation of electrical repulsion. How times do change!"

> Kenneth Sterling, "Caverns Measureless to Man," *Science-Fantasy Correspondent* No. 1 (1975): 37

PAUL A. CARTER   Since *The Time Machine* there have been hundreds, perhaps thousands, of stories written on its central theme. A writer for the science fiction pulps could confidently assume his readers' familiarity with Wells's classic; not only with its specific time-traveling gadget, which was imitated many times over, but—more important—with its mood and point of view. Wells's *fin-de-siècle* pessimism surely influenced John Campbell's "Twilight," for example. It also touched Howard Phillips Lovecraft, who seized upon the radical shock of mental displacement that travel to far-off time might entail; a terror at least as keen as the kind evoked by yawning graveyards, sag-roofed farmhouses, and musty genealogy, which were that writer's usual stock in trade. In his "Commonplace Book" of notes for stories to be written, Lovecraft jotted down one truly hair-raising idea: "In an ancient buried city a man finds a mouldering prehistoric document *in English in his own handwriting.*" That sentence grew into one of Lovecraft's longest and most effective tales, "The Shadow out of Time," published in *Astounding Stories* (June 1936).

If the event in that story really happened, says its narrator, "then man must be prepared to accept notions of the cosmos, and of his own place in the seething vortex of time, whose merest mention is paralyzing." Wrenched back into time by an ancient prehuman civilization that practices time travel as a novel method for doing scholarly research, Lovecraft's hero finds himself among other, similarly kidnapped time travelers from all eons, past and future. Down among his weird captors' library stacks, he talks with— to list some of the human examples only—

> the mind of Yiang-Li, a philosopher from the cruel empire of
> Tsan-Chan, which is to come in 5,000 A.D.; with that of a
> general of the great-headed brown people who held South Africa
> in 50,000 B.C.; with that of a twelfth-century Florentine monk
> named Bartolomeo Corsi; . . . with that of a Roman named Titus
> Sempronius Blaesus, who had been quaestor in Sulla's time; with
> that of Khephnes, an Egyptian of the 14th dynasty . . .; with that
> of a Suffolk gentleman of Cromwell's day, James Woodville; with
> that of a court astronomer of pre-Inca Peru; with that of the
> Australian physicist Nevil Kingston-Brown, who will die in 2,518
> A.D.; . . . and with so many others that my brain cannot hold the
> shocking secrets and dizzying marvels I learned from them.

"To Lovecraft," anthologist Donald Wollheim perceptively wrote (in *The Portable Novels of Science*, 1945), "the millions of years gone by and the millions of years to come are sources of dread, because of his knowledge of the cold cruelty of nature." Mingled with the dread, however, is that other powerful impulse so often expressed in science fiction: the Faustian urge to know all. As Lovecraft's character converses with all these highly knowledgeable people and Things, his sense of estrangement and horror mutates insensibly into fascination.

Paul A. Carter, *The Creation of Tomorrow: Fifty Years of Magazine Science Fiction* (New York: Columbia University Press, 1977), pp. 93–95

DIRK W. MOSIG and DONALD R. BURLESON   As with many of Lovecraft's later works dealing with his fictional concept of a universe peopled even beyond its dimensional confines by intelligences of unthinkable antiquity, *At the Mountains of Madness* immerses the reader in a world view in which mankind is the most recent, the most transient, and the least significant of life forms in the whole scenario of Earth's history. Like the story "The Shadow out of Time" (1936), this novel presents a pseudohistory of our planet involving the early advent, burgeoning, and cataclysmic decline of intelligences whose civilizations spanned stunning periods of time and vanished at periods so remote in Earth's past as to defy even being called "fabulous" in any common understanding of that word. As represented by Dyer and Danforth, man, a mere terrestrial newcomer by comparison, learns of the dim and awesome prehistoric tenancy of the Old Ones, yet is made to feel a profound sense of empathy with his predecessors. The grandeur of the crumbling city is mute testimony to the greatness of the Old Ones; yet it is exceeded by the sense of horror inspired by the sprawling protoplasmic shoggoths below, in realms as dark as Coleridge's "caverns measureless to man." Indeed, it is this continuity with an unimaginable past, this implication that a detestable and now greatly magnified vestige of that past still lurks below after countless aeons to menace overly inquisitive human beings—it is this shocking linkage that gives the novel its unforgettable horror. ⟨. . .⟩

The novel has a strong psychological appeal, touching deep emotions in the reader. Lovecraft himself was haunted all his life by a vague but persistent sense of "adventurous expectancy," a feeling that immediately beyond one's grasp, beneath the prosaic world of appearances and normalcy, lay substrata of wonder. And who can fail to feel, with Dyer and Danforth as they enter the immemorial city beyond the mountain range—a city of this very Earth but untrod by human feet—the excitement of discovery, mingled with awe at the implications of the place for Earth's history and man's motelike place in it? The novel stacks awe upon awe, horror upon horror. The Old Ones and their crumbling citadel are overshadowed by the piping shoggoths, whose immensity fills the cave-riddled mountain range to the very peaks, and these horrors in turn pale in comparison with the unnamed things lying beyond the farther mountain range and only dimly glimpsed, only fearfully guessed at. Whatever wonders there are, there are always more, just beyond clear discernment.

At the Mountains of Madness stirs deep-seated capacities for attraction and repulsion; the reader may shudder at the experiences of Dyer and Danforth on the accursed Plateau while at the same time yearning to be in their shoes. The reader is left, paradoxically, both with a heightened sense of human adventurousness and a curious sense of the unimportance and evanescence of humankind. As is the case with all great artists' work, these sensations, along with other impressions left by the novel, grow in potency with rereading.

Dirk W. Mosig and Donald R. Burleson, "At the Mountains of Madness," *Survey of Science Fiction Literature*, ed. Frank N. Magill (Englewood Cliffs, NJ: Salem Press, 1979), Vol. 1, pp. 98–101

JAMES TURNER   During the final decade of his life Lovecraft's cosmicism became far more complex and profound as he began to incorporate the contemporary scientific thinking of his age into his macabre fiction. The first major story after his return from New York was the 1926 nouvelle "The Call of Cthulhu," which also inaugurated the body of mature work that would become Lovecraft's crowning achievement and to which has been applied posthumously the term "Cthulhu Mythos." The opening paragraph of "The Call of Cthulhu" serves as a virtual prolegomenon for the Mythos tales that would follow:

> The most merciful thing in the world, I think, is the inability
> of the human mind to correlate all its contents. We live on a
> placid island of ignorance in the midst of black seas of infinity,
> and it was not meant that we should voyage far. The sciences,
> each straining in its own direction, have hitherto harmed us little;
> but some day the piecing together of dissociated knowledge will
> open up such terrifying vistas of reality, and of our frightful

position therein, that we shall either go mad from the revelation
or flee from the deadly light into the peace and safety of a new
dark age.

Although Lovecraft often is designated as a founding father of the modern
American horror movement, the preceding scientifically formulated statement will serve to suggest the essential apartness of Lovecraft's cosmic
Cthulhu Mythos from the supernatural occultism, urban paranoia, and abba-
toir extravagances of present-day horror fiction. In these Mythos tales Lovecraft typically would take an element from the old Gothic tradition—perhaps
an authentic New England setting or some aspect of New England lore or
legendry—and reinterpret this element in terms of the scientific theories
(Einstein, Heisenberg, Planck, et al.) of his day. Through a fanciful extension
of contemporary scientific thinking Lovecraft ultimately would resolve his
narrative upon a supernatural—or, more accurately, supramundane—level
of reality, thus revivifying the trappings and appurtenances of old-time
Gothicism through an expressly scientific approach. Here is Lovecraft's own
explanation of the technique, from a 1930 letter: "My big kick comes from
taking reality just as it is—accepting all the limitations of the most orthodox
science—and then permitting my symbolising faculty to *build outward* from
the existing facts; rearing a structure of *infinite promise and possibility* whose
topless towers are in no cosmos or dimension penetrable by the contradicting-
power of the tyrannous and inexorable intellect." An example of this technique is the 1932 story "The Dreams in the Witch House," in which
Lovecraft presented figures of New England legendry—the old Salem witch
Keziah Mason, her evil ratlike familiar, and the infamous Black Man of the
witch cult—and reinterpreted these figures as emissaries from a fourth-
dimensional space-time continuum; the narrative itself is then resolved into
a sequence of oneiric episodes in which this fourth dimension impinges
upon the present world. If "The Dreams in the Witch House" is far from
being a completely satisfactory reading experience, one can only marvel at
Lovecraft's audacity in attempting so formidable a synthesis of New England
black magic and Einsteinian physics!

James Turner, "H. P. Lovecraft: A Mythos in His Own Image," *Foundation* No. 33
(Spring 1985): 59

S. T. JOSHI   It is of some significance that most of the tales of the
so-called Lovecraft Mythos or Cthulhu Mythos involve whole civilisations

of alien entities rather than individual monsters as in "Dagon" or "The Shunned House". This phenomenon immediately compels us to look for sociopolitical implications in the tales in question. What we are presented with in the tales beginning with "The Call of Cthulhu" is a series of *counter-civilisations*—civilisations in many cases as fully evolved as our own but implacably hostile or at least carelessly indifferent to ours. ⟨. . .⟩

It quickly becomes clear that the three civilisations in "The Mound", *At the Mountains of Madness*, and "The Shadow out of Time" are transparent parables for the future development of Western civilisation. It is of some significance that "The Mound", written a few months after the stock market crash of October 1929, is very pessimistic in its account of the gradual decadence of the mound people. ⟨. . .⟩

Initially it appears as if the mound people are true Epicureans, living solely for pleasure and tranquillity: "To see that the mutual encroachments of pleasure-seeking never crippled the mass life of the community—this was all that was desired." Earlier it is even remarked that many "mechanical devices . . . had been abandoned when it was seen that they failed to give pleasure"—a more pitiable expression of Lovecraft's pipe-dream of reversing the march of technology would be difficult to find. But even before the full-fledged decadence of the mound people becomes apparent, a dangerous element enters into their pleasure-seeking:

> Daily life was organised in ceremonial patterns; with games,
> intoxication, torture of slaves, day-dreaming, gastronomic and
> emotional orgies, religious exercises, exotic experiments, artistic
> and philosophical discussions, and the like, as the principal
> occupations.

The narrative tone is very urbane and tolerant here; but the later account of the mound people's decadence picks up on a number of points raised in this passage:

> [Zamacona] felt that the people of Tsath were a lost and
> dangerous race—more dangerous to themselves than they knew—
> and that their growing frenzy of monotony-warfare and novelty-
> quest was leading them rapidly toward a precipice of
> disintegration and utter horror. . . . With the growth of boredom
> and restlessness, he saw, cruelty and subtlety and revolt were
> growing apace. There was more cosmic abnormality, more and
> more curious sadism, more and more ignorance and superstition,

and more and more desire to escape out of physical life into a
half-spectral state of electronic dispersal. ⟨. . .⟩

If "The Mound" is a dire prediction of the future of mankind if mechanisation proceeds at its current pace, At the Mountains of Madness begins to
suggest, tentatively, ways out of the dilemma; but the shift is gradual and
filled with tension. When Dyer remarks that the government of the Old
Ones "was evidently complex and probably socialistic", he quickly backs
down by adding that "no certainties in this regard could be deduced from
the sculptures we saw". Nothing further is really said about the Old Ones'
political system, and it cannot be assumed that Lovecraft was a convert to
socialism at this time—his first grudging acknowledgement of the viability
of socialism had occurred in a letter written just before At the Mountains of
Madness was begun. Like the mound denizens, the Old Ones had rejected
mechanisation:

> Some of the sculptures suggested that they had passed through a
> stage of mechanised life on other planets, but had receded upon
> finding its efforts emotionally unsatisfying.

But this ostrich-act on Lovecraft's part is balanced by the remark that "the
culture was mainly urban". ⟨. . .⟩

Finally, with "The Shadow out of Time", Lovecraft reconciles himself
with both socialism and technology, recognising that the omnipresence of
the latter impels the embracing of the former. It is here that the term
"fascistic socialism" is used, and Peaslee explains its import: "major resources
[were] rationally distributed, and power delegated to a small governing board
elected by the votes of all able to pass certain educational and psychological
tests". It is the Utopia of "Some Repetitions on the Times".

The "decadence" of the Great Race is of the slightest: the only remark
to this effect is the statement that "art . . . had passed its crest and meridian".
It is true that the Great Race will someday have to abandon its cone-shaped
bodies in the face of some nameless peril and usurp the bodies of a future
species; but one supposes that it will be eminently capable of reinstating
its model civilisation at that time. The Great Race's sole function is intel-
lection; and it is this that will allow them, apparently, to defy the Spenglers
of the world and maintain their civilisation permanently at or near its
apogee.

S. T. Joshi, H. P. Lovecraft: The Decline of the West (Mercer Island, WA: Starmont
House, 1990), pp. 143–45

⬙ Bibliography

The Crime of Crimes. 1915.

United Amateur Press Association: Exponent of Amateur Journalism. c. 1916.

Looking Backward. 1920.

The Materialist Today. 1926.

The Shunned House. 1928 (printed but not distributed).

Further Criticism of Poetry. 1932.

The Battle That Ended the Century (with R. H. Barlow). 1934.

The Cats of Ulthar. 1935.

Charleston. 1936.

Some Current Motives and Practices. 1936.

The Shadow over Innsmouth. 1936.

HPL. 1937.

A History of the Necronomicon. 1938.

The Notes & Commonplace Book. [Ed. R. H. Barlow.] 1938.

The Outsider and Others. Ed. August Derleth and Donald Wandrei. 1939.

Fungi from Yuggoth. 1943.

Beyond the Wall of Sleep. Ed. August Derleth and Donald Wandrei. 1943.

Marginalia. Ed. August Derleth and Donald Wandrei. 1944.

Supernatural Horror in Literature. 1945.

Best Supernatural Stories. Ed. August Derleth. 1945.

Something about Cats and Other Pieces. Ed. August Derleth. 1949.

The Lovecraft Collectors Library. Ed. George Wetzel. 1952–55. 7 vols.

The Challenge from Beyond (with C. L. Moore, A. Merritt, Robert E. Howard,
     and Frank Belknap Long). 1954.

The Shuttered Room and Other Pieces. Ed. August Derleth. 1959.

Dreams and Fancies. [Ed. August Derleth.] 1962.

The Dunwich Horror and Others. Ed. August Derleth. 1963, 1984 (ed. S. T.
     Joshi).

Collected Poems. [Ed. August Derleth.] 1963.

At the Mountains of Madness and Other Novels. Ed. August Derleth. 1964,
     1985 (ed. S. T. Joshi).

Selected Letters. Ed. August Derleth, Donald Wandrei, and James Turner.
     1965–76. 5 vols.

Dagon and Other Macabre Tales. Ed. August Derleth. 1965, 1986 (ed. S. T.
     Joshi).

The Dark Brotherhood and Other Pieces. [Ed. August Derleth.] 1966.

Prose Poems. [Ed. Roy A. Squires.] 1969–70. 4 vols.

The Horror in the Museum and Other Revisions. Ed. August Derleth. 1970, 1989 (ed. S. T. Joshi).

Hail, Klarkash-Ton! Being Nine Missives Inscribed upon Postcards to Clark Ashton Smith. [Ed. Roy A. Squires.] 1971.

E'ch-Pi-El Speaks: An Autobiographical Sketch. 1972.

Lovecraft at Last (with Willis Conover). 1975.

The Occult Lovecraft. Ed. Anthony Raven. 1975.

First Writings: Pawtuxet Valley Gleaner 1906. Ed. Marc A. Michaud. 1976.

The Conservative. Ed. Marc A. Michaud. 1976, 1977.

Writings in The United Amateur *1915–1925.* Ed. Marc A. Michaud. 1976.

To Quebec and the Stars. Ed. L. Sprague de Camp. 1976.

The Californian 1934–1938. Ed. Marc A. Michaud. 1977.

Writings in The Tryout. Ed. Marc A. Michaud. 1977.

A Winter Wish. Ed. Tom Collins. 1977.

Uncollected Prose and Poetry. Ed. S. T. Joshi and Marc A. Michaud. 1978–82. 3 vols.

Science versus Charlatanry: Essays on Astrology (with J. F. Hartmann). Ed. S. T. Joshi and Scott Connors. 1979.

Juvenilia 1897–1905. Ed. S. T. Joshi. 1984.

Saturnalia and Other Poems. Ed. S. T. Joshi. 1984.

In Defence of Dagon. Ed. S. T. Joshi. 1985.

Uncollected Letters. Ed. S. T. Joshi. 1986.

Medusa and Other Poems. Ed. S. T. Joshi. 1986.

Commonplace Book. Ed. David E. Schultz. 1987. 2 vols.

European Glimpses. Ed. S. T. Joshi. 1988.

Yr Obt Servt: Some Postcards Sent to Wilfred Blanch Talman. Ed. R. Alain Everts. 1988.

The Vivisector. Ed. S. T. Joshi. 1990.

Letters to Henry Kuttner. Ed. David E. Schultz and S. T. Joshi. 1990.

The Fantastic Poetry. Ed. S. T. Joshi. 1990, 1993.

Letters to Richard F. Searight. Ed. David E. Schultz and S. T. Joshi. 1992.

Autobiographical Writings. Ed. S. T. Joshi. 1992.

Letters to Robert Bloch. Ed. David E. Schultz and S. T. Joshi. 1993.

Miscellaneous Writings. Ed. S. T. Joshi. 1994.

⊞ ⊞ ⊞

George Orwell
1903–1950

GEORGE ORWELL was the pseudonym of Eric Arthur Blair, who was born on June 25, 1903, in Motihari, Bengal, the son of a minor British official in India. When Orwell was two he returned to England with his mother and older sister. The family was able to save enough money to send their only son to St. Cyprian's, an expensive private school near Eastbourne. There Orwell won scholarships to Wellington and, in 1917, to Eton, where he spent four years. Although an excellent (albeit unhappy) student at St. Cyprian's, Orwell showed little interest in his studies at Eton. Instead of going on to university like most of his classmates, he became an officer in the Burmese Imperial Police.

Orwell's five years in Burma were dismal. In his first novel, *Burmese Days* (1934), he painted a highly critical portrait of the British community there. In 1927 he returned to England, penniless and without prospects. For several years he lived in London and then Paris, earning only enough money to feed himself. His experiences among the world of day laborers, itinerant hop-pickers, and restaurant employers were chronicled in his first published book, the novel *Down and Out in Paris and London* (1933).

Although his early ambition was to write "a neat shelf of realistic novels," Orwell's growing involvement in political debate impinged more and more on his literary career as the 1930s progressed. Following two minor novels, he was commissioned in 1936 to write a book-length report on the living conditions of miners in the north of England. This study was published by the Left Book Club as *The Road to Wigan Pier* (1937). The following year Orwell went to Spain to cover the civil war there, and wound up as a captain in the military arm of a syndicalist party fighting against the Falangist insurgents. After many months at the front he was shot through the neck, sustaining a permanent injury to his vocal cords, and returned behind the lines just in time to find that his faction had been denounced by its Communist partners and was being systematically purged. With his wife of one year, Eileen O'Shaughnessy, he escaped across the border to France and returned to England, where he published *Homage to Catalonia* (1938), an account of his Spanish adventure.

In 1939 Orwell published a fourth novel, *Coming Up for Air*, and continued to write political commentary and reviews. Once World War II broke out he joined the Home Guard and began to work for the BBC in its Indian Division, producing presentations of political and literary commentary for broadcast in India. In 1943 he left that position after disputes with his superiors over the censorship of war news and took a position as literary editor of the *Tribune*, a left-wing weekly where he also wrote a column for several years entitled "As I Please." During this time he also composed a brief satirical fable about Stalinism, which after many rejections was published in 1945 as *Animal Farm*. In the same year his wife died suddenly, leaving the chronically ill Orwell to raise their adopted infant son.

Increasingly hampered by pneumonia, Orwell spent his final years on the Outer Hebrides island of Jura, working on his last novel, *Nineteen Eighty-four* (1949). This bitter and compelling dystopian fantasy of the ultimate totalitarian future was an immediate worldwide success, but Orwell failed to live long enough to reap its rewards. After entering a London hospital for treatment of his tuberculosis in late 1949, he married a young editorial assistant, Sonia Brownell, in a bedside ceremony. A month later, on January 21, 1950, he died following severe hemorrhaging in one lung.

In his short life George Orwell managed to leave several works that would inspire and define debate across the political spectrum for decades following. He is now regarded as among the finest essayists in modern English literature, and his *Collected Essays, Journalism and Letters* appeared in four volumes in 1968.

◈ *Critical Extracts*

GRAHAM GREENE   It is a welcome sign of peace that Mr George Orwell is able to publish his 'fairy story' *Animal Farm*, a satire upon the totalitarian state and one state in particular. I have heard a rumour that the manuscript was at one time submitted to the Ministry of Information, that huge cenotaph of appeasement, and an official there took a poor view of it. 'Couldn't you make them some other animal,' he is reported as saying in reference to the dictator and his colleagues, 'and not pigs?'

For this is the story of a political experiment on a farm where the animals, under the advice of a patriarchal porker, get organised and eventually drive out Mr Jones, the human owner. ⟨. . .⟩

It is a sad fable, and it is an indication of Mr Orwell's fine talent that it is really sad—not a mere echo of human failings at one remove. We do become involved in the fate of Molly the Cow, old Benjamin the Donkey, and Boxer the poor devil of a hard-working, easily deceived horse. Snowball is driven out by Napoleon, who imposes his solitary leadership with the help of a gang of savage dogs, and slowly the Seven Commandments become altered or erased, until at last on the barn door appears only one sentence. 'All animals are equal, but some animals are more equal than others.'

If Mr Walt Disney is looking for a real subject, here it is: it has all the necessary humour, and it has, too, the subdued lyrical quality he can sometimes express so well. But is it perhaps a little too real for him? There is no appeasement here.

Graham Greene, [Review of Animal Farm], Evening Standard (London), 10 August 1945, p. 6

GEORGE ORWELL   My recent novel ⟨Nineteen Eighty-four⟩ is NOT intended as an attack on Socialism or on the British Labour Party (of which I am a supporter) but as a show-up of the perversions to which a centralised economy is liable and which have already been partly realised in Communism and Fascism. I do not believe that the kind of society I describe necessarily *will* arrive, but I believe (allowing of course for the fact that the book is a satire) that something resembling it *could* arrive. I believe also that totalitarian ideas have taken root in the minds of intellectuals everywhere, and I have tried to draw these ideas out to their logical consequences. The scene of the book is laid in Britain in order to emphasise that the English-speaking races are not innately better than anyone else and that totalitarianism, *if not fought against*, could triumph anywhere.

George Orwell, Letter to Francis A. Henson (16 June 1949), Collected Essays, Journalism and Letters, ed. Sonia Orwell and Ian Angus (New York: Harcourt, Brace & World, 1968), Vol. 4, p. 502

DIANA TRILLING   Although George Orwell's *Nineteen Eighty-four* is a brilliant and fascinating novel, the nature of its fantasy is so absolutely final and relentless that I can recommend it only with a certain reservation. This is Mr. Orwell's picture of the way the world ends: actually it does not end at all, physically—one would even welcome some well-placed atom bombs—but continues in a perpetual nightmare of living death. ⟨. . .⟩

Here is Mr. Orwell's vision of the future. The fact that the scene of *Nineteen Eighty-four* is London and that the political theory on which Mr. Orwell's dictatorship is based is called Ingsoc, which is Newspeak for English socialism, indicates that Mr. Orwell is fantasying the fate not only of an already established dictatorship like that of Russia but also that of Labor England; and indeed he states very clearly that "by the fourth decade of the twentieth century all the main currents of political thought were authoritarian. . . . Every new political theory, by whatever name it called itself, led back to hierarchy and regimentation." This assimilation of the English Labor government to Soviet communism is surely from any immediate political point of view, unfortunate. On the other hand, whatever our partisanship for the present English revolution as against the present situation in Russia, we must recognize that the generalization in the lesson Mr. Orwell is teaching is a proper one. Even where, as in his last novel, *Animal Farm*, Mr. Orwell seemed to be concerned only with unmasking the Soviet Union for its dreamy admirers, he was urged on by something larger than sectarianism. What he was telling us is that along the path the Russian revolution has followed to the destruction of all the decent human values there have stood the best ideals of modern social enlightenment. It is this idealism he has wished to jolt into self-awareness. In the name of a higher loyalty, treacheries beyond imagination have been committed; in the name of Socialist equality, privilege has ruled unbridled; in the name of democracy and freedom, the individual has lived without public voice or private peace— if this is true of the Soviet Union, why should it not eventually be equally true of the English experiment? In other words, we are being warned against the extremes to which the contemporary totalitarian spirit can carry us, not only so that we will be warned against Russia but also so that we will understand the ultimate dangers involved wherever power moves under the guise of order and rationality.

Diana Trilling, [Review of *Nineteen Eighty-four*], *Nation*, 25 June 1949, pp. 716–17

ALDOUS HUXLEY   The philosophy of the ruling majority in *Nineteen Eighty-four* is a sadism which has been carried to its logical conclusion by going beyond sex and denying it. Whether in actual fact the policy of the boot-on-the-face can go on indefinitely seems doubtful. My own belief is that the ruling oligarchy will find less arduous and wasteful ways of governing and of satisfying its lust for power, and that these ways will resemble those which I described in *Brave New World*. ⟨. . .⟩ Within the next generation I believe that the world's rulers will discover that infant conditioning and narco-hypnosis are more efficient, as instruments of government, than clubs and prisons, and that the lust for power can be just as completely satisfied by suggesting people into loving their servitude as by flogging and kicking them into obedience. In other words, I feel that the nightmare of *Nineteen Eighty-four* is destined to modulate into the nightmare of a world having more resemblance to that which I imagined in *Brave New World*. The change will be brought about as a result of a felt need for increased efficiency. Meanwhile, of course, there may be a large-scale biological and atomic war—in which case we shall have nightmares of other and scarcely imaginable kinds.

Aldous Huxley, Letter to George Orwell (21 October 1949), *Letters of Aldous Huxley*, ed. Grover Smith (London: Chatto & Windus, 1969), pp. 604–5

IRVING HOWE   No other book has succeeded so completely in rendering the essential quality of totalitarianism. *1984* is limited in scope; it does not pretend to investigate the genesis of the totalitarian state, the laws of its economy, or the prospect for its survival; it simply evokes the "tone" of life in a totalitarian society. And since it is not a realistic novel, it can treat Oceania as an *extreme instance*, one that might never actually exist but which illuminates the nature of societies that do exist.

Orwell's profoundest insight is that in a totalitarian world man's life is shorn of dynamic possibilities. The end of life is completely predictable in its beginning, the beginning merely a manipulated preparation for the end. There is no opening for surprise, for that spontaneous animation which is the token of and justification for freedom. Oceanic society may evolve through certain stages of economic development, but the life of its members is static, a given and measured quantity that can neither rise to tragedy nor tumble to comedy. Human personality, as we have come to grasp for it in a class society and hope for it in a classless society, is obliterated; man becomes a function of a process he is never allowed to understand or control. The fetishism of the state replaces the fetishism of commodities. ⟨. . .⟩

But even as Orwell, overcoming the resistance of his own nausea, evoked the ethos of the totalitarian world, he used very little of what is ordinarily called "imagination" in order to show how this ethos stains every aspect of human life. Like most good writers, he understood that imagination is primarily the capacity for apprehending reality, for seeing more clearly and deeply whatever it is that exists. That is why his vision of social horror, if taken as a model rather than a portrait, strikes one as essentially credible, while the efforts of most writers to create utopias or anti-utopias founder precisely on their desire to be scientific or inventive. Orwell understood that social horror consists not in the prevalence of diabolical machines or in the invasion of Martian automatons flashing death rays from mechanical eyes, but in the persistence of inhuman relations among men.

And he understood, as well, the significance of what I can only call the psychology and politics of "one more step." From a bearable neurosis to a crippling psychosis, from a decayed society in which survival is still possible to a totalitarian state in which it is hardly desireable, there may be only "one step." But it is decisive and, for all we know, irrevocable. To lay bare the logic of that social regression which leads to totalitarianism, Orwell had merely to allow his imagination to take . . . one step.

Irving Howe, "Orwell: History as Nightmare," *American Scholar* 25, No. 2 (Spring 1956): 197–99

GEORGE WOODCOCK ⟨. . .⟩ undoubtedly the book that influenced Orwell most ⟨in *Nineteen Eighty-four*⟩ was Zamyatin's *We*, from which Huxley had already borrowed copiously in writing *Brave New World*. ⟨. . .⟩ it was after Orwell had obtained a copy of *We*, of which he already knew by hearsay and which he immediately discussed in the *Tribune*, that he started work on *Nineteen Eighty-four*. ⟨. . .⟩

Between *We* and *Nineteen Eighty-four* the resemblances are so close in both detail and structure as to leave little doubt of Zamyatin's direct influence on Orwell, who admitted it freely. Both authors see Utopia as a possible— even a probable—outcome of twentieth-century technological and political developments. Both assume that if this Utopian future ever arrives, it will involve the destruction of the very idea of freedom, the falsification or destruction of history and the sense of the past, and the reduction of culture to a rudimentary and mechanical function. Both envisage the economic structure of Utopia as collectivist and its political structure as a pyramid controlled by an exclusive elite with the help of an efficient police system. Both foresee radical interference in sexual life, and some form of conditioning to make the individual docile and obedient; such conditioning involves the destruction of privacy, the denial of a natural or spontaneous way of living, the systematic destruction of passionate relationships and of any association that might exist outside the state. In both states literature and music are produced by machine, life is run on strict time schedules, men in helicopters look into windows. In Orwell's Oceania the telescreens in all the rooms enable the citizens to be observed as closely as the "numbers" are observed through the glass walls of Zamyatin's buildings, and the place of the Guardians is taken by the ubiquitous Thought Police, who also operate by scientific methods of torture. Just as "fancy" is the great crime in the United State, so "thought-crime" is unforgivable felony in Oceania. ⟨. . .⟩

Yet in addition to these many points of resemblance, there are some important differences between *We* and *Nineteen Eighty-four*. Zamyatin tended to be preoccupied with the mechanical problems which interested him as an engineer, and the statistical-mathematical outlook shapes both the attitude of his Guardians and the character of the society they construct, a crystalline, higher-mathematical order where men become merely figures in gigantic equations. Orwell, on the other hand, did not have a scientific mind, and the abstractions of mathematics made little appeal to him; hence his anti-Utopia is dominated less by technology than by predominantly cultural and psychological means of tyranny.

Again, there is a sharp difference between Zamyatin's calendar of the future and Orwell's. Zamyatin saw his United State a thousand years ahead. Aldous Huxley's "brave new world," conceived approximately a decade after *We* was completed, lay only six hundred years in the future. Orwell, writing less than thirty years after Zamyatin, shifted his sights even more abruptly; finishing *Nineteen Eighty-four* in 1948, he represented the final submersion of the human personality in the totalitarian nightmare as only thirty-six years ahead, and the scene as the familiar, shabby London of the immediate postwar years, in which only the vast pyramidal strongholds of the new government agencies tower up in menacing indestructibility.

George Woodcock, *The Crystal Spirit: A Study of George Orwell* (Boston: Little, Brown, 1966), pp. 209, 213–15.

MELVYN NEW   In an essay on Arthur Koestler, written in 1944, Orwell noted that the English literary tradition had no good books on totalitarianism because "there is almost no English writer to whom it has happened to see totalitarianism from the inside. . . . England is lacking, therefore, in what one might call concentration-camp literature." *1984* was purposively designed, I believe, to fill that gap, not merely because Orwell had developed an interest in the subject, but because he came to realize that the future of his civilization depended precisely upon its capacity to face fully and honestly the meaning of the camps. Moreover, as with the satires of one of his favorite authors, Swift, *1984* ultimately depends upon implicating the reader in its final judgment; the work is a test, a trial of the reader's capacity to confront Buchenwald and Auschwitz and to join with the author in bearing witness to that horror. ⟨. . .⟩

⟨. . .⟩ Not a prediction of things to come, only partially the warning to the future that most critics acknowledge, *1984* is most of all a witness to the past: a witness to the holocaust which had really happened and which would be too readily forgotten by people unable or unwilling to face the horror. The violators of history are not only in the Ministry of Truth; they are the readers of *1984* who find Orwell's vision "unrealistic," "melodramatic," "pathological." Orwell's long interest in antisemitism culminates in *1984* in an imaginative union with the Jewish victims who had learned in Buchenwald that no vision of what the twentieth century had become to them could be *too* despairing, *too* pessimistic, *too* apocalyptic; and that if any hope at all remained for mankind, if Hitler was not to gain a posthumous victory, it rested solely in the capacity to acknowledge fully the horror of the camps. Irving Howe is tempted in his fine essay to question Orwell's insistence that a totalitarian society can do anything it wants to a man, but he rightfully dismisses the temptation ("I have been uneasily aware that [such questions] might well be irrelevant"), and in doing so reaches the full purpose of *1984*: "There are some writers who live most significantly for their own age; they are writers who help redeem their time by forcing it to accept the truth about itself and thereby saving it, perhaps, from the truth about itself."

Melvyn New, "Orwell and Antisemitism: Toward *1984*," *Modern Fiction Studies* 21, No. 1 (Spring 1975 [George Orwell Number]): 98, 100–101

PATRICK REILLY   *Nineten Eighty-four* has always been a scandal. It was denounced as a surrender to the mysticism of cruelty, a weapon in the Cold War, an item in our own hate-week, a capitalist horror-comic whose author was another lost leader in the tradition of Wordsworth. Its special offence was its alleged renegade politics, its repudiation of all that 1917 stood for. Yet the scandal is in fact far greater, for the book transcends politics to repudiate not just the Revolution but humanism itself. It is not a capitalist horror-comic—the porn manufactured by Big Brother has found a cosier home in the capitalist West than behind the Curtain—but its enemies might well have described it as a religious horror-comic. It enacts a struggle between two religions, humanism, the religion of the past, with Winston as its last advocate, and totalitarian sadism, the religion of the present and, the book's pessimism insists, of the future, with O'Brien its prophet-fanatic.

'Struggle' is, of course, obsequiously honorific. Winston's humanism has as much chance of checking the new savage god as biscuits strewn before tanks. Suspense comes, if at all, not from wondering whether he can elude, far less overthrow, Big Brother, but whether he can sustain defiance to the modest extent of dying for the faith, winning the martyr's crown: 'the object is not to stay alive but to stay human'. Even this limited victory, Winston joining Spartacus and More, Hus and Bonhoeffer, is finally seen as a fantasy, as much a piece of wish-fulfilment as Jack the Giant-Killer. Here the Giant wins; the dissident loses everything except his life in the book's appalling conclusion.

⟨. . .⟩ The real affront to modern pieties is in the implication that the defeat of humanism is somehow disconcertingly related to the death of the God whose obituary the nineteenth-century humanists so authoritatively announced. Some, like Nietzsche and Feuerbach, hailed his demise, but even when regretted, it was not seen as calamitous. George Eliot, having thrown her clod into the grave, consoles the bereaved: since heaven is no longer there to help us, we will, because we must, help and love each other all the more. It is this religion of humanity that Nineteen Eighty-four consigns to the dustbin of discredited mythologies.

Three gods appear in the book: O'Brien's savage deity; the god of traditional religion that Winston rejects; and the god he claims to serve, the spirit of man that will, somehow, finally defeat Big Brother. Instead, Winston is demolished along with his humanist hopes. We can, if we wish, soften this conclusion by seeing it as the debacle of a very flawed individual and a defective creed whose failure leaves the true doctrine intact, thus wrenching the text away from the despair-of-a-dying-man view to that of a cautionary tale for progressives, an optimistic exhortation to those who share the faith not to repeat the blunders. Yet the inadequate Winston is the only liberal champion textually present, the last of his kind, as O'Brien taunts him— is that in itself an implied judgement on the kind he represents? Orwell denounced *Gulliver* as a reactionary, pessimistic book, though Swift did at least include Don Pedro as an exception, a partial corrective, to his vision of universal corruption. There is no Don Pedro in *Nineteen Eighty-four*, simply torturers and victims, who sometimes switch roles, perplexing us as to which is the more revolting.

> Patrick Reilly, "*Nineteen Eighty-four:* The Failure of Humanism," *Critical Quarterly* 24, No. 3 (Autumn 1982): 19–20

BRIAN W. ALDISS   One can see how George Orwell enjoyed writing *1984* for its own sake. I believe the prophetic element to be only part of its attraction, and in any case the prophecy was apotropaic, intended to warn. Thus, the more it succeeded in conveying its warning, the less likely was its picture of the future to become reality. Its success is that it fails to paint a true portrait of the true 1984. However grim we may hold our 1984 to be, it is not Orwell's grimness. We perhaps owe Orwell some gratitude that his widely influential *1984* is not our 1984.

Some commentators have claimed as a weakness the fact that the dialectic of the novel is all with the Party, with O'Brien, with the Thought Police, and that nothing positive is offered by way of opposition. To my mind, such comments show a misreading of the book. In the long line of utopianists, Orwell has an honorable place.

H. G. Wells perceived that for a utopia to exist in a period of rapid communications it had to be worldwide; and for 1911, before the first World War, this was an acute perception. By the late 1940s, after a second World War, Orwell saw that a countervailing paradox was required. His way to happiness on Earth lies in the subversive message which Julia slips Smith in the corridor, a note saying merely "I love you." And utopia, far from being worldwide, has shrunk to a shabby little room over a shop, with a willing girl, a double bed, and plenty of privacy.

Thus have our expectations diminished over the century. ⟨. . .⟩

In a television broadcast made during the Christmas season, 1982, the novelist Anthony Burgess claimed to have read *1984* thirty times. He said of it that it was one of those rare books which tells us what we need to know, which informs us of what reality is.

Like all of Orwell's novels, with the brilliant exception of *Animal Farm*, *1984* is not a masterpiece judged purely as a novel. Judged as a vehicle for putting over what Orwell wished to tell us, for conveying that pungent mixture of squalor, nostalgia, disillusion and analysis of betrayal, it is brilliant.

Although *1984* does not on the surface hold up a mirror to our 1984, I believe that Burgess was right on a more inward plane. In 1948, that drab year best never relived, the novel seemed indeed to be a prediction of the future, exact in each realistic detail. Read in the year of its title, it has turned disconcertingly into a secret history of all our lives. For we have lived in a parallel world of political bullying and hypocrisy, of wars and totalitarianism, of cultural revolutions and anticultural movements, of blind hedonism and wild-eyed shortage. Even if these things have not overcome us, they have marked us. Our shadows—to use the word in a Jungian sense— have conspired with the Thought Police and the Party. What has happened to us here is, in O'Brien's words, "forever."

We see the novel's transformation through time: from prophecy of the future to a parable of our worldly existence, 1948–84.

Brian W. Aldiss, "The Downward Journey: Orwell's *1984*," *Extrapolation* 25, No. 1 (Spring 1984): 9–11

DAPHNE PATAI   In the world of *Nineteen Eighty-four*, although men fear women because they may be spies, in general the assumptions of male centrality and female "otherness" survive intact. Julia's love for Winston makes him healthier, whereas O'Brien's attentions destroy him physically and mentally, but Winston's true alliance ⟨. . .⟩ is with O'Brien, who engages him in combat and recognizes him as a worthy opponent—a recognition that means more to Winston than Julia's love. ⟨. . .⟩

The minor role attributed to women in the novel cannot be interpreted as part of Orwell's strategy of criticizing and laying bare the dynamics of totalitarianism. As readers with a different kind of sensibility, we may be aware that *Nineteen Eighty-four* depicts a masculinized world, but Orwell did not see it this way and never made any sort of critique of the sex-role system. Although there exists within the novel a certain amount of specific information about the Party's control of sexuality and family life, there is also a wealth of detail that merely demonstrates Orwell's habitual disdain for women, evident in all his work. Thus any analysis of sex roles in *Nineteen Eighty-four* has to begin by distinguishing between Party policy toward Party women (the proles are ignored), as articulated in the novel, and Orwell's own attitudes that inadvertently seep into the text. ⟨. . .⟩

The women in Orwell's narrative by and large appear as caricatures: They are Party secretaries, Party fanatics, Party wives like Katharine or the stereotypically helpless housewife Mrs. Parsons. They are also antisex freaks or prole prostitutes. There is no woman character in the novel comparable to Syme or Charrington or O'Brien. Although Goldstein's book explains that the Inner Party is not linked by blood and that no racial discrimination is practiced—"Jews, Negroes, South Americans of pure Indian blood are to be found in the highest ranks of the Party"—no female Inner Party members are mentioned. When Winston sees a man and a woman in the canteen, he assumes that the woman is the man's secretary. In describing Julia's work in Pornosec (which churns out machine-produced pornographic literature for prole consumption), work that is assigned to unmarried girls because they are thought to be less vulnerable than men to the corrupting influences of pornography, Orwell includes the detail that "all the workers in Pornosec, except the heads of the departments, were girls." Although Orwell reveals male dominance to be a continuing feature of life in Oceania, he does not treat this as worthy of analysis and does not raise the issue of its role in a totalitarian society. Women's options in a given society, what access they have to earning their own living and what kind of living that would be compared, for example, to becoming a man's economic dependent in exchange for housework and child-care services; how, in general, society structures women's life paths in comparison with men's—all this has everything to do with the shape of life in that society. But Orwell does not realize this, judging by his lack of attention to this problem in *Nineteen Eighty-four*. Even Julia is a largely unexplored character, seen only in terms of her relationship with Winston.

> Daphne Patai, *The Orwell Mystique: A Study in Male Ideology* (Amherst: University of Massachusetts Press, 1984), pp. 239, 242–43.

MARK CRISPIN MILLER   What is most disconcerting ⟨. . .⟩ about the ending of *Nineteen Eighty-four* is not that Winston Smith has now been made entirely unlike us. In too many ways, the ex-hero of this brilliant, dismal book anticipates those TV viewers who are incapable of reading it: "In these days he could never fix his mind on any one subject for more than a few moments at a time." At this moment, Winston Smith is, for the first time in his life, not under surveillance. The motto, "Big Brother Is Watching You," is now untrue as a threat, as it has always been untrue as an assurance. And the reason why he is no longer watched is that the Oceanic gaze need no longer see through Winston Smith, because he is no longer "Winston Smith," but "a swirl of gritty dust," as primitive and transparent as the Party.

As this Smith slumps in the empty Chestnut Tree, credulously gaping, his ruined mind expertly jolted by the telescreen's managers, he signifies the terminal fulfillment of O'Brien's master-plan, which expresses the intentions not only of Orwell's fictitious Party, but of the corporate entity that, through TV, contains our consciousness today: "We shall squeeze you empty, and then we shall fill you with ourselves." The Party has now done for Winston Smith what all our advertisers want to do for us, and with our general approval—answer all material needs, in exchange for the self that might try to gratify them independently, and that might have other, subtler needs as well. As a consumer, in other words, Orwell's ex-hero really has it made. "There was no need to give orders" to the waiters in the Chestnut Tree. "They knew his habits." Furthermore, he "always had plenty of money nowadays." In short, the Party has paid him for his erasure with the assurance, "We do it *all* for you." And so this grotesque before-and-after narrative ends satirically as all ads end in earnest, with the object's blithe endorsement of the very product that has helped to keep him miserable: "But it was all right, everything was all right, the struggle was finished. He had won the victory over himself. He loved Big Brother."

It is a horrifying moment; but if we do no more than wince at it, and then forget about it, we ignore our own involvement in the horror, and thus complacently betray the hope that once inspired this vision. Surely Orwell would have us face the facts. Like Winston Smith, and like O'Brien and the others, we have been estranged from our desire by Enlightenment, which finally reduces all of its proponents into the blind spectators of their own annihilation. Unlike that Oceanic audience, however, the TV viewer does not gaze up at the screen with angry scorn or piety, but—perfectly enlightened—looks down on its images with a nervous sneer that cannot threaten them, but that only keeps the viewer himself from standing up.

As you watch, there is no Big Brother out there watching you, not because there isn't a Big Brother, but because Big Brother is you, watching.

Mark Crispin Miller, "Big Brother Is You, Watching," *Reflections on America, 1984: An Orwell Symposium*, ed. Robert Mulvihill (Athens: University of Georgia Press, 1986), pp. 197–98

JULIAN SYMONS ⟨*Animal Farm*⟩ was written very quickly, if we bear in mind that he was also working three days a week at *Tribune*, and writing a weekly book column for the *Manchester Evening News*. Quickly and easily, and in a language beautifully fitting to the story. With the exception of an occasional word like 'dissentient' it poses no problems for a child of ten or even younger. We don't know whether parallels between events at Animal Farm and in the Soviet Union were worked out in detail before writing began, but they fit together marvellously well—bearing in mind, of course, that this *is* a fairy story, so that such an event as the attempted invasion of Russia by the Allies after World War I to defeat the Revolution is represented by the Battle of the Cowshed when the attempt by Jones and his allies to recapture the farm is defeated. Yet there is no sense that the parallels are absurdly disproportionate, because of the supreme tact with which the incidents are handled. The touch throughout could hardly be more delicate, something painfully obvious to those who have seen the crude cartoon version. At the end of this sad fairy tale those of Orwell's own political persuasion may weep for the betrayal of revolutionary idealism, but children's tears will be shed for the defeat and death of the good animals and the triumph of the evil.

The charm of the manner and the perfection of the story are undoubted, but a question remains: what is being told us in this allegory, what understanding are we meant to take away from it? The simplest answer is that given by the political Right-wingers ⟨. . .⟩, who have done their best to appropriate Orwell as a prophet whose message was that to disturb the social order always ends in totalitarian dictatorship. That, however, is certainly not the reading of his work Orwell intended. Shortly before his death, much distressed by the way in which American reviewers in particular had greeted *Nineteen Eighty-four* as a polemic against all kinds of Socialism, he issued a statement specifically praising the liberal attitudes and intentions of the British Labour Party government of the time (1949), a statement which was generally ignored. It should not have been disregarded. Orwell remained a Socialist until his death, and *Animal Farm* was not meant to be a parable giving comfort to the Right wing. ⟨. . .⟩

If Right- and Left-wing interpretations are both mistaken, what did Orwell intend us to think after reading the story? He certainly wanted to point up the parallels between reality and fable, something made clear in the introduction to the Ukrainian edition, when he says the scene at the end between the pigs and the farmers referred to the false goodwill shown at the Teheran Conference. His own explanation of the fable's 'meaning', quoted by Peter Davison, was that violent revolutions are always made by power-hungry people, and that if a radical improvement in human living was ever to be effected the masses should 'know how to chuck out their leaders as soon as the latter have done their job'. This unconvincing answer (any power-hungry leader will have made provision against an attempt to chuck him out) does not truly suggest the feeling of the book. Two things are conveyed in it: the exultation felt by the animals on achieving their freedom, and the bitterness of the pigs' betrayal that leads to Napoleon's rule and the establishment of a totalitarian state. It is nowhere implied that *Animal Farm* is unworkable by the animals, only that corruption defeats their aspirations.

Julian Symons, "Introduction," *Animal Farm* by George Orwell (New York: Alfred A. Knopf, 1993), pp. xx–xxii

▣ *Bibliography*

Down and Out in Paris and London. 1933.

Burmese Days. 1934.

A Clergyman's Daughter. 1935.

Keep the Aspidistra Flying. 1936.

The Road to Wigan Pier. 1937.

Homage to Catalonia. 1938.

Coming Up for Air. 1939.

Inside the Whale and Other Essays. 1940.

The Lion and the Unicorn: Socialism and the English Genius. 1941.

Talking to India (editor). 1943.

Animal Farm: A Fairy Story. 1945.

Critical Essays ⟨*Dickens, Dali and Others*⟩. 1946.

James Burnham and the Managerial Revolution. 1946.

The English People. 1947.

Politics and the English Language. 1947.

British Pamphleteers I: From the Sixteenth Century to the French Revolution (editor; with Reginald Reynolds). 1948.

Nineteen Eighty-four. 1949.

Shooting an Elephant and Other Essays. 1950.

England, Your England and Other Essays. 1953.

Collected Essays. 1961.

Collected Essays, Journalism and Letters. Ed. Sonia Orwell and Ian Angus. 1968. 4 vols.

Ten "Animal Farm" Letters to His Agent, Leonard Moore. Ed. Michael Shelden. 1984.

Nineteen Eighty-four: The Facsimile of the Extant Manuscript. Ed. Peter Davison. 1984.

The War Broadcasts. Ed. W. J. West. 1985.

The War Commentaries. Ed. W. J. West. 1985.

Edgar Allan Poe
1809–1849

EDGAR ALLAN POE was born Edgar Poe in Boston on January 19, 1809, the son of traveling actors. Shortly after his birth his father disappeared, and in 1811 his mother died. He was taken into the home of John Allan (from whom Poe derived his middle name), a wealthy merchant living in Richmond, Virginia. In 1815 the Allans took Poe to England, where he attended the Manor House School at Stoke Newington, later the setting for his story "William Wilson." Poe returned to Richmond with the Allans in 1820. In 1826 he became engaged to Elmira Royster, whose parents broke off the engagement. That fall he entered the University of Virginia. At first he excelled in his studies, but in December 1826 John Allan took him out of school after Poe accumulated considerable gambling debts that Allan refused to pay. Unable to honor these debts himself, Poe fled to Boston, where he enlisted in the army under the name of Edgar A. Perry.

Poe began his literary career with the anonymous publication, at his own expense, of *Tamerlane and Other Poems* (1827), which because of its small print run and poor distribution has become one of the rarest volumes in American literary history. In 1829 Poe was honorably discharged from the army. Later that year he published a second collection of verse, *Al Aaraaf, Tamerlane, and Minor Poems*, containing revisions of poems from his first collection as well as new material. This volume was well received, leading to a tentative reconciliation with John Allan. In 1830 Poe entered West Point, but after another falling out with John Allan, who withdrew his financial support, Poe deliberately got himself expelled in 1831 through flagrant neglect of his duties. Nonetheless, he managed before leaving to gather enough cadet subscriptions to bring out his third collection of verse, *Poems* (1831). In 1833 Poe's final attempt at reconciliation was rejected by the ailing John Allan, who died in 1834 without mentioning Poe in his will.

In the meantime Poe's literary career was progressing. Having settled in Baltimore after leaving West Point, Poe won a prize in 1833 from the

Baltimore Saturday Visitor for one of his first short stories, "MS. Found in a Bottle." In 1835 he moved to Richmond to become editor of the recently established *Southern Literary Messenger*, which thrived under his direction. In 1836 Poe felt financially secure enough to marry Virginia Clemm, his fourteen-year-old cousin, but later that year he was fired from the *Messenger*, partly because of what appeared to be chronic alcoholism. In fact, Poe seems to have suffered from a physical ailment that rendered him so sensitive to alcohol that a single drink could induce a drunken state. Poe was later an editor of *Burton's Gentleman's Magazine* (1839–40), *Graham's Magazine* (1841–42), and the *Broadway Journal* (1845–46). In this capacity he wrote many important reviews—notably of Hawthorne, Dickens, and Macaulay— and occasionally gained notoriety for the severity and acerbity of his judgments. In particular he wrote a series of polemics against Henry Wadsworth Longfellow, whom he accused of plagiarism.

Meanwhile Poe continued to write fiction voluminously. His longest tale, *The Narrative of Arthur Gordon Pym*, is dated 1838 but appeared in the summer of 1837 (it has frequently but erroneously been believed to be unfinished); *Tales of the Grotesque and Arabesque*, containing "The Fall of The House of Usher" and other important stories, was published in 1840; and *Tales* appeared in 1845. As a fiction writer Poe wrote not only tales of the macabre and the supernatural ("The Pit and the Pendulum," "The Black Cat," "The Tell-Tale Heart," "Ligeia") but also many humorous or parodic pieces ("King Pest," "Some Words with a Mummy"), prose poems ("Silence—a Fable," "Shadow—a Parable"), and what are generally considered the first true detective stories.

In 1844 Poe moved to New York, and in the following year he achieved international fame with his poem "The Raven," published in *The Raven and Other Poems* (1845). In 1847 Poe's wife Virginia, who had been seriously ill since 1842, died, leaving him desolate. For the few remaining years of his life he helped support himself by delivering a series of public lectures, including "The Poetic Principle" (published posthumously in 1850). Among his publications were the philosophical treatise *Eureka: A Prose Poem* (1848) and the lyric "Annabel Lee" (1849). His *Marginalia* was published serially from 1844 to 1849. After his wife's death Poe had several romances, including an affair with the Rhode Island poet Sarah Helen Whitman, and in 1849 he became engaged for a second time to Elmira Royster (then Mrs. Shelton). Before they could be married, however, Poe died in Baltimore on October 7, 1849, under mysterious circumstances.

Poe can be seen as an important precursor in the field of science fiction. Aside from such a tale as "The Unparalleled Adventure of One Hans Pfaall" (a humorous story about a trip to the moon), there are a number of stories involving the future, in some cases dealing with the destruction of the human race ("The Conversation of Eiros and Charmion," "The Colloquy of Monos and Una," "Mellonta Tauta"). Poe was fascinated with contemporary developments in science, and he utilized such things as mesmerism ("Mesmeric Revelation," "The Facts in the Case of M. Valdemar"), balloon travel ("The Balloon-Hoax"), and artificial intelligence ("Maelzel's Chess-Player") in his tales. *Eureka* can be seen as a grandiose attempt to harmonise modern science and religious mysticism.

◈ Critical Extracts

CHARLES BAUDELAIRE   I wish I could characterize Poe's work very briefly and very categorically, for it is a quite new literature. What gives it its essential character and distinguishes it among all others is, if I may use these strange words, conjecturism and probabilism. My statement may be verified by a consideration of some specific examples. ⟨. . .⟩

"A Descent into the Maelstrom": could one not descend into a bottomless whirlpool while studying the laws of gravity in a new way? ⟨. . .⟩

"Mesmeric Revelation": the author's point of departure has obviously been this: would it not be possible to discover the law which governs distant worlds with the help of the unknown force called magnetism? The beginning is full of grandeur and solemnity. The doctor has mesmerized his patient only to comfort him. "How do you think your present illness will result?"— "I must die."—"Does the idea of death afflict you?"—"No." The patient complains that he is not being questioned properly. "What then shall I ask?" says the doctor. "You must begin at the beginning."—"But where is the beginning?"—(In a very low voice.)—"It is GOD."—"Is not God spirit?"— "No."—"Is God, then, material?"—"No." There follows a very comprehensive theory of matter, of the gradations of matter and of the hierarchy of beings. I published this story in one of the issues of *Liberté de penser* in 1848.

Elsewhere we have the story of a soul which once lived on a planet that had disappeared. The point of departure is: can one, by means of induction and analysis, guess what would be the physical and moral phenomena among the inhabitants of a world which was being approached by a destructive comet? ⟨. . .⟩

In Edgar Poe there is no tiresome snivelling; but everywhere and at all times an indefatigable enthusiasm in seeking the ideal. He has a passion for science like Balzac, who died grieved perhaps at not being a pure scientist. He had written a work called *The Conchologist's First Book* which I have forgotten to mention. He has, like conquerors and philosophers, a compelling yearning for unity; he combines the spiritual with the physical. It could be said that he seeks to apply to literature the processes of philosophy, and to philosophy the methods of algebra. In this constant ascension toward the infinite, one becomes somewhat breathless. The air in this literature is as rarefied as that of a laboratory. In it can be observed continually the glorification of will applying itself to induction and to analysis. It seems that Poe wants to usurp the role of the prophets and to claim for himself a monopoly on rational explanation. Thus the landscapes which sometimes serve as background for his febrile compositions are pale as phantoms. Poe, who scarcely seemed to share the passions of other men, sketches trees and clouds which are like the trees and clouds of a dream, or rather which resemble his strange characters and which are agitated like them by a supernatural and convulsive shudder.

Charles Baudelaire, "Edgar Allan Poe: His Life and Works" (1852), *Baudelaire on Poe*, tr. Lois and Francis E. Hyslop, Jr. (State College, PA: Bald Eagle Press, 1952), pp. 68–71, 80

GEORGE A. WOODBERRY   It is probable that few readers of *Eureka* ever seriously tried to understand its metaphysics. Its power—other than the fascination which some readers feel in whatever makes of their countenances "a foolish face of wonder"—lies in its exposition of Laplace's nebular theory and its vivid and popular presentation of astronomical phenomena. In this physical portion of the essay it has been fancied that Poe anticipated some of the results of later science; but this view cannot be sustained with candor. His own position that matter came from nihility and consisted of centres of force had been put forth as a scientific theory by Boscovitch in 1758–59, had been widely discussed, and had found its way into American text-books. The same theory in a modified form had just been revived and brought to the notice of scientists by Faraday in his lecture in 1844. It has not, however, occupied the attention of first-class scientific men since that time. There may be, in the claim that "the recent progress of scientific thought runs in Poe's lines," some reference to Sir William Thomson's vortex theory of the constitution of atoms, but its resemblance to Poe's theory of vortices is only superficial, for what he puts forth was merely a revival of one of the earliest attempts to explain the Newtonian law, long since abandoned by science. It is true that in several particulars, such as the doctrine of the evolution of the universe from the simple to the complex, Poe's line of thought has now been followed out in detail; these suggestions, however, were not at the time peculiar to Poe, were not originated or developed by him, but on the contrary were common scientific property, for he appropriated ideas, just as he paraphrased statements of fact, from the books he read. He was no more a forerunner of Spencer, Faraday, and Darwin than scores of others, and he did nothing to make their investigations easier.

George A. Woodberry, *Edgar Allan Poe* (Boston: Houghton Mifflin, 1885), pp. 296–97

J. O. BAILEY   Tales of imaginary voyages to the interior of the earth were greatly influenced by a theory set forth by Captain John Cleves Symmes of Ohio. In 1818, Captain Symmes issued a circular to institutions of learning in Europe and America stating that the earth is hollow and open at the poles. In 1823 he petitioned Congress to send an exploring expedition to test his theory and got twenty-five affirmative votes. With James McBride as collaborator he published in 1826 *Symmes's Theory of Concentric Spheres*. 〈. . .〉

Poe's story "MS. Found in a Bottle" (1838) is clearly an experimental fragment from a design to tell of an adventure in the hollow earth. After a collision, the narrator is hurled aboard a strange old vessel on which are men who seem to be the living-dead. It is drawn by irresistible currents toward the South Pole. The story ends abruptly with the description of the ship's behavior in a whirlpool and then its "going down." In the light of Poe's interest in Symmes's theory, it is clear that the ship, which cannot sink, for it is porous and lighter than water, is going down into the interior of the earth. Poe's intention can only be surmised; perhaps at one time he planned to describe the interior of the earth as a spirit-world.

Poe's unfinished *Narrative of Arthur Gordon Pym* is likewise a fragment, describing a voyage destined for adventure in Symmes's hollow earth. The voyage is made up of mutiny, shipwreck, famine, cannibalism, and other horrors, but it draws the narrator, Pym, steadily toward the entrance to the internal world. The story ends—or breaks off—just before the descent, but many parallels with ⟨Captain Adam Seaborn's⟩ *Symzonia* ⟨1820⟩ show that Poe intended to follow the route of that book into the earth. *Arthur Gordon Pym* continually speaks of scientific discoveries that will amaze the world, but does not reach them. One long episode describes the search for islands formerly reported in the fifty-second latitude, but Captain Guy is unable to find them in the location given. Poe is evidently following a suggestion in *Symzonia* that the curvature at the rim distorts latitude, with the intention of finding the islands later in the same (apparent) latitude. *Pym* describes the discovery on an island of the carcass of a strange animal, just as *Symzonia* had done; Pym's party discovers the prow of a canoe, as Seaborn had done. As Seaborn had left a party to take seals, Poe's Captain Guy prepares to leave a party to collect *bêche de mere*. The black islanders discovered, in Poe's story, at the entrance to a white sea apparently represent the exiles from Symzonia, described by Captain Seaborn as blackened by the sun. The islanders' fear of all things white, especially their terror when an explosion on board the *Jane Guy* spurts flame, apparently reflects their fear of the flame-throwing weapons of the internal world. Captain Seaborn interrupts his narrative for several pages to describe a colony of penguins; Poe interrupts his narrative for the same purpose. The warmth of the regions of the south and the strong southward-flowing current into which Pym and Peters are drawn indicate the influence of Symmes's theory.

J. O. Bailey, *Pilgrims through Space and Time: Trends and Patterns in Scientific and Utopian Fiction* (New York: Argus Books, 1947), pp. 40, 42–43

H. BRUCE FRANKLIN   One question which must be asked of those who champion Poe as the father of science fiction, bequeathing to his heirs the great values overlooked by his progenitors, is this: Does the ultimate meaning of Poe's science fiction mislead one as to the ultimate possibilities of the form? Rarely in Poe's science fiction does one find science itself as a subject and nowhere does one find any kind of true scientist as a consequential figure. Poe tends to present technological details about an aerial voyage across the Atlantic or to the moon with little attention to the significance of technology; enumeration of mesmeric passes with little evaluation of scientific as opposed, say, to dramatic psychology; measurement itself rather than the measurement of measurement. Now of course Poe sometimes resisted this tendency, and when we look at "Mesmeric Revelation," *Eureka,* and "Mellonta Tauta" we shall see one reason why Poe did not take existing science seriously: he has an alternative kind of science to offer. Furthermore, much—probably most—other science fiction is even less seriously concerned with science. And there are those—such as Maxim Gorki, Hugo Gernsback, the 1940 Soviet conference on science fiction, and the sympathetic nineteenth-century reviewers of Verne—who argue that the chief value of science fiction is to make available with a sugar-coating of drama some scientific facts and figures. But if science fiction is merely a popularizer of science rather than the literature which, growing with science, evaluates it and relates it meaningfully to the rest of existence, it is hardly worth serious attention. ⟨. . .⟩

Poe, then, may be the father not of science fiction but rather of what is so often associated with the term science fiction—fiction which popularizes science for boys and girls of all ages while giving them the creeps. But perhaps we should not let Poe mislead us with either his rhetorically directed theories about the short story or his extended quibbles about scientific accuracy in fiction (as in the statement affixed to "The Balloon-Hoax"). By ignoring both, one may be able to perceive that the tale of terror can be more than a mere tale of terror and the science in the tales can be more than mere pseudo-science.

> H. Bruce Franklin, "Edgar Allan Poe and Science Fiction," *Future Perfect: American Science Fiction of the Nineteenth Century* (New York: Oxford University Press, 1966), pp. 95–96, 98

DORIS L. FALK   Hawthorne, Melville, Whitman, and, later, Henry James, saw animal magnetism as a force of attraction between minds and wills, an important moral analogue to human interdependence (the "magnetic chain" or "adhesiveness"), or to the potentially destructive influence of one personality upon another. For Poe, however, it is an amoral force operating *within* the mind and body, linking consciousness and "physique," animating both. Within the body, magnetism is the unifying force which prevents dissolution; within the mind it is a unifying and illuminating force, comparable to "imagination" within a poem. The will of the magnetist himself is only a mechanical stimulus like drugs or sensory deprivation, and its power upon the mind of the patient is "psychedelic" rather than psychological or moral. The widened consciousness or the preserved body becomes the theater of the action rather than a motivating force with metaphorical or moral significance. Poe's mesmerists, therefore, have none of the diabolism of Melville's Ahab, holding his "magnet" to Starbuck's brain, or of Hawthorne's Westervelt or James's Tarrant. ⟨. . .⟩

Galvanic electricity and animal magnetism are constantly compared, if not equated, in *The Philosophy of Animal Magnetism by a Gentleman of Philadelphia*, published originally in 1937, and edited in 1928 by Joseph Jackson, who attributed the pamphlet to Poe. While the evidence of Poe's authorship is dubious, the little book elucidates better than any of Poe's known sources—including Chauncey Hare Townshend's *Facts in Mesmerism* (London, 1840)—his own tales, particularly ⟨. . .⟩ "The Facts in the Case of M. Valdemar" and "A Tale of the Ragged Mountains."

The "gentleman of Philadelphia" stated clearly and with lavish italics (all those in the quotations are his) the popular conception which led some contemporary readers to accept the M. Valdemar case as fact:

> The will is a power that sits enthroned about our physical
> natures. . . . But the human brain is the organ upon which the *will*
> acts. This organ seems to be a composition that, like Galvanic
> fluid, sends forth, at the command of the will, an *electro-magnetic*
> *fluid*, to *traverse the nerves—themselves empty tubes*—in order to
> give vitality and action to the muscular system. The galvanic
> experiments, made on dead men, seem to affect muscular action
> in this way. That there is a striking analogy between *galvanic*
> *electricity* and *nervous influence*, is certain.

This analogy underlies all of Poe's mesmeric tales, but not in the simple-minded diagrammatic form which the "gentleman of Philadelphia" explained it for the audience to whom his book is dedicated, "the citizens generally, but more especially the ladies of the United States of America." In Poe's tales the "electro-magnetic fluid" does not simply flow through hose-pipe nerves "in order to give vitality and action to the muscular system." Rather, it is a pervasive organizing principle, accounting for the cohesion of the molecules of the body and the nervous system, as it does for that of the particles of matter and of the units of the cosmos. This concept is implied in "Valdemar" and "Ragged Mountains" but is explicated as philosophy in "Mesmeric Revelation."

Doris L. Falk, "Poe and the Power of Animal Magnetism," *PLMA* 84, No. 3 (May 1969): 537–38

HAROLD BEAVER   All his imaginary trips—by ship, balloon, laudanum, hypnosis—were aimed at setting the soul free from the demands of the body and so from the restraints of normal perception; simultaneously releasing the mind from its own tomb, the prison of its endlessly inturned and ramifying nervous complexes (where Madeleine Usher or Fortunato were buried). For, above all, they express 'the thirst *to know* which is forever unquenchable'—reaching out for knowledge, beyond waking, in sleep; beyond sleep, in death; beyond death, pushed to further and further extremes of consciousness on voyages as dreams, or dreams as voyages ('Out of Space—out of Time'), to a confrontation with the abyss, the whirlpool, the void which is eternity. There are voices of those who have plunged into the ultimate abyss, but survived (like the Norse fisherman); voices that seem to rebound from the fatal impact (like that of Arthur Gordon Pym); voices that hover suspended at the point of transition (like M. Valdemar); voices retrieved from beyond the point of no return (via bottles or Moon-men); voices that continue the quest on the far side of the grave in angelic dialogues among the stars.

Harold Beaver, "Introduction," *The Science Fiction of Edgar Allan Poe*, ed. Harold Beaver (Harmondsworth, UK: Penguin Books, 1976), p. xx

MAURICE J. BENNETT   Poe's endnote ⟨to "The Unparalleled Adventure of One Hans Pfaall"⟩ emerges as a strategic maneuver. By citing some predecessors and suppressing his extensive borrowings from others, he deflects attention from what, in point of originality, are actually the weakest aspects of his own tale. He selects a competition that guarantees his own victory. However, ⟨. . .⟩ the endnote is entirely misleading to the extent that it claims for "Hans Pfaall" an exclusive concern with scientific plausibility. In terms of the literary tradition that he outlines, Poe's significant innovation is not the superior verisimilitude of his tale but his protagonist's unusual motivation and objective. Earlier literary journeys originated in sincere intellectual interests; but Poe's epigraph, ascribed to Tom O'Bedlam, immediately announces a different set of values: "With a heart of furious fancies, / Whereof I am commander, / With a burning spear *and a horse of air*, / To the wilderness I wander." The public concerns of the other narratives have been exchanged here for the radical subjectivity of madness—in Poe, often a metaphor for the hypertrophy of imagination. Pfaall's voyage is not undertaken to satisfy scientific curiosity but to gratify his imagination and to relieve him of social responsibility. For instance, with business failure and the necessity of supporting his family, he claims that "my burdens at length became intolerable, and I spent hour after hour reflecting upon the most convenient method of putting an end to my life." The accidental discovery of a book on speculative astronomy inspires him with the idea of a means of escape more "imaginative" than mere suicide:

> It was not, however, that to life itself I had any positive disgust,
> but I was harasssed beyond endurance by the adventitious miseries
> attending my situation. In this state of mind, wishing to live, yet
> wearied with life . . . I determined to depart, yet live—to leave
> the world, yet continue to exist—in short, to drop enigmas, I
> resolved, let what would ensue, to force a passage, if I could, *to the
> moon*.

Pfaall thus commits a figurative suicide by effectively removing himself from the "adventitious" circumstances of earthly existence and by attaining another, a higher reality.

Maurice J. Bennett, "Edgar Allan Poe and the Literary Tradition of Lunar Speculation," *Science-Fiction Studies* 10, No. 2 (July 1983): 143

BRIAN W. ALDISS and DAVID WINGROVE   Certainly Poe shows remarkable prescience. For instance, in a neglected story, "The Colloquy of Monos and Una", he perceives certain laws of conservation which were only widely acknowledged in the 1960s. In this potted history of a technologically overwhelmed future, he says, "Meantime huge smoking cities arose, innumerable. Green leaves shrank before the hot breath of furnaces. The fair face of nature was deformed as with the ravages of some loathsome disease. . . ." He also makes the equation between global pollution and global ageing: "Prematurely induced by intemperance of knowledge, the old age of the world drew on."

In a letter, he said, "I live continually in a reverie of the future." But those stories which are most like science fiction are least like stories, more resembling essays or conversations, and often tumbling into the facetious (one of Poe's besetting sins, linked with a habit of giving characters names like von Underduk), as if he found his material intractable.

He may use scientific flavouring, much as Lawrence Durrell does in our day; but this makes him no more a science fiction writer than it does Durrell—in fact, rather less, when we remember the latter's *Numquam*, with its transvestite Frankenstein motif.

There are excellent stories which are kin to science fiction: "MS. Found in a Bottle", featuring a splendid 'Flying Dutchman', which has often been turned into a derelict spaceship; "William Wilson", with a doppelganger, which has often been turned into an android since Poe's time; but Flying Dutchmen and doppelgangers are not in themselves science fiction and were only later smuggled into the genre. Poe wrote stories in which scientific or quasi-scientific theories are present, as mesmerism is in the horrific "The Facts in the Case of M. Valdemar". That story is his most successful science fiction.

"M. Valdemar" concerns the hypnotizing of a sick man. He dies, but his soul cannot leave his decaying body until the hypnotic bond is released. Poe's biological details are good, his manner cool and clinical. He regarded mesmerism as a strange but legitimate new science. But the emotional charge of the story, which is the well-spring of its horrifying success, comes from the fact that Poe is here treading on his favourite unhallowed ground, the territory between life and death.

Brian W. Aldiss and David Wingrove, "Something Monomaniacal: Edgar Allan Poe," *Trillion Year Spree: The History of Science Fiction* (New York: Atheneum, 1986), p. 59

WILLIAM J. SCHEICK   Poe's interest in human psychology and biology, particularly as they correspond to his knowledge of physics, is manifest as well in a critically neglected feature of his work: how his notions about human perception relate to his ideas about optics. Even a cursory exposure to Poe's fiction leaves a strong impression of his recurrent emphasis on the eye, whether it be a horse's human-looking eye in "Metzengerstein" (1832), the seemingly pupilless eye of the subject of "Berenice" (1835), the deep well-like eyes of the heroine of "Ligeia" (1838), the luminous eyes of Roderick in "The Fall of the House of Usher" (1839), the entrancing eye of the artist's dying bride and model in "The Oval Portrait" (1842), the fiery feline eye in "The Black Cat" (1843) or the veiled, pale eye of the victim in "The Tell-Tale Heart" (1843). In Poe's time there was, among philosophers and scientists, a consensus that sight was the most comprehensive and engaged of the five senses. In detailing the relationship between Poe's ideas about human perception and his understanding of optics, the depth of his knowledge of certain scientific information and the role of this knowledge in his fiction can be better appreciated. To date, the function of optics in Poe's works has not been immediately self-evident. Coming to terms with his thought about perception discloses features of his symbolism and shows how he found scientific authority to support his aesthetic management of optical concepts.

William J. Scheick, "An Intrinsic Luminosity: Poe's Use of Platonic and Newtonian Optics," *American Literature and Science*, ed. Robert J. Scholnick (Lexington: University Press, 1992), pp. 79–80

GARY WESTFAHL   In establishing the broad parameters of his SF history, ⟨Hugo⟩ Gernsback first described the time from the Middle Ages to 1800 as a kind of anticipatory era of "Proto SF" (to use the usual modern term):

> Scientifiction is not a new thing on this planet. While Edgar Allan Poe probably was the first to conceive the idea of a scientific story, there are suspicions that there were other scientifiction authors before him. Perhaps they were not such outstanding figures in literature, and perhaps they did not write what we understand today as scientifiction at all. Leonardo da Vinci . . . while he was not really an author of scientifiction, nevertheless had enough prophetic vision to create a number of machines in his own mind that were only to materialize centuries later. . . .
>
> There may have been other scientific prophets, if not scientifiction writers, before his time, but the past centuries are so beclouded, and there are so few manuscripts of such literature in

existence today, that we cannot really be sure who was the real
inventor of scientifiction.

In the eleventh century there also lived a Franciscan monk,
the amazing as well as famous Roger Bacon (1214–1294). He . . .
foresaw many of our present-day wonders. But as an author of
scientifiction, he had to be extremely careful, because in those
days it was not "healthy" to predict new and startling inventions.
(*Amazing Stories*, June 1926)

Interestingly, Gernsback did not dismiss this period on the grounds that
there existed insufficient awareness of "science," either as a concept or in
its particulars; instead, he argued, while there were sporadic individuals in
those times who possessed sufficient scientific knowledge and imagination
to write, they lacked a satisfactory—and safe—literary outlet for their visions.

The second era of SF, which might be termed its development period,
began in the 19th century with the works of Edgar Allan Poe. In Gernsback's
first editorial for *Amazing Stories*, he offered this capsule history:

Edgar Allan Poe may well be called the father of "scientifiction."
It was he who really originated the romance, cleverly weaving
into and around the story, a scientific thread. Jules Verne, with
his amazing romances, also cleverly interwoven with a scientific
thread, came next. A little later came H. G. Wells, whose
scientifiction stories, like those of his forerunners, have become
famous and immortal. (*Amazing Stories*, April 1926)

The works of Poe, Verne, and Wells were in Gernsback's eyes the most
important progenitors of SF; indeed, the statement that qualifies as Gernsback's very first definition of SF is simply a list of their names: "By 'scientifiction' I mean the Jules Verne, H. G. Wells, and Edgar Allan Poe type of
story—a charming romance intermingled with scientific fact and prophetic
vision" (ibid.). And these three names are continually the focus of Gernsback's surveys of older SF; introducing *Air Wonder Stories*, for example, he
said, "Years ago, Edgar Allan Poe wrote his immortal 'Unparalleled Adventure of One Hans Pfaal [sic],' as well as 'The Balloon Hoax.' Later, the
illustrious Jules Verne gave the world his 'Five Weeks in a Balloon.' Still
later, H. G. Wells startled us with his incomparable 'The War in the Air.'
All of these famous stories, it should be noted, fall in the class of scientific
action . . ." (*Air Wonder Stories*, July 1929).

Gary Westfahl, " 'The Jules Verne, H. G. Wells, and Edgar Allan Poe Type of
Story': Hugo Gernsback's History of Science Fiction," *Science-Fiction Studies* 19, No.
3 (November 1992): 341–42

◈ *Bibliography*

Tamerlane and Other Poems. 1827.

Al Aaraaf, Tamerlane, and Minor Poems. 1829.

Poems. 1831.

The Narrative of Arthur Gordon Pym of Nantucket. 1838.

The Conchologist's First Book; or, A System of Testaceous Malacology. 1839.

Tales of the Grotesque and Arabesque. 1840. 2 vols.

Prospectus of The Penn Magazine. 1840.

Prose Romances: The Murders in the Rue Morgue; The Man That Was Used Up. 1843.

Tales. 1845.

The Raven and Other Poems. 1845.

Mesmerism "in Articulo Mortis" ⟨"The Facts in the Case of M. Valdemar"⟩. 1846.

Prospectus of The Stylus. 1848.

Eureka: A Prose Poem. 1848.

Works. Ed. Rufus W. Griswold. 1850–56. 4 vols.

Tales of Mystery and Imagination. 1855.

Works. Ed. John H. Ingram. 1874–75. 4 vols.

Works. Ed. Richard Henry Stoddard. 1884. 8 vols.

Works. Ed. Edmund Clarence Stedman and George Edward Woodberry. 1894–95. 10 vols.

Complete Works. Ed. James A. Harrison. 1902. 17 vols.

Last Letters to Sarah Helen Whitman. Ed. James A. Harrison. 1909.

Complete Poems. Ed. J. H. Whitty. 1911.

Poems. Ed. Killis Campbell. 1917.

Letters. Ed. Mary Newton Stanard. 1925.

Best Known Works. Ed. Hervey Allen. 1931.

Complete Poems and Stories. Ed. Arthur Hobson Quinn. 1946. 2 vols.

Letters. Ed. John Ward Ostrom. 1948 (2 vols.), 1966.

Selected Prose, Poetry, and Eureka. Ed. W. H. Auden. 1950.

Literary Criticism. Ed. Robert L. Hough. 1965.

Poems. Ed. Floyd Stovall. 1965.

Collected Works. Ed. Thomas Ollive Mabbott et al. 1969–78. 3 vols. (incomplete).

The Science Fiction of Edgar Allan Poe. Ed. Harold Beaver. 1976.

Collected Writings. Ed. Burton R. Pollin et al. 1981– .

The Annotated Edgar Allan Poe. Ed. Stephen Peithman. 1981.
Poetry and Tales. Ed. Patrick Quinn. 1984.
Essays and Reviews. Ed. G. R. Thompson. 1984.

Mary Shelley
1797—1851

MARY WOLLSTONECRAFT SHELLEY was born in London on August 30, 1797, the only daughter of the philosopher William Godwin and the writer Mary Wollstonecraft. Her mother died giving birth to her, and in 1808 Godwin took a second wife, whom Mary passionately disliked. In 1812 Godwin sent Mary to live in Dundee, where she remained, except for brief visits, until 1814. During one of these visits, at the end of 1812, Mary met Percy Bysshe Shelley and his wife Harriet. After meeting a second time in 1814, Percy and Mary fell in love and left England together, traveling through France, Switzerland, Germany, and Holland. In 1815, after they had returned to England, Mary gave birth to a daughter, who died less than two weeks later; of their four children only one, Percy (b. 1819), was to survive infancy. Shelley and Mary Godwin were married in 1816, shortly after Harriet Shelley's death by drowning.

In 1817 Mary Shelley published anonymously the *History of a Six Weeks' Tour*, cowritten with Percy. The following year her most famous work—and one of the most famous novels of the nineteenth century—was published: *Frankenstein; or, The Modern Prometheus*. It was the product of a contest among Mary Shelley, Percy Shelley, Lord Byron, and John William Polidori as to who could write the most frightening tale; Mary's was the only one brought to a conclusion, although Polidori produced the able short story "The Vampyre." *Frankenstein* was published anonymously, as were several of Mary's later books, and was thought to be the work of a man until the revised edition appeared in 1831.

Shortly after the publication of *Frankenstein*, Mary and Percy left for Italy, where on July 28, 1822, Shelley was drowned in the Bay of Spezia during a heavy squall. Because Mary did not wish to surrender her only remaining child, Percy, to Shelley's father, Sir Timothy, the latter refused to give any financial support, and it became necessary for Mary to support herself by writing. Between Shelley's death and her own in 1851 she produced five novels: *Valperga* (1823), *The Last Man* (1826), *The Fortunes of Perkin*

Warbeck (1830), *Lodore* (1835), and *Falkner* (1837). She also wrote five
volumes of biographical sketches of "eminent literary and scientific men" for
Lardner's Cabinet Cyclopedia (1835–38); a two-volume travel book, *Rambles in
Germany and Italy in 1840, 1842 and 1843* (1844); and a number of poems,
essays, and short stories, mostly published in the periodical *Keepsake*. Mary
Shelley edited and published her husband's *Poetical Works* (4 vols., 1839)
and his *Essays, Letters from Abroad, Translations and Fragments* (2 vols.,
1840). She died in London on February 1, 1851.

    Frankenstein is considered by many to be the first authentic work of
science fiction, in that it conceives of a possible advance in the science of
biology that might make possible the creation of a composite animate entity
from disparate human parts. This idea has subsequently been used many
times in fiction, and it may also have inspired the notion of androids, or
humanlike machines. *The Last Man* is a striking exemplar of the "last man
on earth" theme, which has also been widely used by writers of science
fiction and fantasy.

◈ *Critical Extracts*

SIR WALTER SCOTT   A more philosophic and refined use of the
supernatural in works of fiction, is proper to that class in which the laws
of nature are represented as altered, not for the purpose of pampering the
imagination with wonders, but in order to shew the probable effect which
the supposed miracles would produce on those who witnessed them. In
this case, the pleasure ordinarily derived from the marvellous incidents is
secondary to that which we extract from observing how mortals like ourselves
would be affected,

> By scenes like these which, daring to depart
> From sober truth, are still to nature true. ⟨. . .⟩

    In the class of fictitious narrations to which we allude, the author opens
a sort of account-current with the reader; drawing upon him, in the first
place, for credit to that degree of the marvellous which he proposes to
employ; and becoming virtually bound, in consequence of this indulgence,
that his personages shall conduct themselves, in the extraordinary circumstances in which they are placed, according to the rules of probability, and

the nature of the human heart. In this view, the *probable* is far from being laid out of sight even amid the wildest freaks of imagination; on the contrary, we grant the extraordinary postulates which the author demands as the foundation of his narrative, only on condition of his deducing the consequences with logical precision.

We have only to add, that this class of fiction has been sometimes applied to the purpose of political satire, and sometimes to the general illustration of the powers and workings of the human mind. Swift, Bergerac, and others, have employed it for the former purpose, and a good illustration of the latter is the well known *Saint Leon* of William Godwin. In this latter work, assuming the possibility of the transmutation of metals and of the *elixir vitæ*, the author has deduced, in the course of his narrative, the probable consequences of the possession of such secrets upon the fortunes and mind of him who might enjoy them. *Frankenstein* is a novel upon the same plan with *Saint Leon;* it is said to be written by Mr Percy Bysshe Shelley, who, if we are rightly informed, is son-in-law to Mr Godwin; and it is inscribed to that ingenious author.

In the preface, the author lays claim to rank his work among the class which we have endeavoured to describe.

> The event on which this fiction is founded has been supposed by Dr Darwin, and some of the physiological writers of Germany, as not of impossible occurrence. I shall not be supposed as according the remotest degree of serious faith to such an imagination; yet, in assuming it as the basis of a work of fancy, I have not considered myself as merely weaving a series of supernatural terrors. The event, on which the interest of the story depends, is exempt from the disadvantages of a mere tale of spectres or enchantment. It was recommended by the novelty of the situations which it developes; and, however impossible as a physical fact, affords a point of view to the imagination for the delineating of human passions more comprehensive and commanding than any which the ordinary relations of existing events can yield.
>
> I have thus endeavoured to preserve the truth of the elementary principles of human nature, while I have not scrupled to innovate upon their combinations. The *Iliad*, the tragic poetry of Greece,—Shakspeare, in the *Tempest* and *Midsummer Night's Dream*,—and most especially Milton, in *Paradise Lost*, conform to this rule; and the most humble novellist, who seeks to confer or receive amusement from his labours, may, without presumption,

apply to prose fiction a license, or rather a rule, from the adoption
of which so many exquisite combinations of human feeling have
resulted in the highest specimens of poetry.

Sir Walter Scott, "Remarks on *Frankenstein, or the Modern Prometheus*," *Blackwood's Edinburgh Magazine* 2, No. 12 (March 1818): 613–15

PERCY BYSSHE SHELLEY   The novel of *Frankenstein; or, the Modern Prometheus*, is undoubtedly, as a mere story, one of the most original and complete productions of the day. We debate with ourselves in wonder, as we read it, what could have been the series of thoughts—what could have been the peculiar experiences that awakened them—which conduced, in the author's mind, to the astonishing combinations of motives and incidents, and the startling catastrophe, which compose this tale. There are, perhaps some points of subordinate importance, which prove that it is the author's first attempt. But in this judgment, which requires a very nice discrimination, we may be mistaken; for it is conducted throughout with a firm and steady hand. The interest gradually accumulates and advances towards the conclusion with the accelerated rapidity of a rock rolled down a mountain. We are led breathless with suspense and sympathy, and the heaping up of incident on incident, and the working of passion out of passion. We cry "hold, hold! enough!"—but there is yet something to come; and, like the victim whose history it relates, we think we can bear no more, and yet more is to be borne. Pelion is heaped on Ossa, and Ossa on Olympus. We climb Alp after Alp, until the horizon is seen blank, vacant, and limitless; and the head turns giddy, and the ground seems to fail under our feet.

This novel rests its claim on being a source of powerful and profound emotion. The elementary feelings of the human mind are exposed to view; and those who are accustomed to reason deeply on their origin and tendency will, perhaps, be the only persons who can sympathize, to the full extent, in the interest of the actions which are their result. But, founded on nature as they are, there is perhaps no reader, who can endure anything beside a new love story, who will not feel a responsive string touched in his inmost soul. The sentiments are so affectionate and so innocent—the characters of the subordinate agents in this strange drama are clothed in the light of such a mild and gentle mind—the pictures of domestic manners are of the most simple and attaching character: the father's is irresistible and deep.

Nor are the crimes and malevolence of the single Being, though indeed withering and tremendous, the offspring of any unaccountable propensity to evil, but flow irresistibly from certain causes fully adequate to their production. They are the children, as it were, of Necessity and Human Nature. In this the direct moral of the book consists; and it is perhaps the most important, and of the most universal application, of any moral that can be enforced by example. Treat a person ill, and he will become wicked. Requite affection with scorn;—let one being be selected, for whatever cause, as the refuse of his kind—divide him, a social being, from society, and you impose upon him the irresistible obligations—malevolence and selfishness. It is thus that, too often in society, those who are best qualified to be its benefactors and its ornaments, are branded by some accident with scorn, and changed, by neglect and solitude of heart, into a scourge and a curse.

Percy Bysshe Shelley, "On *Frankenstein*" (1818), *Athenaeum*, 10 November 1832, p. 730

MARY SHELLEY   In the summer of 1816 we visited Switzerland and became the neighbours of Lord Byron. At first we spent our pleasant hours on the lake or wandering on its shores; and Lord Byron, who was writing the third canto of *Childe Harold*, was the only one among us who put his thoughts down upon paper. These, as he brought them successively to us, clothed in all the light and harmony of poetry, seemed to stamp as divine the glories of heaven and earth, whose influences we partook with him.

But it proved a wet, ungenial summer, and incessant rain often confined us for days to the house. Some volumes of ghost stories translated from the German into the French fell into our hands. 〈. . .〉

'We will each write a ghost story,' said Lord Byron, and his proposition was acceded to. 〈. . .〉 I busied myself *to think of a story*—a story to rival those which had excited us to this task. One which would speak to the mysterious fears of our nature and awaken thrilling horror—one to make the reader dread to look round, to curdle the blood, and quicken the beatings of the heart. If I did not accomplish these things, my ghost story would be unworthy of its name. I thought and pondered—vainly. I felt that blank incapability of invention which is the greatest misery of authorship, when dull Nothing replies to our anxious invocations. 'Have you thought of a story?' I was asked each morning, and each morning I was forced to reply with a mortifying negative. ⟨. . .⟩

Many and long were the conversations between Lord Byron and Shelley, to which I was a devout but nearly silent listener. During one of these, various philosophical doctrines were discussed, and among others the nature of the principle of life, and whether there was any probability of its ever being discovered and communicated. They talked of the experiments of Dr Darwin (I speak not of what the doctor really did, or said that he did, but as more to my purpose, of what was then spoken of as having been done by him), who preserved a piece of vermicelli in a glass case till by some extraordinary means it began to move with voluntary motion. Not thus, after all, would life be given. Perhaps a corpse would be reanimated; galvanism had given token of such things: perhaps the component parts of a creature might be manufactured, brought together, and endued with vital warmth.

Night waned upon this talk, and even the witching hour had gone by before we retired to rest. When I placed my head on my pillow, I did not sleep, nor could I be said to think. My imagination, unbidden, possessed and guided me, gifting the successive images that arose in my mind with a vividness far beyond the usual bounds of reverie. I saw—with shut eyes, but acute mental vision—I saw the pale student of unhallowed arts kneeling beside the thing he had put together. I saw the hideous phantasm of a man stretched out, and then, on the working of some powerful engine, show signs of life, and stir with an uneasy, half-vital motion. Frightful must it be; for supremely frightful would be the effect of any human endeavour to mock the stupendous mechanism of the Creator of the world. His success would terrify the artist; he would rush away from his odious handiwork, horror-stricken. He would hope that, left to itself, the slight spark of life which he had communicated would fade; that this thing which had received such imperfect animation would subside into dead matter, and he might sleep in the belief that the silence of the grave would quench forever the transient existence of the hideous corpse which he had looked upon as the cradle of life. He sleeps; but he is awakened; he opens his eye; behold, the horrid thing stands at his bedside, opening his curtains and looking on him with yellow, watery, but speculative eyes.

I opened mine in terror. The idea so possessed my mind that a thrill of fear ran through me, and I wished to exchange the ghastly image of my fancy for the realities around. I see them still: the very room, the dark parquet, the closed shutters with the moonlight struggling though, and the sense I had the glassy lake and white high Alps were beyond. I could not so easily get rid of my hideous phantom; still it haunted me. I must try to think of something else. I recurred to my ghost story—my tiresome, unlucky ghost story! Oh! If I could only contrive one which would frighten my reader as I myself had been frightened that night!

Swift as light and as cheering was the idea that broke in upon me. 'I have found it! What terrified me will terrify others; and I need only describe the spectre which had haunted my midnight pillow.' On the morrow I announced that I had *thought of a story*. I began that day with the words, 'It was on a dreary night of November,' making only a transcript of the grim terrors of my waking dream.

Mary Shelley, "Author's Introduction to the Standard Novels Edition" (1831), *Three Gothic Novels*, ed. Peter Fairclough (Harmondsworth: Penguin, 1968), pp. 260–64

ROBERT M. PHILMUS   The clue to the Faustian nature of the conflict between Frankenstein and his monster lies in their being necessarily dependent on one another in their relation as creator-and-destroyer and in their seesawing roles as master-and-slave, pursuer-and-pursued. The monster hints that together they represent man's potential: "Was man, indeed, at once so powerful, so virtuous and magnificent, yet so vicious and base? He appeared at one time a mere scion of the evil principle, and at another as all that can be conceived of as noble and godlike." But the contrast between them is not so striking as the impulse that involves each in the destiny of the other and points to an unconscious sympathy of creator and creature. Frankenstein himself, by failing to act decisively or effectively, vicariously shares in the monster's acts of destruction, as if the monster itself were some essential part of his own nature—an active "evil principle" that has been separated from him in bringing the monster to life—a principle corresponding to that part of him which attracts him to death and has led him "to examine the cause and progress of decay, and forced him to spend days and nights in vaults and charnel-houses." In fact, his own sensations of guilt come from the feeling that somehow he has willed the murders. "I felt as if I was about the commission of a dreadful crime, and avoided with shuddering anxiety any encounter with my fellow-creatures," he says before fleeing to discover that his monster has strangled Clerval. And after the event he reflects that "Clerval, my friend and dearest companion, had fallen a victim to me and the monster of my creation."

Yet self-knowledge is something that Frankenstein is always fleeing from. He seeks to lose himself in the external world ⟨. . .⟩ For Frankenstein, the impulse to go beyond the recognized limits of human power points to his Faustian desire to transcend the limits of human nature, in this instance by overcoming death. And his creature is the "monstrous Image" of himself because it shares the same rebellious impulse against the conditions of its existence.

This similarity of impulse also indicates a profound dialectical involvement of creature and creator. That Frankenstein should repeatedly identify himself with his monster, that he should accuse himself, almost proudly, of being responsible for the murders that it commits—"I, not in deed, but in effect, was the true murderer"—all this implies that the monster is the agent of his own clandestine wishes. His desire is not only what he confesses it to be, to learn "the secrets of heaven and earth," but also, in so doing, to attain power over the lives of his fellow creatures. The creation of the monster does not satisfy that desire, because the monster soon shows signs of having a consciousness and will of its own, and refuses to submit to its creator. The acts of the monster, however, represent an alternative access to the power Frankenstein has been seeking; and the monster is in no way constrained to repress the destructive impulses that give it power over human life and allow it to possess the imagination of its creator. Thus the dialectic of power that Frankenstein submits to when he undertakes his Faustian purpose leads to the diabolical conclusion that murder is a means of dominating absolutely the life of another creature.

Robert M. Philmus, "Old Myths and New; or, Faustus Redivivus," *Into the Unknown: The Evolution of Science Fiction from Francis Godwin to H. G. Wells* (Berkeley: University of California Press, 1970), pp. 87–89

ELLEN MOERS   Mary Shelley was a unique case, in literature as in life. She brought birth to fiction not as realism but as Gothic fantasy, and thus contributed to Romanticism a myth of genuine originality: the mad scientist who locks himself in his laboratory and secretly, guiltily works at creating human life, only to find that he has made a monster. ⟨. . .⟩

That is very good horror, but what follows is more horrid still: Frankenstein, the scientist, runs away and abandons the newborn monster, who is and remains nameless. Here, I think, is where Mary Shelley's book is most interesting, most powerful, and most feminine: in the motif of revulsion against newborn life, and the drama of guilt, dread, and flight surrounding birth and its consequences. Most of the novel, roughly two of its three volumes, can be said to deal with the retribution visited upon monster and creator for deficient infant care. *Frankenstein* seems to be distinctly a *woman's* mythmaking on the subject of birth precisely because its emphasis is not upon what precedes birth, not upon birth itself, but upon what follows birth: the trauma of the afterbirth. ⟨. . .⟩

Birth is a hideous thing in *Frankenstein*, even before there is a monster. For Frankenstein's procedure, once he has determined to create new life, is to frequent the vaults and charnel houses and study the human corpse in all its loathsome stages of decay and decomposition. "To examine the causes of life," he says, "we must first have recourse to death." His purpose is to "bestow animation upon lifeless matter," so that he might "in the process of time renew life where death had apparently devoted the body to corruption." Frankenstein collects bones and other human parts from the slaughterhouse and the dissecting room, and through long months of feverish and guilty activity sticks them together in a frame of gigantic size in what he calls "my workshop of filthy creation." ⟨. . .⟩

Death and birth were ⟨. . .⟩ as hideously intermixed in the life of Mary Shelley as in Frankenstein's "workshop of filthy creation." Who can read without shuddering, and without remembering her myth of the birth of a nameless monster, Mary's journal entry of March 19, 1815, which records the trauma of her loss, when she was seventeen, of her first baby, the little girl who did not live long enough to be given a name. "Dream that my little baby came to life again," Mary wrote; "that it had only been cold, and that we rubbed it before the fire, and it lived. Awake and find no baby. I think about the little thing all day. Not in good spirits." (*"I thought, that if I could bestow animation upon lifeless matter, I might in process of time renew life where death had apparently devoted the body to corruption."*)

Ellen Moers, "Female Gothic," *Literary Women* (Garden City, NY: Doubleday, 1976), pp. 93, 95–96

LEE STERRENBURG   Since ⟨*The Last Man*⟩ first appeared in 1826, reviewers and critics have often sought out the autobiographical meanings of Mary Shelley's disaster novel. The work has been described as a dispirited postmortem on Percy Shelley and Lord Byron, both of whom died in the early 1820's. The two deceased poets appear in the novel, thinly disguised, as Adrian, Earl of Windsor, and Lord Raymond. Both characters perish in the course of the story. They do so in a manner recalling the deaths of their real-life counterparts. Like Percy Shelley, Adrian drowns at sea; like Lord Byron, Lord Raymond dies while attempting to aid a Greek revolution against the Turks. The novel, in fact, is so obviously a *roman à clef* that critics sometimes tend to see it as little else. One early reviewer, citing Mary Shelley's personal involvement in her story, snidely asked why she did not write a novel about being *"the last Woman"* because then "she would have known better how to paint her distress at having nobody left to talk to." ⟨. . .⟩

Mary Shelley does more in *The Last Man* than memorialize the personalities of Percy Shelley and Lord Byron. Her novel is intellectually ambitious. Formally, it combines confession and anatomy. In part, the novel is an anatomy or encyclopedic survey of a number of political positions, including utopianism, Bonapartism, and revolutionary enthusiasms of various kinds. *The Last Man* deals with politics, but ultimately it is an antipolitical novel. The characters in the novel discuss and try to enact various reforming and revolutionary solutions, but all such endeavors prove to be a failure in Mary Shelley's pessimistic and apocalyptic world of the future.

The antipolitical import of *The Last Man* might not fully reveal itself, however, until we look seriously at Mary Shelley's disease metaphors. Mary Shelley often engages political issues on the level of metaphor. She works dialectically, adapting old metaphors to new ends. In *Frankenstein* (1818), she grapples with the conflicting heritages of William Godwin, Mary Wollstonecraft, and Edmund Burke by recasting a familiar political metaphor, the parricidal monster who destroys his own creator. She does something analogous to this in *The Last Man*. She takes up a set of nature metaphors— diseases and plagues—which previous writers had used as hopeful symbols of the revolutionary process. She reinterprets those symbols in a pessimistic and apocalyptic way and, in so doing, rejects the meliorative political views of her parents' generation. ⟨. . .⟩

⟨. . .⟩ The plague ⟨in *The Last Man*⟩ enables her to survey the past heroic age from a consistent point of view; it enables her to comment on the ideas and metaphors of her forerunners; and it also enables her to suggest, by implication, some of the genocidal atrocities of the Greek revolution. It also places her as an artistic forerunner of modern science fiction. The structure of her novel, with its isolated narrator-witness who is surrounded by disasters and holocausts, looks forward to such works as H. G. Wells's *Time Machine* and *War of the Worlds*. Mary Shelley may well have been responding to a sense of personal grief when she wrote *The Last Man*, but she translated her personal suffering into an ambitious, historically significant anatomy of the revolutionary age.

Lee Sterrenburg, "*The Last Man*: Anatomy of Failed Revolutions," *Nineteenth-Century Fiction* 33, No. 3 (December 1978): 327–28, 346–47

JOHN J. PIERCE   It doesn't take a great deal of insight to realize that Shelley is equating science with sorcery ⟨in *Frankenstein*⟩, at least for the purposes of her story. If the creation of artificial life is a controversial idea today, how much more so must it have been in her time, when even innovations like anesthesia were seen by some as blasphemous? There was and is a strong intellectual and literary tradition that science is tainted by the same hubris as that which motivated outright sorcery—see C. S. Lewis' *The Abolition of Man* (1947), for example. And the romantic movement was a revolt against "rationalism" as perceived by its exponents.

Shelley clearly drew some of her inspiration from closer to home, however. Her father, William Godwin, was the author of *St. Leon* (1799), in which the hero is given the secret of eternal life and learns its price. Immortality alienates him from friends and loved ones, none of whom can profit from his gift, and he spreads misery wherever he goes. In the end, he must realize that "magic dissolves the whole principle and arrangement of human action, subverts all generous enthusiasm and dignity, and renders life itself loathsome and intolerable."

Substitute "science" for "magic" and you have in a nutshell the theme of what became a whole school of gothic science fiction that is still influential. Critics may argue whether Shelley really meant to portray science as original sin and scientists as sinners—but the public has long since made up its mind. Gothic sf has sometimes been given other names; Isaac Asimov calls it "Faustian" after the figure of legend who dealt with the Devil for forbidden knowledge and power. But the thematic essentials have never changed.

"Science" replaced the supernatural as the basis for the gothic theme of sin and retribution, but only because changing times had made Galvani a

more credible model than Faust for Shelley's transgressor of the laws of God
and nature. The atmosphere of *Frankenstein* remains one not of science, but
of sorcery. One hardly imagines Victor Frankenstein as a member of the
Royal Society, that open fellowship of science which Francis Bacon helped
inspire. Nor is there any castle full of scientific apparatus; in fact, we learn
nothing about the "instruments of life" by which he brings his creature into
being. Frankenstein practices his black arts in secret, and he knows them
for what they are; he does not mean the world to learn what it is not meant
to know.

"I meddled in things that Man must leave alone," says Claude Rains at
the end of the film version of *The Invisible Man* (1933), directed by the
very James Whale who brought *Frankenstein* to the screen. Often has that
line, or one like it, been repeated in Hollywood's melodramas of "scientific"
experiments gone wrong! Yet Hollywood never explicitly sets forth another
thematic essential of pure gothic sf: the personal nature of sin and retribution.
Frankenstein's monster is never really a threat to the world at large or even
to the neighborhood peasantry: It is Frankenstein's own doom, aimed only
at him and those dear to him—his fiancée is murdered when he refuses to
provide a mate for the creature.

> John J. Pierce, "Embryonic Science Fiction," *Foundations of Science Fiction: A Study
> in Imagination and Evolution* (Westport, CT: Greenwood Press, 1987), pp. 21–22

GREGORY O'DEA   ⟨. . .⟩ even as this awareness of historical creation and its problems began to grow and take on weight in the eighteenth
and early nineteenth centuries, alternative forms of history—and especially
speculative or creative history—began to appear. More than traditional
histories, these works address the theoretical issues of narrative representa-
tion and reader reception, and find a partial solution to the dilemma of
"distinction" versus "immediacy" in the then-nascent literary form of futuristic fiction. ⟨Edward⟩ Gibbon had already formulated the historian's difficulty
in metaphor; his meditation on the legend of the Seven Sleepers brings
him almost to the edge of the futuristic genre, and near to a type of discourse
which attempts in part to solve the dilemma he describes. Writing a history
of the future, for example, allows the speculative historian to shift the time
locus of the reader, and thus the work's influence upon the reader. No longer
does the reader reside in the "new world," trying to grasp a sense of the

"old" with distinction and immediacy; instead, the reader of futuristic fiction inhabits the "old" world, retaining "a lively and recent impression" of it, while the "new world" is exhibited in the detailed language of fictional description. It is this detailed, recognizably fictional discourse that addresses the dilemma of distinction and immediacy. ⟨. . .⟩ While traditional historians puzzle over creative history, speculative historians actually rely upon it; by an imaginative leap, they begin writing of events still to come rather than those already past, and present the reader with a "lively conception" ⟨David Hume⟩ of the "new world" in all its detail, rather than with "faint and languid conception" ⟨Hume⟩ of the "old" world, without immediate particulars.

Mary Shelley turns to such meditations on a number of occasions, notably in those works of short fiction and historical speculation that treat the subjects of reanimation and extended life. In "Roger Dodsworth: The Reani- mated Englishman" (written in 1826, published posthumously in 1863), Shelley compares the story of the Seven Sleepers to Dodsworth's suspended animation, and like Gibbon she is aware of the subject's fictional possibilities: "If philosophical novels were in fashion," she writes, "we conceive an excellent one might be written on the development of the same mind in various stations, in different periods of the world's history." Here Shelley extends Gibbon's notion of "two memorable eras" to "various stations" and several "different periods," and remarks on the historiographic and instructive value of conscious reincarnation: "While the love of glory and posthumous reputation is as natural to man as his former attachment to life itself, he must be, under such a state of things, tremblingly alive to the historic records of his honor or shame." Winzy, the superannuated narrator of "The Mortal Immortal: A Tale" (1834), also mentions the Seven Sleepers, but only in happy contrast to his own condition: "thus to be immortal would not be so burthensome: but, oh! the weight of never-ending time— the tedious passage of the still-succeeding hours!" Unlike the Seven Sleepers or Dodsworth, Winzy is burdened by living through history, but enduring (rather than sleeping through or annihilating) the tiresome years between memorable eras. To use Gibbon's terms, Dodsworth thus "unite[s] the most distant revolutions" in history, while Winzy "observ[es] the gradual, but incessant, change of human affairs."

In neither of these tales does Shelley attempt to record history; rather, she offers speculation about what history might be, given fantastic historians like Dodsworth and Winzy. In this she is undoubtedly informed by the similar considerations of philosophical romance and history in such speculative works as Walter Savage Landor's *Imaginary Conversations* (1824–28), and by P. B. Shelley's more theoretical statements in *A Defense of Poetry* (1821). In the latter work, P. B. Shelley contrasts "story" (or chronicle history) with poetry. Story is "a catalogue of detached facts, which have no other bond of connexion than time, place, circumstance, cause and effect"; as an account it is merely "partial," and "applies only to a definite period of time, and a certain combination of events which can never again recur." Poetry, by contrast, is "the very image of life expressed in its eternal truth." If Mary Shelley is concerned with speculative history, it is because she wishes to reinform history with poetry: to offer distinction and immediacy, and to make history's actors, events, writers, and readers "tremblingly alive" with "eternal truth."

> Gregory O'Dea, "Prophetic History and Textuality in Mary Shelley's *The Last Man*," *Papers on Language and Literature* 28, No. 3 (Summer 1992): 287–89

◈ Bibliography

History of a Six Weeks' Tour through a Part of France, Switzerland, Germany and Holland (with Percy Bysshe Shelley). 1817.

Frankenstein; or, The Modern Prometheus. 1818. 3 vols.

Valperga; or, The Life and Adventures of Castruccio, Prince of Lucca. 1823. 3 vols.

Posthumous Poems by Percy Bysshe Shelley (editor). 1824.

The Last Man. 1826. 3 vols.

The Fortunes of Perkin Warbeck: A Romance. 1830. 3 vols.

Lodore. 1835. 3 vols.

Falkner. 1837. 3 vols.

Poetical Works by Percy Bysshe Shelley (editor). 1839. 4 vols.

Essays, Letters from Abroad, Translations and Fragments by Percy Bysshe Shelley (editor). 1840. 2 vols.

Rambles in Germany and Italy in 1840, 1842 and 1843. 1844. 2 vols.

The Choice: A Poem on Shelley's Death. Ed. H. Buxton Forman. 1876.

Tales and Stories. Ed. Richard Garnett. 1891.

Letters, Mostly Unpublished. Ed. Henry H. Harper. 1918.

Proserpine and Midas: Mythological Dramas. Ed. André Henri Koszul. 1922.

Harriet and Mary: Being the Relations between P. B., Harriet and Mary Shelley and T. J. Hogg as Shown in Letters between Them (with others). Ed. Walter Sidney Scott. 1944.

Letters. Ed. Frederick L. Jones. 1944. 2 vols.

Journal. Ed. Frederick L. Jones. 1947.

My Best Mary: Selected Letters. Ed. Muriel Spark and Derek Stanford. 1953.

Matilda. Ed. Elizabeth Nitchie. 1959.

Shelley's Posthumous Poems: Mary Shelley's Fair Copy Book (editor). Ed. Irving Massey. 1969.

Collected Tales and Stories. Ed. Charles E. Robinson. 1976.

Letters. Ed. Betty T. Bennett. 1980–88. 3 vols.

Journals. Ed. Paula R. Feldman and Diana Scott-Kilvert. 1987. 2 vols.

The Mary Shelley Reader. Ed. Betty T. Bennett and Charles E. Robinson. 1990.

◈ ◈ ◈

Olaf Stapledon
1886–1950

WILLIAM OLAF STAPLEDON was born in Wallasey, England, on May 10, 1886, but spent his first six years in Port Said, Egypt. He attended Abbotsholme School in Uttotexter and then studied modern history at Balliol College, Oxford. After receiving his B.A. in 1909 he taught at the Manchester Grammar School and later worked in shipping offices in Liverpool and Port Said. In 1913 he received his M.A. from Balliol College and became a lecturer on history and literature for the Workers' Educational Association (WEA) and the University of Liverpool's extramural program. He published his first book, a collection of poems entitled *Latter-Day Psalms,* in 1914.

During World War I Stapledon, a pacifist, served in France and Belgium with the Friends Ambulance Unit from July 1915 to January 1919. He married Agnes Zena Miller in June 1919; they had two children and settled down in a home in West Kirby. In 1920 Stapledon received a Ph.D. in philosophy from the University of Liverpool and began to lecture on industrial history, literature, philosophy, and psychology for the WEA and the University Extension Board at the University of Liverpool; he continued as a lecturer for most of his life. In 1929 his second book, *A Modern Theory of Ethics,* appeared.

Stapledon then turned his attention to science fiction. His first novel was *Last and First Men* (1930), a pseudohistory of the infinitely distant future that became the first volume of an informal trilogy including *Last Men in London* (1932) and *Star Maker* (1937). *Odd John* (1935) is the tale of a modern superman. Stapledon did not entirely abandon philosophical work, writing several books of social criticism (*Waking World,* 1934; *Saints and Revolutionaries,* 1939; *New Hope for Britain,* 1939) and an ambitious work of popular philosophy, *Philosophy and Living* (1939). None of these works, however, achieved the popularity of his science fiction novels.

At the outbreak of World War II Stapledon, a lifelong socialist, modified his pacifist stance, recognizing that the threat to world civilization represented by Hitler must be overcome before the spiritual development of humanity Stapledon sought could occur. His novel *Darkness and the Light* (1942) proposes two alternative futures for civilization, depending on whether humanity follows the forces of "darkness" (ignorance and savagery) or of "light" (knowledge and spiritual evolution). *Sirius* (1944), about a dog who receives hormone injections and develops human intellectual powers, is his last major work of science fiction, although the war novel *Death into Life* (1946) and the short novel *The Flames* (1947) both contain science-fictional elements. The last work published in his lifetime, *A Man Divided* (1950), is a psychological novel about split personality containing many autobiographical vignettes.

Stapledon became a full-time professor at the University of Liverpool in 1939. In 1949 he achieved notoriety by being the only English representative of the Cultural and Scientific Conference for World Peace, held in New York and sponsored by the Communist party. Olaf Stapledon died in Cheshire on September 6, 1950.

◈ *Critical Extracts*

ALGERNON BLACKWOOD   *Last and First Men*, if too over-loaded to be breathless, casts a sparkling bird's-eye-view back over the progress of humanity from a point two thousand million years beyond to-day. The author lives in Neptune. Though this sounds over fantastic, it is all so plausible, almost possible, that the mind and judgment are captivated to a degree few murders could achieve. Mr. Stapledon calls it humbly an "essay in myth creation"; it can only be glanced at here.

Through the rise and fall of countless civilizations we taste the vast diversity of mind's possible modes. Progress has been prodigious. So immense is the scale that a million years serves as a unit. Civilizations as far beyond our own as we are beyond the cave-men vanish utterly, only to be reconstructed. Scientific invention has become as startling as the development of Super Brains. Men possess, for instance, "astronomical minds"; they use instruments able to detect the existence of mind elsewhere in the universe, though not necessarily to understand it, since it is often far beyond their own. Universal telepathy has been acquired, producing a racial consciousness that inhibits war or strife. Time in two dimensions is a commonplace, and this "supra-temporal experience" makes possible the projection of vision into any locality of space-time desired. Not only does the past lie wide open, but men can contribute to it, although they cannot alter it. A Mission to the Stone Age is not nonsense, and some of our inspired minds today may thus owe their "singularity" to assistance from the distant future. Out of this racial consciousness, moreover, individuals rise at rare moments "into eternity," where past and future are both accessible. Here, at any rate, are ideas and suggestions more truly thrilling than any murder. Humanity, meanwhile, has long since migrated *en masse* to Venus, their astronomical minds having foreseen exactly when the moon, steadily approaching, must split up and crash upon the earth. But Venus has first been provided with vegetation and its excessive moisture driven off. For men need oxygen in the right proportion. Interatomic energy supplies all the heat and power needed, and the ability to alter the orbit of the earth is also turned to account. An invasion from Mars, and trouble with the inhabitants of Venus, are vividly described; so, too, is the later migration to Neptune, when the disintegration of the sun is foreseen a few million years in advance. To escape the murderous heat, the outermost planet is chosen as the safest place to move to. Finally, the inevitable extinction of humanity is envisaged.

There is no escape. The story rises to a majestic climax. The doomed men do not sit down and weep; they think of others, not of themselves. Using the sun's radiation as energy, they scatter space with the germs of life—on the chance that these may lodge somewhere and humanity may start again. The curtain falls on this gallant attempt to send the seed of life on its trans-galactic voyage of millions of years, "seed intricate enough to bear the potentialities of life and special development."

Algernon Blackwood, "Cosmic Thrillers," *Time and Tide*, 20 December 1930, pp. 1606–7

OLAF STAPLEDON   A book of mine, *Last and First Men*, has received a certain amount of attention, and nearly every review has contained some reference to yourself. Recently I have come to feel that if you happened to notice the book, a copy of which the publishers must have sent you, you might wonder why I had not the grace to make some acknowledgment of your influence. Of course it cannot matter to you whether a new writer admits his debt or not; and anyhow you may not have seen the book or the reviews. All the same I should like to explain. Your works have certainly influenced me very greatly, perhaps even more than I supposed when I was writing my own book. But curiously enough I have only read two of your scientific romances, *The War of the Worlds* and "The Star." If I seem to have plagiarized from any others, it was in ignorance. Your later works I greatly admire. There would be something wrong with me if I did not. They have helped very many of us to see things more clearly. Then why, I wonder, did I not acknowledge my huge debt? Probably because it was so huge and obvious that I was not properly aware of it. A man does not record his debt to the air he breathes in common with everyone else.

> Olaf Stapledon, Letter to H. G. Wells (16 October 1931), cited in Robert Crossley, "The Correspondence of Olaf Stapledon and H. G. Wells, 1931–1942," *Science Fiction Dialogues,* ed. Gary K. Wolfe (Chicago: Academy, 1982), p. 35

H. G. WELLS   I like your book tremendously. *Star Maker* and *Star-Begotten* ought to help each other. They give admirable opportunity for the intelligent reviewer. Essentially I am more positivist and finite than you are. You are still trying to get a formula for the whole universe. I gave up trying to swallow the Whole years ago.

> H. G. Wells, Letter to Olaf Stapledon (22 June 1937), cited in Robert Crossley, "The Correspondence of Olaf Stapledon and H. G. Wells, 1931–1942," *Science Fiction Dialogues,* ed. Gary K. Wolfe (Chicago: Academy, 1982), p. 41

E. W. MARTIN   Like Plato of old, Stapledon is anxious to impart his meaning as myth. In the preface to *Last and First Men,* he writes: "Our aim is not merely to create aesthetically admirable fiction. We must achieve neither mere history, nor mere fiction, but myth. A true myth is one which, within the universe of a certain culture (living or dead) expresses richly, and often perhaps tragically, the highest aspirations possible within that culture." The myth is a tragic myth; it pictures the failure of man to achieve the Utopia he seeks. It is necessary to face tragic situations, and in this book the treasures of the spirit are finally surrendered by fatalists who see that all hope for man is lost. Such a book as this is not easy to read, and, in reading it, one realizes that even more than Aldous Huxley, Stapledon is a writer of tracts and not a novelist. His main concern is not to produce a work of art or to tell a tale, but to give form to his ideas, to invest them with the universal excellence which is the pleasure of the stoic.

> E. W. Martin, "Between the Devil and the Deep Sea: The Philosophy of Olaf Stapledon," *The Pleasure Ground: A Miscellany of English Writing*, ed. Malcolm Elwin (London: Macdonald, 1947), pp. 213–14

BASIL DAVENPORT   Olaf Stapledon's first novel, *Last and First Men*, was written in 1930, when modern science-fiction (dating from the foundation of *Amazing Stories*, the first magazine in the field, in 1926) was only four years old. His last, *A Man Divided*, appeared in 1950. For twenty years he produced a series of science-fiction novels which reveal one of the few truly creative intelligences that have ever tried the medium—yet most of them have never been published in America, and, except for a handful of enthusiasts, are unknown in this country at first-hand. At second-hand, Stapledon's ideas and inventions turn up constantly. He has been an inspiration to good writers and a veritable quarry of hacks. The mutant who is both a prodigy and a monster; the dog whose intelligence is equal to man's; the ruin of a world by an atomic chain-reaction; the superman who is not the oppressor of *Homo sapiens* but his potential savior and actual victim; alien intelligences which are not even animal; controlled evolution and artificial brains—in a field so wide and unpruned and one which depends so much on the actual findings of science, which are open to everyone, it is not possible to be absolutely sure that any given book has not been anticipated by another, but certainly I first came on all these ideas in Stapledon, and have constantly come on them since, sometimes in a recognizably Stapledonian form. ⟨. . .⟩

One theme that runs through all his work is of course "the tragic disorder of our whole terrestrial hive." He understands how much of man's misery he brings on himself, and how much of it he could avert—*if* he could! His last novel, *A Man Divided*, is about a man who suffers from a sort of divine schizophrenia; at times he is the mean sensual man, acting under the pressures of all the taboos and false values he has been taught, and all the petty self-seeking motives which he has learned to disguise from himself; then, for months at a time, he sees through all these pretences and falsities with angelic clarity, and acts for the Good, as Socrates said all men must if they could perceive clearly what the Good was. *A Man Divided* is one of Stapledon's weakest novels; yet there is something fine in the thought of Stapledon, at the end of his life, reining in his imagination from galaxies and aeons, to try to give once more the eternal unheeded message of how good life might be if man could learn to act sensibly and unselfishly.

Basil Davenport, "The Vision of Olaf Stapledon," *To the End of Time: The Best Science Fiction of Olaf Stapledon*, ed. Basil Davenport (New York: Funk & Wagnalls, 1953), pp. vii, ix

---

STANISLAW LEM   In contrast to the traditional image of the almost completely lifeless physical universe, in which the sparks of living consciousness vegetate in solitude on certain planets, Stapledon (in *Star Maker*) depicts a panpsychozoic universe, in which the primal nebulae, the stars, the galaxies, the planet-inhabiting nations are all endowed with soul. The telepathic community of all the civilizations, stars, gas-clouds, fusing together in spiritual unity high above the level of mundane, existential matters, is strongly reminiscent of the community of saints. But Stapledon does not describe the actual contents of these panpsychic connections, where they lead and to what purpose. Instead, he announces that human language is incapable of articulating them. We are dealing therefore with the concept of the ortho-evolution of a panpsychism, according to which the positive, desirable gradient of the development of the universe is the "intermingling" of all the existing minds within it with all the others. This, then, is the highest value, the magnificent product that the universe bears forth with the greatest pain and effort, through the work of a myriad stars. It is the culmination the universe strives towards.

But why should this Pancosmic Yoga be the final stage of cosmogonic evolution? Why does this development begin with the lower stages? Why does the Star Maker begin Its work with such terrible, Sisyphusian, indirect means to create the panpsychic harmony, instead of creating it all at once? None of this can be known. Did It intend things to be this way, or was It compelled? The answer: silence. Stapledon thus raises the typical dilemmas and antinomies of every religion to a cosmic scale, elevating them from an earthly plane and earthly scale of magnitude to the dimensions of the fictive universe. He directs the traditional drama by manipulating not-entirely-traditional figures and symbols.

Thus, although *Star Maker* is an artistic and intellectual failure, at least the author was defeated in a titanic battle. The road Stapledon travelled from his novel about "Superior Man"—via the history of humanity—to the book that tells the "universal history of the cosmos" is clearly visible. Stapledon's book is a completely solitary creation. No other work in fantastic literature has begun from similar premises. For this reason, it defines the boundaries of the SF imagination.

> Stanislaw Lem, "On Stapledon's *Star Maker*" (1970), tr. Istvan Csercsery-Ronay, Jr., *Science-Fiction Studies* 14, No. 1 (March 1987): 6–7

SUSAN GLICKSOHN   Stapledon uses the modern concept of the artificial creation of a superman ⟨in *Last and First Men*⟩ to chart the spiral path of man's development. The First Men, ourselves, are destroyed by chance and imperfection. The Second Men, a product of natural evolution, achieve a remarkably high level of civilization, only to be destroyed by their bacterial war with the Martians. The Third Men finally evolve lacking man's "finer mental capacities"; they decide to breed "a man who is nothing but man," but the resulting creature of pure intellect is nothing but a monstrous brain, "a bump of curiosity equipped with the most cunning hands." Realizing his own limitations, he in turn develops the Fifth Men, whose spiritual development is the highest yet attained. Yet the imminent destruction of the Earth forces this race to migrate to Venus, where it is slowly destroyed and brutalized by harsh conditions and guilt over the murder of the Venusians. The Sixth Men, totally engaged in a struggle for survival, nevertheless create their version of a perfect human—the Flying Men. These, however, inevitably fall because of their own limited natures and a plague of biological defects. The remaining flightless cripples are "strictly pedestrian, mentally and physically"; however they, too, are forced to develop a new form of man, one capable of migrating to Neptune to escape the heat of the sun's coming explosion. An unfavourable environment and innate flaws cause a slow brutalization of this race, too; yet eventually the Fourteenth Men emerge, on a level with the First and, like them, destroyed by their inability to "transcend their imperfect spiritual nature." Yet once again, "unaided nature" creates a new race, the equals of the Second Men, whose descendants steadily "advance to full humanity." While Nature was partly responsible for much of the previous evolutionary movements, the triumph of the Eighteenth Men is a triumph of eugenics. The "designers" of the race not only produced a perfect physical type, but developed "distinct and specialized brains" able at last to achieve a true "unity of individual minds." Thus the Racial Awakening and the reconciliation of loyalty to man and loyalty to fate are made possible. Stapledon's twentieth century concern with the future of social and scientific developments is inseparable from his vision of man's future as a slow upward movement to full humanity.

Susan Glicksohn, " 'A City of Which the Stars Are Suburbs,' " SF: The Other Side of Realism: Essays on Modern Fantasy and Science Fiction, ed. Thomas Clareson (Bowling Green, OH: Bowling Green University Popular Press, 1971), pp. 338–39

ERIC S. RABKIN   Odd John (1935) is the fountainhead of all those SF works, like A. E. van Vogt's Slan (1940), Theodore Sturgeon's More Than Human (1953), and Robert A. Heinlein's Stranger in a Strange Land (1961), which show mankind stepped up to a higher consciousness in which individuals can merge their thinking with that of their fellows in order to achieve a new order of mind, a group mind. Like the protagonists in those other novels, and like Frankenstein's demon, John is persecuted for his oddity and superiority; indeed, John is finally destroyed. Just as Frankenstein's demon offers to leave the inhabited parts of the Earth once he has a bride, so John does in fact leave the main habitations of ordinary man, only to have man follow him just as Victor pursued his hardy creation. The novel is the story of John's growth, his education, his acquisition of a fortune, his search for other "supernormals," and his failed attempt to establish a supernormal colony. Odd John, like Sirius, is the story of an alienated creature's futile efforts to enjoy a sense of community.

Odd John's supernormality is revealed as a mutation, a gene which is quite old and widely dispersed in the population, but which rarely breeds true. One feels that the 30 or so supernormals met in the novel are the full complement alive in the world. These "fantastic" creatures are able to learn a new language by merely reading first a grammar and then a dictionary; they can move boulders and even blizzards by thought-control; and they can maintain world-wide telepathic contact. Some of the deceased supernormals can even communicate with Odd John from their own eras. Yet the whole goal of this powerful colony of supernormals is to advance the "spirit" because of a "growing sense that there's something all wrong with modern solely-scientific culture."

At one point, like Jesus, John banishes himself to the wilderness for a "process of getting clean in spirit." In John's case, the process begins when he abandons all his clothing and utensils and does not end until he has constructed for himself shelter and clothing and even managed to fell a symbolic stag by leaping down on it and stabbing it to death with a sharpened stick. He can then say, almost prophesying his own epitaph, that "it is a great strength to have faced the worst and to have *felt* a feature of beauty." Through John, we are given again a fictional proof, here a proof of Stapledon's pervasive belief that good and evil become irrelevant in a new spiritual context of rightness and beauty. When six national powers attempt to destroy John's colony, the colonists, instead of subduing the world, as they might, elect not to thwart their own spiritual growth by attention to martial matters. Instead, they blow up their island and themselves, leaving only the book the reader holds in his hand as a record and a guidepost. Just as we are to learn tolerance through Sirius's death, so we are to see that tolerance comes from a sense of the transcendent, a sense bodied forth in the death of the supernormals.

> Eric S. Rabkin, "The Composite Fiction of Olaf Stapledon," *Science-Fiction Studies* 9, No. 3 (1982): 239–40

LESLIE FIEDLER   To be sure, A *Man Divided* insofar as it is a story of a single man possessed turn and turn about by two souls, the grosser of which finally takes over completely, reminds us of Robert Louis Stevenson's haunting symbolist fantasy *Dr. Jekyll and Mr. Hyde*.

In Stapledon's novel, however, Victor Cadogan-Smith/Vic Smith is not like Jekyll/Hyde produced in a laboratory by an experimenter who seems more black magician than real scientist. He is a product of "nature," with a psychological etiology rather than experimental physical origin; and his story therefore resembles a case history of "multiple personality" or manic depression, rather than a nightmare expressing the dark ambivalence common to us all. Stapledon's novel is in some sense also an "allegory," a rather perfunctorily fictionalized version of a generalization to be found throughout his work: in *Philosophy and Living*, for instance, and in *Sirius*, where the man-dog reflecting on the "tyrant species," observes, "They were cunning brutes . . . but not nearly so consistently intelligent as he had thought. They were always slipping back into subhuman dullness. . . ." But in this respect, too, it differs, to its disadvantage, from *Dr. Jekyll and Mr. Hyde*, which came to its author in a series of cryptic images, and therefore resists all reductive efforts to interpret it.

In any event, if *A Man Divided* is in one respect something less than *Dr. Jekyll and Mr. Hyde*, in another it is something more. Not only is it a study of psychic splitting, but it is also a didactic essay on a variety of subjects ranging from education to the occult, an autobiography, a love story, and a meditation on growing old.

> Leslie Fiedler, *Olaf Stapledon: A Man Divided* (New York: Oxford University Press, 1983), pp. 205–6

BRIAN W. ALDISS   We may call H. G. Wells's early scientific romances science fiction with a clear conscience. It is more debatable whether Stapledon's first novel, *Last and First Men* (1930), and *Star Maker* (1937) so qualify. They are Stapledon's attempt to blend fiction and philosophy. Wells's imagination was untainted by metaphysics, though politics finally eclipsed it; but Stapledon read Modern History while up at Balliol from 1905–09, and most of his fictions strive to iron themselves out into the progressions of historicity, complete with time-charts.

These two vast works, best regarded as a unity, are *sui generis*. The preface to *Last and First Men* warns that this 'is not a prophecy; it is a myth, or an essay in myth.' Even sterner is the disclaimer at the portals of *Star Maker*: 'Judged by the standards of the Novel, it is remarkably bad. In fact, it is no novel at all.'

The Novel has proved itself unexpectedly capacious, but the Immanent Will does seem to demand a less convivial stage on which to enact the rages of the ages. The rages which energise the gaunt structures of *Last and First Men* and *Star Maker* are, basically, religious faith against atheism and the quest for individual fulfillment versus the needs of the community, whether terrestrial or stellar. Modern rages, one might call them.

With their emphasis on spiritual suffering, catastrophe to come, and the surrealist mutations of shape which mankind must undergo in submission to the Creator, those great glacial novels, together spanning the thirties, now appear oddly characteristic of their day.

In many respects, Stapledon himself is markedly of his time. As were many men of his generation, he was torn by religious doubt; he was a non-combatant in the 1914–1918 war, and had some trouble in fitting himself, essentially a Victorian, into post-war society. Along with other intellectuals of his day, he flirted with pacifism and promiscuity. He had strong leanings towards Communism without ever becoming a member of the Party. Like many writers outside the swim of London literary society, he knew few other authors, and was critically disregarded.

It could also be said that the central premise of his work, that mankind is irrelevant to the purposes of the universe, is unpalatable to believer and unbeliever alike. It is precisely for that unpalatability, so variously, so swoopingly expressed, as if in contradiction to itself, that his admirers honour him.

> Brian W. Aldiss, "The Immanent Will Returns," *The Pale Shadow of Science* (Seattle, WA: Serconia Press, 1985), pp. 52–53

BRIAN STABLEFORD   The plot of *Sirius* is principally concerned with an inner conflict between his inherited nature and the culture imposed upon him by his upbringing. This conflict is evolved in connection with the various ways in which he has to try to fit into the human world, seeming at various stages to be a sheepdog or a family pet or the companion of a clergyman, while in reality being something else altogether. In the end, the world is alerted to his strangeness and becomes implacably hostile to him, except for his beloved Plaxy, who is so closely bound to him by spiritual and physical ties that the two constitute a unique and special atom of community, frequently referred to as Sirius-Plaxy.

Much is made in the course of the story of the violence innate in Sirius's character. When he first discovers hunting it strikes him as 'the main joy of life' and it is observed that 'he felt its call almost as a religious claim upon him'. It is this violence which is ultimately implicated in his downfall, because he eventually kills a man—albeit in the face of extreme provocation. As his personal philosophy develops, he has to come to terms with this innate violence, and its analogues in mankind. He is aided in this by reading H. G. Wells, whose opinion he once cites regarding the imperfect socialisation of the human species. His attempts to imagine God lead him, as might be expected, to brief moments of ecstatic vision when he catches frustrating but nevertheless enlightening glimpses of the essence of universal Nature. Once, he is comforted by a sudden conviction that instead of the universal Tiger he had suspected there is actually a universal Master—a much more comforting ideal—but he cannot cling to this conviction and doubt reclaims him. All he has, in the end, is his commitment to 'the spirit' and the urge to make a plea (which falls on deaf ears) for the destiny of mankind to be entrusted to people who can awake from their customary stupidity.

In the end, Sirius, like the protagonist of *Star Maker*, has to take what comfort he can from his one intimate relationship, which is the only spiritual anchorage that he has. His acceptance of this, however, is not the resignation which it appears to be in the earlier story, because in his case it requires such an astonishing triumph over circumstance. Domesticity and love, so easily achieved by human beings, are very different when they are the achievement of a human and a mutated dog. Sirius's final dying affirmation that Sirius-Plaxy has been worthwhile thus carries a paradoxical conviction which is present nowhere else in Stapledon's work.

> Brian Stableford, "Olaf Stapledon," *Scientific Romance in Britain 1890–1950* (New York: St. Martin's Press, 1985), pp. 214–15

ROBERT CROSSLEY   ⟨. . .⟩ "Science and Literature" ⟨a manuscript essay in the Stapledon Archive at the Sydney Jones Library, University of Liverpool⟩ ponders the cultural significance of the new hybrid of scientific literature (Stapledon had not yet learned to call this hybrid "science fiction"). In 1937 the body of literature that was genuinely scientific seemed to him "v. small," but he was ready to name its distinctive virtues. He describes the new form functionally in terms now taken for granted in science fiction criticism but still fresh in the mid-1930s as "critical" and "speculative." Scientific literature provides a corrective to "the *specialist's fallacy*," a target he subdivides to include "abstraction, materialism, determinism, magnitude, myopic detail." He distinguishes it from the literature of escape and from literature that responds narrowly to the current moment and finds a place for it within what he calls "creative literature." As science infiltrates the literary imagination, fiction's prophetic powers are enhanced, and Stapledon indicates the two extrapolative directions such fiction can take: toward the visionary splendor of utopianism and the celebration of human potentiality or toward the literature of disaster and "*revulsion* against science."

Stapledon's climactic arguments concern the epistemological and spiritual effects of science's influence on literature. The new fiction, he says, encourages a "*natural piety* toward the universe for its aloofness, for its potentiality," and it contributes to the "atrophy" of Alexander Pope's dictum that "the proper study of mankind is man." Because scientific literature tends philosophically to the "weakening of human interest," its "literary style" shifts in the direction of the "unemotional, unrhetorical, dry, concise, abstract." In this litany of stylistic markers that concludes the lecture notes we find a distinctively Stapledonian approach to the language of science fiction. The stylistic terms Stapledon uses do not at all fit either Wells's lively, colloquial storytelling or the unsophisticated purple prosiness of the fiction in American pulp magazines. But these terms describe accurately one side of Stapledon's style. His own fictions typically alternate between dispassionate and evocative language, between the clinical record and the startling metaphor, between the conceptual and the lyrical, between the numerical austerity of an astronomer's star catalogue and the sonorous grandeur of a Homeric catalogue. Stylistically his works behave in exactly the way one would expect of that symbiotic kind of text called science fiction.

> Robert Crossley, "Olaf Stapledon and the Idea of Science Fiction," *Modern Fiction Studies* 32, No. 1 (Spring 1986): 27–28

PATRICK A. McCARTHY   In historical terms, Stapledon's works generally operate on two levels. There is of course a sense of historical engagement, even urgency: in the preface to *Last and First Men*, for example, Stapledon says that he has "tried to make the story relevant to the change that is taking place today in man's outlook," and in the prefaces to *Star Maker* and *Darkness and the Light* he feels compelled to apologize for writing what some writers might regard as a waste of paper or, at best, a "distraction." Moreover, the extended analysis, in *Last Men in London*, of the origins of World War I is surely an attempt to place the modern mentality within the context of a particular historical and evolutionary process, while the future histories of *Last and First Men* and *Darkness and the Light* offer Stapledon great opportunities to concentrate on historical development at the expense of the more typically Modernist focus on individual life. Even the protagonists of *Odd John* and *Sirius*, who receive what is for Stapledon a very thorough development of individual character, are seen primarily as by-products or exempla of evolutionary processes, so that they exist within a very clearly defined biological and historical context.

At the same time—and with Stapledon there is always an "at the same time"—in these novels, the study of the temporal is generally important not for its own sake but as a means of gaining entree to the eternal. In fact, to be entirely wrapped up in the present moment is to lose the heightened perspective that Stapledon always sought—what the narrator of *Last Men in London* calls a "Neptunian" perspective. Moreover, the historical focus of *Last and First Men* is itself subverted by the narrative strategies adopted in that novel, for as John Huntington has shown, "the important sequence of the novel is not that of history or even that of the progress of humanity's higher stages, but rather the baffling order of awarenesses that the narrator (rather than history itself) imposes on the reader. Any suggestion of historical pattern that may emerge is either shattered by an unexpected and unpredictable event which leaves 'mere continuity' as the only order possible, or rendered trivial by the narrator's compressions and elisions." This emphasis on the disorientation of the reader is surprisingly similar to the tactics adopted often in modern poetry and fiction, where the intent is to undermine the reader's comfortable relationship to the text—a relationship made more comfortable by the notions of historical progress that Stapledon rejects. Indeed, the purely time-bound or historical viewpoint is an aspect of the mental slumber that Stapledon describes at the opening of *Last and First Men* and that he refers to in key sections of *Star Maker* and other books. Its converse is the "awakening" of the human—and later the cosmic—spirit into a detached, almost divine, perspective. This is Stapledon's nearest equivalent to the epiphanic moment in Joyce, the moment at which the individual object is stabilized in the imagination so that its form appears "radiant" and eternal; but whereas Joyce stresses the perception of a common object or event, Stapledon aims at the total form of the spirit in both its evolving and its completed aspects.

Patrick A. McCarthy, "Stapledon and Literary Modernism," *The Legacy of Olaf Stapledon: Critical Essays and an Unpublished Manuscript*, ed. Patrick A. McCarthy, Charles Elkins, and Martin Harry Greenberg (Westport, CT: Greenwood Press, 1989), pp. 42–43

▦ *Bibliography*

Latter-Day Psalms. 1914.

A Modern Theory of Ethics: A Study of the Relations of Ethics and Psychology. 1929.

Last and First Men: A Story of the Near and Far Future. 1930.

Last Men in London. 1932.

Waking World. 1934.

Odd John: A Story between Jest and Earnest. 1935.

Star Maker. 1937.

New Hope for Britain. 1939.

Saints and Revolutionaries. 1939.

Philosophy and Living. 1939. 2 vols.

Darkness and the Light. 1942.

Beyond the "Isms." 1942.

Sirius: A Fantasy of Love and Discord. 1944.

Old Man in New World. 1944.

Seven Pillars of Peace. 1944.

Death into Life. 1946.

Youth and Tomorrow. 1946.

The Flames: A Fantasy. 1947.

Worlds of Wonder: Three Tales of Fantasy ⟨The Flames, Death into Life, Old Man in New World⟩. 1949.

A Man Divided. 1950.

To the End of Time: The Best of Olaf Stapledon. Ed. Basil Davenport. 1953.

The Opening of the Eyes. Ed. Agnes Z. Stapledon. 1954.

Nebula Maker. 1976.

4 Encounters. 1976.

Far Future Calling: Uncollected Science Fiction and Fantasies. Ed. Sam Moskowitz. 1979.

Nebula Maker and 4 Encounters. 1983.

Talking across the World: The Love Letters of Olaf Stapledon and Agnes Miller 1913–1919. Ed. Robert Crossley. 1987.

H. G. Wells
1866–1946

HERBERT GEORGE WELLS was born at Bromley, Kent, on September 21, 1866. His father owned a china shop, and his mother was a lady's maid. Although he received little formal education and had been apprenticed to a draper, Wells became an assistant teacher at the Midhurst Grammar School at the age of seventeen. A year later he won a scholarship to study biology at the Normal School of Science in London, where one of his teachers was Thomas Henry Huxley. In 1888 he was awarded a B.Sc. from London University.

Suffering from ill health, Wells spent several difficult years as a teacher. His 1891 marriage to his cousin Isabel Mary Wells did not prove successful, and several years later he eloped with his student Amy Catherine ("Jane") Robbins, whom he married in 1895. Even after his marriage, however, Wells continued to have affairs with other women, reflecting his philosophical advocacy of sexual freedom. Among his liaisons was one with Rebecca West, who in 1914 gave birth to a son by Wells, Anthony West, himself a well-known writer and author of a biography of his father.

While still a teacher Wells began working on the side as a journalist. In 1895 he published his first novel, *The Time Machine*. This immediately successful book was quickly followed by several other works of science fiction: *The Wonderful Visit* (1895), *The Island of Dr. Moreau* (1896), *The Invisible Man* (1897), *The War of the Worlds* (1898), and *When the Sleeper Wakes* (1899).

Attracted to socialism since his student days, Wells joined the Fabian Society in 1903, while in his fiction he began to produce realistic comedies of lower-middle-class life in such novels as *Love and Mr. Lewisham* (1900), *Kipps* (1905), and *The History of Mr. Polly* (1910). The wide range of his social concerns was manifested in other novels such as *Ann Veronica* (1909), about an emancipated woman who defies conventional morality in her personal life, and *Tono-Bungay* (1909), about the dissolution of traditional English society and the ascendancy of a new kind of amoral bourgeois entrepreneur. At the same time Wells continued to write works of science fiction and fantasy, such as *The First Men in the Moon* (1901), *The Food of the Gods* (1904), *In the Days of the Comet* (1906), *The War in the Air* (1908), and many short stories.

Wells's restless desire for social reform impelled him to turn more and more to nonfiction work of a speculative, sociological, or philosophical nature. Even before joining the Fabians he had written several books expressing his vision of society's potential to evolve toward utopia, including *Anticipations of the Reaction of Mechanical and Scientific Progress upon Human Life and Thought* (1901) and *A Modern Utopia* (1905). As Wells became more involved with the Fabians and, eventually, at odds with them, he began to write books presenting his own concept of socialism, such as *New Worlds for Old* (1908) and *First and Last Things* (1908).

World War I made Wells a less optimistic thinker, and he began to believe that society could improve only if human beings adapted to their changing environment. To help achieve this end he took to writing didactic works in a popular style, such as the two-volume *Outline of History* (1920), *The Science of Life* (1929–30; with Julian Huxley and G. P. Wells), and *The Work, Wealth, and Happiness of Mankind* (1931), as well as speculative works such as *The Shape of Things to Come* (1933), *The Fate of Homo Sapiens* (1939), and *The New World Order* (1940). His last book, *Mind at the End of Its Tether* (1945), expresses an extreme pessimism regarding the human prospect.

H. G. Wells died on August 13, 1946. His memoirs were published in 1934 as *Experiment in Autobiography*.

◈ Critical Extracts

ISRAEL ZANGWILL   Countless are the romances that deal with other times, other manners; endless have been the attempts to picture the time to come. Sometimes the future is grey with evolutionary perspectives, with previsions of a post-historic man, bald, toothless and fallen into his second infancy; sometimes it is gay with ingenious fore-glimpses of a renewed golden age of socialism and sentimentality. In his brilliant little romance *The Time Machine* Mr. Wells has inclined to the severer and more scientific form of prophecy—to the notion of a humanity degenerating inevitably from sheer pressure of physical comfort; but this not very novel conception, which was the theme of Mr. Besant's *Inner Houses*, and even partly of Pearson's *National Life and Character*, Mr. Wells has enriched by the invention of the Morlocks, a differentiated type of humanity which lives underground and preys upon the softer, prettier species that lives luxuriously in the sun, a fine imaginative creation worthy of Swift, and possibly not devoid of satirical reference to "the present discontents." There is a good deal of what Tyndall would have called "scientific imagination" in Mr. Wells' further vision of the latter end of all things, a vision far more sombre and impressive than the ancient imaginings of the Biblical seers. The only criticism I have to offer is that his Time Traveller, a cool scientific thinker, behaves exactly like the hero of a commonplace sensational novel, with his frenzies of despair and his appeals to fate, when he finds himself in danger of having to remain in the year eight hundred and two thousand seven hundred and one; nor does it ever occur to him that in the aforesaid year he will have to repeat these painful experiences of his, else his vision of the future will have falsified itself—though how the long dispersed dust is to be vivified again does not appear. Moreover, had he travelled backwards, he would have reproduced a Past which, in so far as his own appearance in it with his newly invented machine was concerned, would have been *ex hypothesi* unveracious. Had he recurred to his own earlier life, he would have had to exist in two forms simultaneously, of varying ages—a feat which even Sir Boyle Roche would have found difficult. These absurdities illustrate the absurdity of any attempt to grapple with the notion of Time; and, despite some ingenious metaphysics, worthy of the inventor of the Eleatic paradoxes, Mr. Wells' *Time Machine*, which traverses time (viewed as the Fourth Dimension of Space) backwards or forwards, much as the magic carpet of the *Arabian Nights* traversed space, remains an amusing fantasy.

Israel Zangwill, "Without Prejudice," *Pall Mall Magazine* No. 29 (Sept. 1895): 153

J. D. BERESFORD   *The War of the Worlds* (1898), although written in the first person, is in some ways the most detached of all these fantasies; and it is in this book that Mr. Wells frankly confesses his own occasional sense of separation. "At times," says the narrator of this history, "I suffer fron the strangest sense of detachment from myself and the world about me, I seem to watch it all from the outside, from somewhere inconceivably remote, out of time, out of space, out of the stress and tragedy of it all." That sense must have remained with him as he wrote the account of the invading Martians, so little passion does the book contain. The vision, however, is clear enough and there is more invention than in many of the other romances. The picture of the Martians themselves develops in one direction the theory of human evolution expressed in *The Man of the Year Million*. The expansion of the brain case, and the apotheosis of pure intellect, devoid, so far as we can judge, of any emotional expression, are the steadily biological deductions that we should expect from the Wells of this period. The fighting machines of these incomprehensible entities, the heat ray and the black smoke, are all excellent conceptions; and the narrative is splendidly graphic. But only in the scenes with the curate, when the narrator is stirred to passionate anger, and in his later passages with the sapper, do we catch any glimpses of the novelist intrigued with the intimate affairs of humanity. Even the narrator's brother, in his account of the escape with two women in a pony-carriage, has become infected with that sense of detachment. The two women are strongly differentiated but leave little impression of personality.

The fact that I have made this comment on lack of passion in describing one of these earlier romances is indicative of a particular difference between Mr. Wells' method in this sort and the method of the lesser writer of fantasias. The latter, whatever his idea, is always intent on elaborating the wonder of his theme by direct description. Mr. Wells is far more subtle and more effective. He takes an average individual, identifies him with the world as we know it, and then proceeds gradually to bring his marvel within the range of this individual's apprehension. We see the improbable, not too definitely, through the eyes of one who is prepared with the same incredulity as the reader of the story, and as a result the strange phenomenon, whether fallen angel, invisible man, converted beast or invading Martian, takes on the shape of reality. That this shape is convincing is due to the brilliance of Mr. Wells' imagination and his power of graphic expression; the lesser writer might adopt the method and fail utterly to attain the effect; but it is this conception of the means to reach the intelligence and sense of the average reader that chiefly distinguishes these romances from those of such writers as Jules Verne. Our approach to the wonderful is so gradual and so natural that when we are finally confronted with it, the incredible thing has become inevitable and expected. Finally, it has become so identified with human surprise, anger and dismay that any failure of humanity in the chief person of the story reacts upon our conception of the wonderful intrusion among familiar phenomena.

J. D. Beresford, *H. G. Wells* (London: Nisbet & Co., 1915), pp. 29–32

H. G. WELLS   For the writer of fantastic stories to help the reader to play the game properly, he must help in every possible unobtrusive way to *domesticate* the impossible hypothesis. He must trick him into an unwary concession to some plausible assumption and get on with his story while the illusion holds. And that is where there was a certain slight novelty in my stories when they first appeared. Hitherto, except in exploration fantasies, the fantastic element was brought in by magic. Frankenstein even, used some jiggery-pokery magic to animate his artificial monster. There was trouble about the thing's soul. But by the end of last century it had become difficult to squeeze even a momentary belief out of magic any longer. It occurred to me that instead of the usual interview with the devil or a magician, an ingenious use of scientific patter might with advantage be substituted. That was no great discovery. I simply brought the fetish stuff up to date, and made it as near actual theory as possible.

As soon as the magic trick has been done the whole business of the fantasy writer is to keep everything else human and real. Touches of prosaic detail are imperative and a rigorous adherence to the hypothesis. Any *extra* fantasy outside the cardinal assumption immediately gives a touch of irresponsible silliness to the invention. So soon as the hypothesis is launched the whole interest becomes the interest of looking at human feelings and human ways, from the new angle that has been acquired. One can keep the story within bounds of a few individual experiences as Chamisso does in *Peter Schlemil*, or one can expand it to a broad criticism of human institutions and limitations as in *Gulliver's Travels*. My early, profound and lifelong admiration for Swift, appears again and again in this collection, and it is particularly evident in a predisposition to make the stories reflect upon contemporary political and social discussions. It is an incurable habit with literary critics to lament some lost artistry and innocence in my early work and to accuse me of having become polemical in my later years. That habit is of such old standing that the late Mr Zangwill in a review in 1895 complained that my first book, *The Time Machine*, concerned itself with 'our present discontents'. *The Time Machine* is indeed quite as philosophical and polemical and critical of life and so forth, as *Men Like Gods* written twenty-eight years later. No more and no less. I have never been able to get away from life in the mass and life in general as distinguished from life in the individual experience, in any book I have ever written. I differ from contemporary criticism in finding them inseparable.

> H. G. Wells, "Introduction," *The Scientific Romances of H. G. Wells* (London: Victor Gollancz, 1933), pp. viii–ix

ANDRÉ MAUROIS   Jules Verne sought to prove nothing, whereas in Wells the marvellous is always utopian and satiric in essence, and there is always a moral intention. *The Time Machine,* we are told, suggests the responsibility of man towards humanity; *The Wonderful Visit,* the restricted horizon of most men's outlook, in contrast to that of a being free from all the normal constraints of humanity; *The Island of Dr Moreau* showed the bestial side of man's existence; *The Invisible Man,* the danger of power uncontrolled by moral sense; *The War of the Worlds,* the danger of intelligence being developed at the expense of sympathy.

> André Maurois, "H. G. Wells," *Prophets and Poets,* tr. Hamish Miles (New York: Harper & Brothers, 1935), p. 79

GEORGE ORWELL   A generation ago every intelligent person was in some sense a revolutionary; nowadays it would be nearer the mark to say that every intelligent person is a reactionary. In this connection it is worth comparing H. G. Wells's *The Sleeper Awakes* with Aldous Huxley's *Brave New World,* written thirty years later. Each is a pessimistic Utopia, a vision of a sort of prig's paradise in which all the dreams of the "progressive" person come true. Considered merely as a piece of imaginative construction *The Sleeper Awakes* is, I think, much superior but it suffers from vast contradictions because of the fact that Wells, as the arch-priest of "progress," cannot write with any conviction *against* "progress." He draws a picture of a glittering, strangely sinister world in which the privileged classes live a life of shallow gutless hedonism, and the workers, reduced to a state of utter slavery and subhuman ignorance, toil like troglodytes in caverns underground. As soon as one examines this idea—it is further developed in a splendid short story in *Stories of Space and Time*—one sees its inconsistency. For in the immensely mechanised world that Wells is imagining, why should the workers have to work harder than at present? Obviously, the tendency of the machine is to eliminate work, not to increase it. In the machine-world the workers might be enslaved, ill-treated and even underfed, but they certainly would not be condemned to ceaseless manual toil; because in that case what would be the function of the machine? You can have machines doing all the work or human beings doing all the work, but you can't have both. Those armies of underground workers, with their blue uniforms and their debased, half-human language, are only put in "to make your flesh creep." Wells wants to suggest that "progress" might take a wrong turning; but the only evil he cares to imagine is inequality—one class grabbing all the wealth and power and oppressing the others, aparently out of pure spite. Give it quite a small twist, he seems to suggest, overthrow the privileged class—change over from world-capitalism to Socialism, in fact—and all will be well. The machine-civilisation is to continue, but its products are to be shared out equally. The thought he dare not face is that the machine itself may be the enemy. So in his more characteristic Utopias (*The Dream, Men Like Gods*, etc.), he returns to optimism and to a vision of humanity, "liberated" by the machine, as a race of enlightened sunbathers whose sole topic of conversation is their own superiority to their ancestors.

George Orwell, *The Road to Wigan Pier* (London: Victor Gollancz, 1937), pp. 234–35

H. E. BATES   Poe, as I have pointed out, anticipated the nineteenth-century hunger for dream worlds and scientific fantasy, but satisfied it only partially. Wells satisfied it completely. In an age when naturalism was the most advanced of literary fashions Wells was not interested in naturalism; in the short stories, at any rate, he was not interested in life as it was. "It is always about life being altered that I write, or about people developing schemes for altering life," he himself says. "And I have never once 'presented' life. My apparently most objective books are criticism and incitements to change." To the restless desire to invert life, to turn it inside out, Wells brought a kind of impishness; and it is significant that in the hands of good cartoonists he is often portrayed with something of the attitude of a small boy holding a pin behind his back. With that pin Wells caused, indeed, any amount of delicious and exciting havoc in the flat, complacent, three-dimensional world of his time. Wells was unwilling to exclude the wildest improbability about life on earth. Supposing it were ten-dimensional instead of three? Supposing men could be made invisible? Supposing a man walked through a door and disappeared? Supposing we were not the only human beings in the cosmic world? Supposing men could fly? It is first in the abundance of such ideas, rather than their startling newness, and then in his manipulation of them into credible narratives, that Wells excels. For clearly other people before Wells must have wondered if a man could suddenly disappear, or if men could fly, or if there were living creatures on other stars. For the task of making such ideas credible Wells possessed no other apparatus than that possessed by every writer in the world: words. Ideas, as most writers know, are two a penny. It is only by the translation of these ideas into words of a certain credible order that they can be given ephemeral value for another person.

H. E. Bates, *The Modern Short Story* (Boston: The Writer, 1941), pp. 107–8

JORGE LUIS BORGES   Before Wells resigned himself to the role of sociological spectator, he was an admirable storyteller, an heir to the concise style of Swift and Edgar Allan Poe; Verne was a pleasant and industrious journeyman. Verne wrote for adolescents; Wells, for all ages. There is another difference, which Wells himself once indicated: Verne's stories deal with probable things (a submarine, a ship larger than those existing in 1872, the discovery of the South Pole, the talking picture, the crossing of Africa in a balloon, the craters of an extinguished volcano that lead to the center of the earth); the short stories Wells wrote concern mere possibilities, if not impossible things (an invisible man, a flower that devours a man, a crystal egg that reflects the events on Mars, a man who returns from the future with a flower of the future, a man who returns from the other life with his heart on the right side, because he has been completely inverted, as in a mirror). I have read that Verne, scandalized by the license permitted by *The First Men in the Moon*, exclaimed indignantly, *"Il invente!"*

The reasons I have given seem valid enough, but they do not explain why Wells is infinitely superior to the author of *Hector Servadac*, and also to Rosney, Lytton, Robert Paltock, Cyrano, or any other precursor of his methods. Even his best plots do not adequately solve the problem. In long books the plot can be only a pretext, or a point of departure. It is important for the composition of the work, but not for the reader's enjoyment of it. That is true of all genres; the best detective stories are not those with the best plots. (If plots were everything, the *Quixote* would not exist and Shaw would be inferior to O'Neill.) In my opinion, the excellence of Wells' first novels—*The Island of Dr. Moreau*, for example, or *The Invisible Man*—has a deeper origin. Not only do they tell an ingenious story; but they tell a story symbolic of processes that are somehow inherent in human destinies. The harassed invisible man who has to sleep as though his eyes were wide open because his eyelids do not exclude light is our solitude and our terror; the conventicle of seated monsters who mouth a servile creed in their night is the Vatican and is Lhasa. Work that endures is always capable of an infinite and plastic ambiguity; it is all things for all men, like the Apostle; it is a mirror that reflects the reader's own traits and it is also a map of the world. And it must be ambiguous in an evanescent and modest way, almost in spite of the author; he must appear to be ignorant of all symbolism. Wells displayed that lucid innocence in his first fantastic exercises, which are to me the most admirable part of his admirable work.

Jorge Luis Borges, "The First Wells," (1946), *Other Inquisitions 1937–1952*, tr. Ruth L. C. Simms (Austin: University of Texas Press, 1964), pp. 86–87

BERNARD BERGONZI   The significance of *The Invisible Man* in terms of Wells' fictional development is that, for the first time in his romances, we are shown a recognizable society in being which engages our sympathy and interest for its own sake. Instead of seeing a society, albeit a small one, through the eyes of a strange visitor, as in *The Wonderful Visit*, we see the strange visitor—to begin with—through the eyes of the society. And, as Wells emphasizes, it is a smug, settled and apparently prosperous community. Later, Griffin is to disturb its peace in the farcical events of Whit Monday when he goes berserk and inflicts widespread—if minor— damage to property and injury to its inhabitants. Thematically, *The Invisible Man* relates those romances in which the interest is centered in the heuristic perceptions of a single figure—the Time Traveller, the Angel, Prendick— to *The War of the Worlds*, where attention is focused on society as whole as it is subject to the unwelcome attentions of not one but a multitude of alien visitations.

Bernard Bergonzi, *The Early H. G. Wells: A Study of the Scientific Romances* (Toronto: University of Toronto Press, 1961), pp. 116–17

MARK R. HILLEGAS   *The First Men in the Moon* is, of course, a
classic example of a very old genre, the cosmic voyage, whose defining
conventions were established in the seventeenth century under the impact
of the new astronomy. Although Wells knows and uses the whole tradition,
his most important indebtedness, as Coleman Parsons and Marjorie Nicolson
have shown, is to the conception of the moon in Kepler's *Somnium*—a
porous moon with great caverns in which the lunar creatures hide from the
extremes of temperatures, with the so-called craters as entrances to the
world inside. But Wells forges this anew in the furnaces of his imagination,
and indeed he takes most of the old conventions of the cosmic voyage and
infuses them with a new poetic vitality. This is apparent in the narrative
of the beautiful, silent journey through star-dusted space and the landing
on the moon at the dawn of a lunar day. Wells's imagination is also evident
in the description of the moon's interior, with its blue-lit passageways and
tunnels lying above the great swirling, luminescent central sea that laps
around the lunar core.

We have been so caught up in the journey through space and the landing
on the moon that we are now ready to accept Wells's description of the
civilization of the Selenites, his vivid picture of the great anthill which is
the interior of the moon. The idea of the Selenites as ants, albeit intelligent,
and the moon as an anthill is a brilliant foreshadowing of the giant World
States of twentieth-century anti-Utopias.

One implied criticism of human life in *The First Men in the Moon* is a
paradox of the twentieth century which Wells presents but cannot resolve:
how, in an age of science and technology, can the world achieve economic,
social, political stability and efficiency and, at the same time, not dehumanize
the individual by completely controlling him? Wells describes here the
ultimate in "specialization," a word which means in the context of the book
the thorough adaptation of the organism to its function in society.

"In the moon," Cavor observes, "every citizen knows his place. He is
born to that place, and the elaborate discipline of training and education
and surgery he undergoes fits him at last so completely to it that he has
neither ideas nor organs for any purpose beyond it." And so the moon is a
forerunner of the twentieth-century *Brave New World*, a state in which
each individual is, by physical, psychological, and chemical means, irresistibly adapted to his position and even comes to hate those who are not like
him.

Mark R. Hillegas, *The Future as Nightmare: H. G. Wells and the Anti-Utopians* (New
York: Oxford University Press, 1967), pp. 51–52.

DARKO SUVIN   *The Time Machine* (1895), Wells's programmatic and (but for the mawkish character of Weena) most consistent work, shows his way of proceeding to his ultimate horizon. The horizon of sociobiological regression leading to cosmic extinction, simplified from Darwinism into a series of vivid pictures in the Eloi, the giant crabs, and the eclipse episodes, is established by the Time Traveller's narration as a stark contrast to the Victorian after-dinner discussions in his comfortable residence. The Time Machine itself is validated by an efficient forestalling of possible objections, put into the mouth of schematic, none too bright, and reluctantly persuaded listeners, rather than by the bogus theory of the fourth dimension or any explanation of the gleaming bars glimpsed in the machine. Similarly, the sequence of narrated episodes gains much of its impact from the careful foreshortening of ever larger perspectives in an ever more breathless rhythm. Also, the narrator-observer's gradually deepening involvement in the Eloi episode is marked by cognitive hypotheses that run the whole logical gamut of sociological SF. From a parodied Morrisite model ("Communism," says the Time Traveller at first sight) through the discovery of degeneration and of persistence of class divisions, he arrives at the anti-Utopian form most horrifying to the Victorians—a run-down class society ruled by a grotesque equivalent of the nineteenth-century industrial proletariat. Characteristically, the sociological perspective then blends into biology. The laboring and upper classes are envisioned as having developed into different races or indeed species, with the Morlocks raising the Eloi as cattle to be eaten. In spite of a certain contempt for their effeteness, the Time Traveller quickly identifies with the butterfly-like upper class Eloi and so far forsakes his position as neutral observer to engage in bloody and fierce carnage of the repugnant spider-monkey-like Morlocks, on the model of the most sensationalist exotic adventure stories. His commitment is never logically argued, and there is a strong suggestion that it flows from the social consciousness of Wells himself, who came from the lower middle class, which lives on the edge of the "proletarian abyss" and thus "looks upon the proletariat as being something disgusting and evil and dangerous" ⟨Christopher Caudwell⟩. Instead, the Time Traveller's attitude is powerfully supported by the prevailing imagery—both by animal parallels, and by the pervasive open-air green and bright colors of the almost Edenic garden (associated with the Eloi) opposed to the subterranean blackness and the dim reddish glow (associated with the Morlocks and the struggle against them). Later in the story these menacing, untamed colors lead to the reddish black eclipse, symbolizing the end of the Earth and of the solar system. The bright pastoral of the Eloi is gradually submerged by the encroaching night of the Morlocks, and the Time Traveller's matches sputter out in their oppressive abyss. At the end, the unforgettable picture of the dead world is validated by the disappearance of the Time Traveller in the opaque depths of time.

Darko Suvin, "Wells as the Turning Point of the SF Tradition," *The Metamorphosis of Science Fiction* (New Haven: Yale University Press, 1979), pp. 211–13

FRANK McCONNELL   Moreau's island is a totalitarian regime— perhaps the first really totalitarian regime imagined by Western man. And Wells is never more brilliant than in understanding the connection between romantic aspiration and tawdry, bestial, murderous practice that underlies so many totalitarianisms. "Each time I dip a living creature into the bath of burning pain," Moreau says, "I say, This time I will burn out all the animal, this time I will make a rational creature of my own." The fatal paradox of his desire is that in his quest for rational perfection he creates a nightmarish world of monsters: in his attempts to burn out the animal, he only disfigures the animals into pathetic caricatures of humanity, but burns out, without even knowing it, the humanity that leavens his own overwhelming intelligence.

Wells ⟨. . .⟩ was no stranger to the complexities of biological science, and was neither frightened nor revolted—as were many of his literary colleagues—by the necessary rigors of the laboratory and dissecting room. So that *Doctor Moreau*, for all its "mad scientist" overtones, cannot be read simply as an anti-scientific, anti-experimentalist potboiler. Yet it is a very dark book. And part of its darkness is also part of a theme Wells begins to sound here and never really finishes sounding until the end of his career. As passionately as he believes in science, he believes in the reality of the ordinary world, the world we see around us, the good things of the Earth and their inalienable right to survive, regardless of human beliefs about their usefulness or efficiency. Moreau is cast into despair when the mere instinctual animal reasserts itself within the grisly handiwork of his surgical sculpture. And the final chapters of the book, describing the reversion of the whole island of beast folk after Moreau's death, is one of Wells' richest and broadest satires of the pretensions of self-confidently "civilized" men and women. Nevertheless, the return of the beast in the beast folk is in its way the one, measured, victory imagined in this novel; for it asserts something Wells tried to make himself believe throughout his life—that evolution itself is not a blind mistake, that Earth as it is given us by cosmic, geological history is not simply a massive blunder, and that we might be saved just because the creation which has produced us is ultimately benevolent. We know that Moreau is *wrong*, in other words. But that does not prove—though all our desire is to believe so—that the nature against which he struggles is right.

> Frank McConnell, *The Science Fiction of H. G. Wells* (New York: Oxford University Press, 1981), pp. 92–93

STANISLAW LEM   The young man composing *The War of the Worlds* was gifted with a rare sociological comprehension in creating his work without any experience of war. It is precisely those who have experienced modern Fascistic total war—including attempts to secure the complete destruction of the conquered—who *recognised* in this 'fictional' work what they themselves had undergone: unforgettable scenes of chaotic mass retreat; social disintegration; the rapid destruction of a way of life and of national traditions; the reduction to ashes of what we believe to be fundamental human rights; how in such social agony symptoms of dishonourable meanness conjoin with equally unlimited heroism; and to what extreme attitudes this complete calamity leads. Wells managed, epically, to reach out from his own time, intuitively, to both individual and collective responses within a crushed culture, and not simply to the conditions experienced in a society defeated in war—which has, ultimately, some bounds to its attendant cruelty. A work which is able to attain such subsequent validation of what were, when it was written, hypothetical representations, must be counted as great literature.

> Stanislaw Lem, "H. G. Wells's *The War of the Worlds*," tr. John Coutouvidis, Franz Rottensteiner, R. J. Elis, and Rhys Garnett, *Science Fiction Roots and Branches*, ed. Rhys Garnett and R. J. Ellis (London: Macmillan, 1990), pp. 19–20

BRIAN ALDISS   *The War of the Worlds* remains a disturbing book. Readers are not especially invited to sympathize, as we might expect to sympathize, with the inhabitants of London in their hour of crisis. We cannot sympathize with the Martians, although a telling moment of pathos comes when they are dying. Mankind survives: but its survival is hardly determined by mankind.

Wells' moral sensibility is at work here. He may agree with Darwin that "mankind has risen by slow and interrupted steps . . . to the highest standard as yet attained by him in knowledge, morals, and religion"; but Wells, throughout life, was never going to concede those standards were sufficiently high. He had his differences with Darwin, as he had with almost everyone. Indeed, the conclusion he drew from the morass of London in which he lived was that standards of knowledge, morals, and religion were desperately low. Wells had not tasted the comfortable Whig background enjoyed by the Darwin family. He never forgot his humble origins, or the humble origins of the human race. The animal in us still had to struggle for survival.

In the course of Wells's narrative, men are likened to a great variety of creatures—to dodos, ants, frogs, bees, rabbits, sheep, and rats. The narrator himself is at one point reduced to "an animal among animals." We are reminded of that earlier novel, *The Island of Dr. Moreau*, in which the narrator says, "I could not persuade myself that the men and women I met were not another, still passably human, Beast People, animals half-wrought in the outward image of human souls, and that they presently would begin to revert, to show first this bestial mark then that."

These reminders of the uncomfortable unity of life all work towards its climax: "By the toll of a billion deaths, man has wrought his birthright of the earth, and it is his against all comers . . ."

Wells sets a snare for us. The reason we are not invited to sympathize with the stricken humans is because we have no sympathy for the invaders either. What the Martians are, we may become. In the Martians we see demonstrated—just as we did with the Eloi and Morlocks in *The Time Machine*—the Darwinian principle. Given the inherited effects of use and disuse, given changed conditions of life, we could become as the Martians. *Le Martien, c'est moi* . . .

Brian Aldiss, "Introduction to *The War of the Worlds* (Part 1)," *New York Review of Science Fiction* 5, No. 2 (October 1992): 8–9

◈ Bibliography

Text-Book of Biology. 1893. 2 vols.

Honours Physiography (with R. A. Gregory). 1893.

Select Conversations with an Uncle, Now Extinct, and Two Other Reminiscences. 1895.

The Time Machine: An Invention. 1895.

The Wonderful Visit. 1895.

The Stolen Bacillus and Other Incidents. 1895.

The Island of Dr. Moreau. 1896.

The Wheels of Chance: A Holiday Adventure. 1896.

The Plattner Story and Others. 1897.

The Invisible Man: A Grotesque Romance. 1897.

Certain Personal Matters: A Collection of Material, Mainly Autobiographical. 1897.

Thirty Strange Stories. 1897.

The War of the Worlds. 1898.

When the Sleeper Wakes: A Story of the Years to Come. 1899.

Tales of Space and Time. 1899.

Love and Mr. Lewisham. 1900.

The First Men in the Moon. 1901.

Anticipations of the Reaction of Mechanical and Scientific Progress upon Human Life and Thought. 1901.

The Discovery of the Future. 1902.

The Sea Lady: A Tissue of Moonshine. 1902.

Mankind in the Making. 1903.

Twelve Stories and a Dream. 1903.

The Food of the Gods, and How It Came to Earth. 1904.

A Modern Utopia. 1905.

Kipps: The Story of a Simple Soul. 1905.

In the Days of the Comet. 1906.

The Future in America: A Search After Realities. 1906.

Faults of the Fabian. 1906.

Socialism and the Family. 1906.

Reconstruction of the Fabian Society. 1906.

This Misery of Boots. 1907.

Will Socialism Destroy the Home? 1907.

New Worlds for Old. 1908.

The War in the Air, and Particularly How Mr. Bert Smallways Fared While It
    Lasted. 1908.

First and Last Things: A Confession of Faith and Rule of Life. 1908.

Tono-Bungay. 1909.

Ann Veronica: A Modern Love Story. 1909.

The History of Mr. Polly. 1910.

The New Machiavelli. 1911.

The Country of the Blind and Other Stories. 1911.

Floor Games. 1911.

The Door in the Wall and Other Stories. 1911.

The Labour Unrest. 1912.

Marriage. 1912.

War and Common Sense. 1913.

Liberalism and Its Party: What Are We Liberals to Do? 1913.

Little Wars. 1913.

The Passionate Friends. 1913.

An Englishman Looks at the World: Being a Series of Unrestrained Remarks upon
    Contemporary Matters. 1914.

The World Set Free: A Story of Mankind. 1914.

The Wife of Sir Isaac Harmon. 1914.

The War That Will End War. 1914.

The Peace of the World. 1915.

Boon: The Mind of the Race, the Wild Asses of the Devil, and the Last Trump:
    Being a Selection from the Literary Remains of George Boon, Appropriate
    to the Times. 1915.

Bealby: A Holiday. 1915.

The Research Magnificent. 1915.

What Is Coming? A Forecast of Things After the War. 1916.

Mr. Britling Sees It Through. 1916.

The Elements of Reconstruction. 1916.

War and the Future: Italy, France, and Britain at War. 1917.

God the Invisible King. 1917.

A Reasonable Man's Peace. 1917.

The Soul of a Bishop: A Novel (with Just a Little Love in It) about Conscience
    and Religion and the Real Trouble of Life. 1917.

In the Fourth Year: Anticipations of a World Peace. 1918.

Joan and Peter: The Story of an Education. 1918.

British Nationalism and the League of Nations. 1918.

The Undying Fire: A Contemporary Novel. 1919.

History Is One. 1919.

The Outline of History: Being a Plain History of Life and Mankind. 1920.

Russia in the Shadows. 1920.

The Salvaging of Civilisation. 1921.

The New Teaching of History. 1921.

Washington and the Hope of Peace. 1922.

What H. G. Wells Thinks about The Mind in the Making *by James Harvey Robinson.* 1922.

The Secret Places of the Heart. 1922.

University of London Election: An Electoral Letter. 1922.

A Short History of the World. 1922.

Men Like Gods. 1923.

Socialism and the Scientific Motive. 1923.

To the Electors of London University, University General Election, 1923. 1923.

The Labour Ideal of Education. 1923.

The Story of a Great Schoolmaster: Being a Plain Account of the Life and Ideas of Sanderson of Oundle. 1924.

The Dream. 1924.

A Year of Prophesying. 1924.

Works (Atlantic Edition). 1924. 28 vols.

Christina Albert's Father. 1925.

The World of William Clissold: A Novel at a New Angle. 1926.

Two Letters to Joseph Conrad. 1926.

Mr. Belloc Objects to The Outline of History. 1926.

Short Stories. 1927.

Democracy under Revision. 1927.

Playing at Peace. 1927.

Meanwhile: The Picture of a Lady. 1927.

Wells' Social Anticipations. Ed. Henry W. Laidler. 1927.

The Way the World Is Going: Guesses and Forecasts of the Years Ahead. 1928.

The Open Conspiracy: Blue Prints for a World Revolution. 1928.

Mr. Blettsworthy on Rampole Island. 1928.

The Book of Catherine Wells. 1928.

The King Who Was a King: The Book of a Film. 1929.

The Common Sense of World Peace. 1929.

Adventures of Tommy. 1929.

Imperialism and the Open Conspiracy. 1929.

The Science of Life: A Summary of Contemporary Knowledge about Life and Its Possibilities (with Julian Huxley and G. P. Wells). 1929–30. 3 vols.

The Autocracy of Mr. Parham: His Remarkable Adventure in This Changing World. 1930.

The Way to World Peace. 1930.

The Problem of the Troublesome Collaborator. 1930.

Settlement of the Trouble Between Mr. Thring and Mr. Wells. 1930.

What Are We to Do with Our Lives? 1931.

The Work, Wealth, and Happiness of Mankind. 1931. 2 vols.

After Democracy: Addresses and Papers on the Present World Situation. 1932.

The Bulpington of Blup. 1932.

What Should Be Done Now? 1932.

Scientific Romances. 1933.

Stories of Men and Women in Love. 1933.

The Shape of Things to Come: The Ultimate Resolution. 1933.

Seven Famous Novels. 1934.

Experiment in Autobiography: Discoveries and Conclusions of a Very Ordinary Brain Since 1866. 1934. 2 vols.

The New America: The New World. 1935.

Things to Come. 1935.

The Anatomy of Frustration: A Modern Synthesis. 1936.

The Croquet Player. 1936.

The Idea of a World Encyclopaedia. 1936.

Man Who Could Work Miracles. 1936.

Star Begotten: A Biological Fantasia. 1937.

Brynhild. 1937.

The Camford Visitation. 1937.

The Brothers. 1938.

World Brain. 1938.

Apropos of Dolores. 1938.

The Holy Terror. 1939.

Travels of a Republican Radical in Search of Hot Water. 1939.

The Fate of Homo Sapiens. 1939.

The New World Order. 1940.

The Rights of Man; or, What Are We Fighting For? 1940.

Babes in the Darkling Wood. 1940.

The Common Sense of War and Peace: World Revolution or War Unending? 1940.

All Aboard for Ararat. 1940.

Two Hemispheres or One World? 1940.

Guide to the New World: A Handbook of Constructive World Revolution. 1941.

You Can't Be Too Careful: A Sample of Life 1901–1951. 1941.

The Outlook for Homo Sapiens. 1942.

Science and the World-Mind. 1942.

Phoenix: A Summary of the Inescapable Conditions of World Reorganization. 1942.

A Thesis on the Quality of Illusion in the Continuity of Individual Life of the Higher Metazoa, with particular Reference to the Species Homo Sapiens. 1942.

The Conquest of Time. 1942.

The New Rights of Man. 1942.

Crux Ansata: An Indictment of the Roman Catholic Church. 1943.

The Mosley Outrage. 1943.

'42 to '44: A Contemporary Memoir upon Human Behaviour During the Crisis of the World Revolution. 1944.

The Happy Turning: A Dream of Life. 1945.

Mind at the End of Its Tether. 1945.

The Desert Daisy. Ed. Gordon N. Ray. 1957.

Henry James and H. G. Wells: A Record of Their Friendship, Their Debate on the Art of Fiction, and Their Quarrel. Ed. Leon Edel and Gordon N. Ray. 1958.

Arnold Bennett and H. G. Wells: A Record of a Personal and a Literary Friendship. Ed. Harris Wilson. 1960.

George Gissing and H. G. Wells: Their Friendship and Correspondence. Ed. Royal A. Gettmann. 1961.

Journalism and Prophecy 1893–1946. Ed. W. Warren Wagar. 1964.

Hoopdriver's Holiday. Ed. Michael Timko. 1964.

The Wealth of Mr. Waddy. Ed. Harris Wilson. 1969.

Early Writings in Science and Science Fiction. Ed. Robert M. Philmus and David Y. Hughes. 1975.

H. G. Wells's Literary Criticism. Ed. Patrick Parrinder and Robert M. Philmus. 1980.

H. G. Wells in Love: Postscript to an Experiment in Autobiography. Ed. G. P. Wells. 1984.

The Man with a Nose and the Other Uncollected Short Stories Ed. J. R. Hammond. 1984.

The Definitive Time Machine. Ed. Harry M. Geduld. 1987.
A Critical Edition of The War of the Worlds. Ed. David Y. Hughes and Harry
     M. Geduld. 1992.
The Island of Doctor Moreau: A Variorum Text. Ed. Robert M. Philmus. 1993.